"*Who Says You Can't? You Do* is the ultimate book for personal growth. It helps you find clarity within yourself regardless of where you are in life."

—Torrey Smith, Philadelphia Eagles,
Super Bowl XLVII champion

"*Who Says You Can't? You Do* offers clear and actionable steps for developing a winner's mental state and ultimately to live a fuller and more successful life. I highly recommend this book!"

—Natalie Eva Marie, WWE pro wrestler and actress

"Making my way through a lifetime of self-help books, finally a text which executes practical use of how to apply the switch to an intelligent and positive lifestyle. Daniel's enthusiasm leaps out of the pages like he is personally behind your cause. Compelling reading!"

—Helen Kapalos, senior news presenter, Network Ten

"Daniel is someone who amazes you with his personal experiences and knowledge. Don't let his age fool you: Daniel possesses the clear and positive understanding of how the world works, and the effects that certain behavior can have on a person's self-esteem. His passion and thoughtful commentary should be shared with everyone."

—Ahron Young, bureau chief, Sky News

"Daniel has uncanny intuition of the core issues driving the challenges people face. He possesses the skill to gently guide them to a new and empowering perspective. His intelligence and vibe is contagious. Daniel has the capacity to understand and respect each person's situation, yet at the same time he challenges them to move beyond their obstacles and achieve what they want in life."

—Toby O'Brien, senior psychologist, Sydney, Australia

"[Daniel's] encouragement and strategies to push past known limits are second to none, truly genius. If only the world had more people like Daniel in it."

—Angela Jacobsen, celebrity nanny and author of
Baby Love: Angela Jacobsen's A to Z

"Thank you for writing this manual for life. I basically use it as a bible."

—Kaleigh, Toronto, Canada

"I'm twenty-six and from the UK. In 2015 I was diagnosed with severe anxiety and depression. I was rushed to the hospital from panic attacks caused by stress and the same year I was told that I had skin cancer and needed an operation to cut it out, all this coupled with the stress of daily living just got too much for me to handle. It affected my relationship, my home life, my work life, and, to be honest, everything that I touched. I started drinking and smoking to help ease the stresses, I went to numerous CBT classes and therapy sessions, but nothing was working.

"I decided one day to take matters into my own hands before I lost control. I stopped the medication the doctors put me on for my depression, I stopped going to the classes, and I looked for ways to help myself. This is how I came across your book. It's taken me eight months to finish the book but that's because I took the leap, I took the challenge, and I stuck to the tasks you so kindly set out. Don't get me wrong—I'm far from "fixed"; however, since turning the first page in 2016 I've never looked back. At times it was hard and a struggle to even open the book as I was always so negative toward anything in my life. But I kept finding myself drawn back to it. Your book and story has guided me through some pretty dark times, and for that I can't thank you enough. Since reading your book I have managed to stop smoking completely, I now drink one to two drinks only when out at social events, and this year I am starting my journey of fitness—both body and mind. With each chapter it just felt like you understood, and that it was okay to have bad or off days as long as I kept moving forward. I would confidently say that my depression has disappeared. The anxiety still rears its ugly head now and again but from reading your book I am able to understand it more and shift my focus onto a more positive path.

"I know that there is still plenty more work to be done and every day teaches us something new, and because of you I now find that exciting instead of worrying what tomorrow will bring. You ought to know that you have helped me in ways that I cannot thank you enough for."

—Jonathan, Cheshire, England

"Thank you for being you. I've just finished your book and I'm crying with joy because I'm on a journey after separating from a man I continue to love. Reading the final chapters in your book has urged me to stay positive and to continue to visualize, meditate every day, and stay focused on my thoughts and actions. I'm soul-searching and have decided to change my career and travel because I need to breathe fresh air. . . . People think I am trying to escape but I want to experience something different and put something back into my community. Thank you for the amazing book once again, and I'm looking forward to my adventure."

—Lorna, London, England

"I wanted to tell you your book has helped me out so much in life. I've gone through some traumatic experiences and until recently, via reading your book and a lot of self-discovery, had never made the connection with how my actions, thoughts, and emotions all shape my life. If I'm not paying attention to these I'm also not paying attention to myself and my dreams. I've been stuck in a job I dislike for far too long and am currently taking steps toward working for my dream company. I study and practice the ideas you speak of in your book daily and have been making it a priority, and my life is changing for the better every day! The work is so hard, but so fulfilling, and I know the payoff will be extraordinary. When I have tough days I always turn back to your book and your words to put me right back on track."

—Haley, Sydney, Australia

"I just wanted to share the difference you have made in my life. I'm a twenty-six-year-old woman from Sydney, and I must say I have settled so much in my life, especially my career! Just like you, I felt so lost and took it out on drugs and alcohol EVERY week. It just wasn't healthy anymore and I was in a very dark place. I almost lost my relationship because of this.

"Anyways, I worked for my previous employer for the last three years with my colleagues, working my nine-to-five (sometimes even longer) butt off and getting paid peanuts. My boss chucked so many unnecessary tasks at me. I felt obliged to do these things, and my boss felt as though I had to prove my self-worth to the company. It was honestly the most toxic working environment. Everyone was backstabbing and bitching about each other. But all I could think about is that I needed this job to support my family.

"After reading your book and doing much self-reflection and self-appreciation, I've come to realize my self-worth. Now, I am happily working for a bigger company that gives me such genuine support and flexibility and not the typical nine-to-five job. I am happily traveling interstate and soon will be overseas (just as I've always dreamed of). During this transition, I was reading your book. So just wanted to thank you for all your help."

—Andrea, New South Wales, Australia

"Thank you so much for putting this masterpiece together, and sharing your personal experiences with me, and for all of the insight. I just finished high school this year, and I am waiting to start college next year, so this current period of my life has been vital. That is why I am so glad I came across your book when I did. I now look at things that I used to do, and I wonder why I ever had certain thoughts or let certain things bother me.

"Your book has been key to my emotional growth as well as my financial growth. In Step 3 there is a task that challenged us to take action on something to get the ball rolling. The task I chose to do was creating my business cards and my business email. Since then, I now have eight clients, which just blows my mind. So thank you so much for the push because since then I have progressed quite a bit, and I don't plan on slowing down."

—Luke, Buenos Aires, Argentina

"Over the last two years I have experienced hard times that have really tested me. I have buried two people in my life, one way too young, and recently went through a breakup with someone that I thought I was going to marry. I kind of stumbled onto your book, but at the right time when I was really struggling to find the strength to just get out of bed. I am still going through the process but as I find time to read each chapter in your book I feel encouraged, and hopeful for better days. Thank you for taking the time to write a book like this that can and will continue to help many people for years to come."

—Nathan, Rhode Island, USA

"I have a lot of troubles in my life from being abused to now being in the middle of leaving my boyfriend who has been on drugs for the past two years. I forgot who I was and what I wanted in life and put all my energy into trying to fix my boyfriend. I have decided to let go of the relationship and focus on myself. This book is really helping with that. I wanted to get in touch with you because I feel hopeless and alone and no one seems to understand what it's like living with an addict. I thank you for creating this book. It has changed my life."

—Lacey, Ontario, Canada

"Before your book, I wasn't really a person who spent a lot of time reading. See, the thing is that when I look back at who I was before this inside revolution, I don't recognize myself.

"I used to be one of those troublemakers who didn't actually know what she wanted, but just did what she did for the attention. Of course, I knew right from wrong, but at the time I was in a 'circle of expectation' where I was seen as this 'clown' who was supposed to make people laugh and wasn't ever taken seriously. My happiness depended on those people I called friends, so whenever I changed schools (which was often), I was always in search of that happiness. . . .

"I started college and began discovering a lot, questioning everything, and spending time on trying new things. As I read your book, I started finding meaning in what I was trying to discover by myself, and started believing in myself and taking more action in my life.

"Your book made me make some hard decisions about friendship. It made me look at life in a more peaceful way. I started the book with a lot of questions that I thought people would help me answer, but now I realize I already have the answers to most of them within myself. I would love to thank you from the bottom of my heart for sharing your knowledge! I can't explain how much it inspired me."

—Nada, Copenhagen, Denmark

"When I started reading your book, I was in my second year of business, a new startup, and things weren't going too well at the time, very bad actually. But I always had one thing in mind, belief!

"My advisors told me my business wasn't going to work and to cut my losses now!! But there was something inside that told me to keep on fighting, and I did. Your book has helped me to keep on fighting through the tough times.

"As you know, when starting up a business it's long hours and 200 percent commitment, plus I also have a family, two kids and an unbelievable partner, and I was taking them for granted and spending no time with them at all.

"Your book has not only made me realize that the best things in life are free, like my family, health, true happiness, and love. But it has also given me massive confidence within myself to achieve anything I want. It's shown me leadership, honesty, kindness, and love.

"Every morning I get myself in my state of mind, I visualize how the day is going to pan out. No matter what obstacles I'm faced with, big or small, I know I will get over them.

"It's been ten months since I've introduced your methodology into my life and, oh my God, it's been the best thing I've ever done!! Not only has it had a massive effect on my life, but I'm passing the energy through to my family, friends, and work colleagues. Last Christmas I bought ten copies of your book as presents for my family, and they love it.

"Business is going fantastically well, which I always knew it would. We've got a small team of six and every one of them is well into the book. What the book has taught me is to invest time into people, and I have implemented these teachings right throughout the company, and it is working and working very well!

"Thank you for being you—I never thought I'd be emailing an author of a book to tell them how much I've learned."

—Mike, Liverpool, England

"You saved my life."

—Jeanie, Georgia, USA

WHO SAYS YOU CAN'T?
YOU DO

DANIEL CHIDIAC

HARMONY
BOOKS • NEW YORK

Originally published in Australia by DC Group Global in 2012.

Library of Congress Cataloging-in-Publication Data has been applied for.

ISBN 978-0-525-57361-6
Ebook ISBN 978-0-525-57362-3

PRINTED IN THE UNITED STATES OF AMERICA

Book design by Andrea Lau
Cover design by Jessie Sayward Bright
Cover photograph by Mark Weiss/The Image Bank/Getty Images (pencil)

10 9 8 7 6 5 4 3 2 1

First US Edition

CONTENTS

WHO SAYS YOU CAN'T? YOU DO

INTRODUCTION

"There are powers inside of you which, if you could
discover and use, would make you everything you
ever dreamed or imagined you could become."

—ORISON SWETT MARDEN

Why do you act the way you do? Why are some people highly
motivated while others can't be bothered to get up and find the
TV remote? What makes the difference in people's lives? How do
you change your approach and outlook when the world seems to
be crashing down around you? How do you create your life the
way you want it? What are the strategies that have worked for the
most successful people in history? How do you build a trusting
relationship with yourself, one that will ensure you achieve what
you set out for?

The burning desire to search for these answers has become
my life's passion. And the search has revealed to me an infinite
source of intelligence and wisdom that waits patiently within every
human. For so many individuals, that fighting spirit has dimmed
over time, worn down by hardship, frustration, and disappointment. I am committed to showing people how to recapture that
spirit.

It's obvious that we all have visions of what we wish our life would be, but very few of us ever get to experience that life. Why not? Could it be reluctance to search deeper? Could it merely be not knowing how? Could it be psychological or emotional barriers that prevent our true powers from being displayed? The sad reality is that most people will go through life dreaming of another life that seems out of reach. The hope and faith in their own ability will be clouded by the stress and worry of everyday life.

> "Where there is no vision, the people perish."
> —PROVERBS 29:18

Not so long ago, I found myself in one of life's uncertain moments. I was in my room on my knees, experiencing the physical and emotional effects of a big weekend on drugs. I had no job, no sense of direction, and had lost all hope in my ability to shape my destiny. I felt worthless to myself and the world. Just like everyone else, I wanted my life to mean something; to have the ability to make a difference in people's lives and live by a purpose that inspired my every move; to fulfill my own desires, contribute to society, and wake up in the morning actually looking forward to the day!

And since that point, when I felt like a failure, I have embarked on a journey to find out **why some people are living an extraordinary life while others are never really fulfilled.** Through this journey I have modeled the most successful people known to man, traveled overseas to meet with leaders who have the strongest mindsets on the planet, interacted with exceptional achievers, coached people all the around the globe, from professional athletes to TV personalities, but most importantly I have delved deeply into the human mind and emotion—and let me assure you, all the fulfilled individuals I have met have similar attributes. Have you ever wondered why only a few people are living their dream, and the vast majority are not? Those people who live a successful, fulfilled life think in a similar way, feel in a certain way, and act according to those patterns. Yes, they are very different in many ways, but the core nature of their existence is very similar. Surprisingly, I also discovered that they, too, had to learn and practice those patterns and principles. And yes, these patterns and principles are available to anyone, not just a select few.

One important truth that I learned is that every experience happens for a reason: to lead us to a point where we are to make a decision, which will ultimately determine how we live out the rest of our life. Wherever you are in your life, whatever your achievements are, or whatever you have set up to conquer, you are reading this book to make that very decision—one that will give you a fulfillment that you never knew existed; one that will drive you to that level you want to reach; one that will offer that healthy lifestyle you dream about, attract that person you have searched for your whole life, or strengthen the relationship you are in. One that will guide you to achieve things you once thought impossible and master your financial state. One that will give you control of your emotions, break fears you thought would last forever, and propel you to wake up every day with an outlook on life that guides every step you take. A decision that ensures you hit the targets you aim for.

Now, as much as this book is about how to make that crucial decision, it's also to create direction in your life, so that every decision will be made with the knowledge and strategies that are certain to elevate you to a level that will inspire others. It doesn't matter what level you currently consider yourself to be at, there is always room for growth.

Just like any journey, this book contains steps . . .

THE 1ST STEP: SELF-DISCOVERY—THE KNOWLEDGE TO EM-POWER YOUR LIFE FOREVER will do just that. Everyone I have come in contact with has shown interest in self-discovery but has said that they wouldn't know where to start. This step is the most crucial in forming a lasting understanding of yourself and enhancing the ability to create change in an instant.

THE 2ND STEP: ENERGY—THAT FUNDAMENTAL FORCE explains how to properly use that vast energy within your being. We all know that the more energy we direct toward something, the faster it happens. Most people expend all their energy on things that are actually destroying their life rather than enriching it. This is the ultimate guide to distinguish between the two and provide the knowledge that will raise your awareness forever.

THE 3RD STEP: THE SYSTEM OF ACHIEVEMENT is the ground-work of everything you set out to achieve. I would never include anything in this book that I did not myself practice and use with my clients, and that did not have a basis in the practices used by the greatest in history. The detailed strategy in this section will give you the arsenal to excel. It will show you in a step-by-step process how to overcome any challenge in business, help you find what you are passionate about, and create the clarity and emotional charge that is needed to succeed.

THE 4TH STEP: STEER YOUR RELATIONSHIPS will show you how to take immediate control of your relationship situation. Is your ship sailing smoothly or rockily, or is it yet to set sail? Whether you are currently struggling in your relationship and want to let go or striving to enhance it, this is your guide. It has also been designed for those who have been looking for their dream partner but are unsure how to attract him or her.

THE 5TH STEP: CREATE A HEALTHY PHYSICAL EXISTENCE gives you the mind-set and strategy to take charge of your health. We can all agree that our health is definitely one of the most important things in life. If it isn't to you, then you probably need to read this section more than anyone. Without a healthy body, your life is not successful, period. I am qualified in personal training and have used my knowledge from previous clients to show the most effective ways to attain that body you want, but more important, the sense of feeling great about yourself. There is also detailed information about how the mind affects your body in every way imaginable.

THE 6TH STEP: AWAKEN YOUR MIND, UNCHAIN YOUR HEART supports the magnitude of being consciously awakened, self-aware, and enlightened to the world around you. This journey through your emotional state will scientifically and morally prove how we are all one in essence. It looks at how your actions affect not only your own life but the world at large. Walk with me as I go on my spiritual journey through Thailand to meet and stay with one of the most respected monks in the country. This step takes you through the vast influence we have on youth, from our children, nephews, and nieces, to the kid on the street! Nothing drives you more than being awakened to your role in this world.

THE 7TH STEP: FIND FULFILLMENT: A REAL SUCCESS is the ultimate advantage one can have. No life is successful without fulfillment. Do not be mistaken: a great achiever is not always fulfilled. True success is fulfillment. Find out what makes us truly happy and knock down the social myth that has influenced our heart to believe that happiness is synthetic. That system has failed many throughout history, so don't allow yourself to be fooled any longer. True fulfillment does exist!

That said, it would be absurd to attempt to minimize the enormity of the life-changing content in this book. I don't want any aspect of this journey to be tainted by an introduction that attempts to sum its power up in a few paragraphs. While this is a fun and interactive read, it does not sugarcoat anything. It is real, raw, and direct in its approach. It has the potential to bring out the absolute greatest qualities you have always had within you. Be ready to be intrigued, fascinated, and amazed. Not by this book, but by your own power.

"Man's mind, stretched by a new idea,
never goes back to its old dimensions."
—OLIVER WENDELL HOLMES JR.

BEFORE I TURNED MY TIDE

> "The ultimate measure of a man is not where he
> stands in moments of comfort, but where he stands
> at times of challenge and controversy."
> —MARTIN LUTHER KING JR.

Growing up as a child I always dreamed of a better life. Others were less fortunate than me, but I had a typical want: to escape the world as I knew it, and what surrounded me every day. I remember thinking big from a young age, yet there always seemed to be something that prevented me from believing it would ever be my reality. As most kids do, I would watch people on TV, listen to singers, or see businessmen and wish I could achieve like that. My parents always attempted to create a happy environment for me and were always supportive, although kids see things differently than their parents hope at times.

My father had two sides. He could be extremely hard on one hand and yet the most loving person I know on the other. Through his hard side he taught me a lot, though, particularly that giving up just doesn't cut it. Second was never good enough, and he expected the most out of everything I committed to. It was tough to handle at times, yet I now see the massive effect those teachings had on me. His "never give up" attitude is something that will stay cemented in me forever. As for my mother, she never had a doubt or really questioned me. My parents didn't have much money when I was growing up, and that was difficult to see. They are both unconditionally loving people, and for that I am ever indebted to them. Even so, I still didn't like to stay at home or abide by their rules.

"It's not what you own in this world,
it's what legacy you leave behind that matters."

—MY MOTHER

I began to find comfort in my grandfather and my auntie. When my parents moved from my grandparents' home, I decided to stay put rather than move with them. I looked up to my grandfather as a role model because of his strong connection with his family, and while he had money and external respect, most notable was his sense of fulfillment. He seemed at peace with the world and used his strong mind to deal with all his family's issues. On a daily basis he would go down to the local church and still serve as an altar boy. Years later, I realized that was what fulfilled him, rather than his money or esteem.

One of the hardest moments of my life was when my grandfather was diagnosed with cancer. As a twelve-year-old, I would kneel in the shower, crying and praying to God to cure him. Without realizing it at the time, I was trying to cure myself of the emotional pain and suffering I was about to endure. After three long years, my grandfather finally gave up his battle with cancer. My own battle in life was just beginning. The world around me seemed to crumble. The rock of the family was gone, and a deep sense of loss would follow me for many years to come.

Living in a working-class suburb of Melbourne, I thought my opportunities were limited. Anger toward the world really started to build up. I chose to run instead of facing it. I began losing all sense of direction, and became a troublemaker. Nearly getting kicked out of school, getting into vicious fights, and having little respect for the world were becoming my way of life.

My friends at the time seemed to show me a lot of love. We would hang out in the backstreets all night just thinking how we would get our next laugh. We had no boundaries when chasing that next laugh, including authority. I was on a one-way road to self-destruction. I knew all along that what I was doing wasn't a true reflection of me, but I was living the way I thought I had to. I guess it was for attention, acceptance, praise, recognition, selfish satisfaction, and every other feeling that leads to unhappiness.

> "There can be no happiness if the things we believe
> in are different from the things we do."
> —FREYA STARK

There was a bridge near my house where I would look out and reflect. I was only about fourteen at the time, but I would analyze the cars as they drove past. I was fascinated by how everyone seemed to be in their own world, driving to their own destination, yet we are all part of the same "big world." A Mercedes-Benz would be followed by an old Toyota, and I would try to figure out why the tables weren't turned. Why did this woman get to drive a car like that, and the other guy didn't? Was it by chance? I would think, *But we are in the same world.* I'd question whether the person in the Mercedes was really happier than the other guy. I was intrigued by human emotion and different ways of life, but more important, by answers. How did our lives affect our feelings? At the time it was just idle wondering, but the interest always remained. I always felt that I was here to affect the world. Little did I know my actions were affecting the world all along, but I guess it's common for people not to realize their power, for good or bad.

A few years went by and not much had changed. I met a girl who would be my girlfriend for three years, and I based my happiness around her presence. Things were great at the start, then just seemed to crumble, and so did most of my life. We would fight, and things turned into a real disaster. I found out that she was cheating on me. Even though our relationship was on the rocks, her cheating left me feeling empty.

I couldn't eat or sleep; every ounce of energy revolved around reminding me of this deep pain I was experiencing. I felt as if she hadn't finished in my life yet, and I told myself that I needed her in order to live. We got back together, but after a while the feelings started to fade. When I got back together with her, I was buying into this lie that I needed the comfort of knowing that she still loved me. I now realize it was a selfish act. I was trying to protect myself. Making the decision to leave was the hardest one I've ever had to make and was a real test of strength. I just knew there were things I had to do in life and I needed to do them on my own. Looking back, I don't think I was ever really in love with who she was, but in love with filling my emotional gaps with her presence.

After losing all contact with my ex-girlfriend, I lost contact with what I believed happiness was. Once again, I began to look for external things to complete me. I didn't understand what I was doing, but more important, I was blind to the fact that complete happiness can only be attained within one's self. Off I went on another journey to outside happiness.

I began to live a party lifestyle. Took up smoking, drinking heavily, and experimenting with drugs. I lived for the weekends. I was doing a commerce degree at university, but I knew that was not what I wanted out of life. As I sat in a lecture one day with about three hundred other students, my mind was racing. All I could think about was how I would be competing with these other people for a job that I didn't even want. I knew I had two options right there: stay and live a life I'd never be happy with, or take the leap of faith straight into the unknown without having a clue what I wanted to do.

I stood up, picked up my books, walked out, and never looked back. My parents wanted me to finish the degree, but I just knew that I didn't want to live my life by what social expectation deems appropriate. I didn't have a clear vision as to what I really wanted out of life, I just knew I didn't want to be where I was. I started working for a marketing company, left that, then got a full-time sales job. I had an uncanny ability to excel in both occupations and was promoted as the youngest sales coach in the company even though I had only been there for six months. But there was only one problem: It didn't fulfill me!

During this time I partnered with my brother and we began a clothing importing business. Still unsure about my true passion, I was never 100 percent committed. I worked at it, but it was only to try and generate money, because that's where I thought happiness lay. With another one of my assumptions about life's greatness gone, I was exhausting all avenues, and the truth was close to showing itself once again. This time it would have no mercy.

I was close to nineteen at the time, flying to Italy and reading books on negotiation. Not something the average teenager does, so I definitely have no regrets. Looking out of the plane window, I would think about where my life was headed. **What is all of this? What does it all mean? What am I doing here?** I wouldn't give these questions too much energy as I thought my time needed to be better spent. I now see that that belief was far from the truth. Instead of answering those questions, I would mentally reenact the scenario of me walking into the boardroom, surrounded by international businessmen, trying to get the best deal. I was nervous, anxious, but amazingly excited at the same time. I knew that I was never going to live a life that was less than what I knew I deserved. I was never willing to settle or accept that I couldn't be my own boss or live that dream life.

By the age of twenty-one I had been to Europe five times for the business. I always put on a happy face when I told people about it, which gave me some satisfaction. I thought I had found happiness by showing off this great lifestyle I pretended to be living. Every time someone asked me how I was, I would say, "Loving life." What these people didn't know is by that stage, I was addicted to drugs; couldn't make a relationship work; I was broke; mentally, emotionally, and spiritually spent; and I had no sense of direction. I would hang out all night smoking dope just to try and cloud the confusion of my inner self. It's like putting a thousand Band-Aids over a fresh wound. It doesn't matter how many you put on top, the wound is still there, as fresh as always.

Who knew all along? I did. I was lying to myself. **But I had the ability to know my own truth—a gift we all have.**

I knew I was lost and would call out to a God I didn't even really feel or understand to light up the path for me and show me the right direction. Did I ever doubt God's presence? Of course I did, especially at the times when I was so low. But who was I to turn to? I had already invested all of my energy into things that I thought would make me happy.

People began to come into my life and I would hear them talk about real happiness. I guess they were always there; my mind just chose to take some notice of them now. I repeat, I would hear them. If I were really interested, I would have listened, but I didn't. I couldn't imagine such fulfillment, so I would reject them just as quickly. I would argue and come up with so many different excuses and get frustrated as they would throw my lies back at me with the question, "Well, are you really happy?" Funnily enough, I would say yes. Every time I said it, I knew I was lying. I was scared to venture out of my fear, as weird as that sounds. I felt my truth arising more, that deep voice inside. But I didn't act upon it, because I guess I didn't have the faith that it could change my life. Even though I always knew I was a good person deep down, I would keep doing things that said otherwise, and it would confuse me even more.

Things were arising that would make me question everything I was doing. The hardest part was questioning those actions I had previously taken subconsciously. One particular night I hit what I thought was my lowest point. After another big weekend on a cocktail of drugs, I hadn't slept for forty-eight hours. I was mentally and physically exhausted. This was no ordinary "comedown." No words can ever describe the feeling of emptiness. I thought, *This is it.* I was at the end of hope. I was wishing the ground would just open up and swallow me. Standing in my bedroom, numb to everything around me, and having thoughts that it would be easier if I were dead, I felt as if there was nowhere to turn. A deep sadness and fear came over me, like a child locked in a dark room, but a thousand times worse. I broke down, got on my knees, and screamed out to God, saying, "Where the hell are you now?" I was so low that I felt I had to reach up to touch the bottom. Choked up and tears blurring my sight, I stood up only to be facing myself in the mirror. Through the tears, my reflection looked deformed, until I wiped them away. My face became clearer and the most overwhelming feeling came over me—an experience so awakening and enlightening that it would change my life forever. I stood there staring at myself for twenty minutes. I finally realized the person I had wanted to be my whole life was looking straight back at me. And so our journey begins . . .

YOUR PERSONAL CONTRACT:

I, _____,
declare that I must master my life in every area. I will no longer
settle for a life that is less than what I know I deserve. I have had
enough experience to know one side of life, and now it's **my time
to shine.** I will commit myself to enrich the quality of my life from
what it is now. I will persist under any circumstance to act upon
the tasks in this book, which are going to empower me forever. I
will not leave any task undone. I will relentlessly work to empower
my life and push beyond my known limits.

I AM responsible for shaping my destiny, and I trust my ability to
see this book through. I understand that the only way to real success is by having a great State of Mind, and I'm willing to work vig-
orously to create and enhance it. I am ready to LIVE MY LIFE in
the never-ending cycle of self-growth and use the unlimited power
within my being.

I am ready to attain a burning desire, compelling visions, and a
passion for life that rises above all else.

Signed: _____

Date: _____

1ST STEP
Self-Discovery—The Knowledge to Empower Your Life Forever

Absolute Power of Questioning

"The definition of insanity is doing the same thing
over and over again and expecting different results."

—ALBERT EINSTEIN

GREAT QUESTIONS = GREAT ANSWERS

Regardless of your age, if you are breathing, then you are always ready for change. It might be in a relationship, a career, an old habit, an anger issue, or something that is really affecting your life. I want you to choose an issue and ask yourself, **"Everything I have come to know in the last eighteen, twenty-two, forty-five, or even sixty-five years, what impact has it had in this particular area of my life? Am I happy where I am? Have I attained fulfillment? Do I feel lost and confused?"**

Now think back to how many times you have asked yourself those same questions. Do you see a pattern in your previous answers and your current ones? Unfortunately, most continue on a circular train track their whole life and are never able to implement real change. First, they don't build a belief in change, instead reminding themselves of why they think they can't change; and second, some people just don't know how to approach it. We are always gathering knowledge in life, but learning requires rapid action. You could watch someone change a car tire twenty times over, but unless you get down and do it, your knowledge is never tested, and you never learn. It seems a lot of us believe we are taking appropriate action yet still feel as if we have failed. This is why we must direct that energy in a way that is going to be effective and implement lasting change.

A lot of us have absorbed a lesson that if we change, then we are not being true to ourselves. Even our friends will have a dig at us and say things like "You've changed" in a hurtful tone. This stance overlooks two truths: Change is extremely powerful, and more important, it's inevitable. Nothing remains the same. Every new moment, you are a new person, even physically. Not one single cell in your body has remained the same since you were born. This means we are always "becoming." But what you are becoming depends on you. The challenge is that most people aren't becoming what they want.

Something must change in order to grow, right? Whether it is financially, physically, emotionally, or mentally, the same rule applies. **Proper questioning is the basis for directing change toward our immediate growth.** It allows us to broaden the way we think and stop being narrow-minded, dismissing the false belief that "there is only one option."

Maybe you're asking yourself questions, but they're disempowering ones, and they're creating the same experiences. Stay away from such questions . . .

Why can't I do that?

Why am I so unlucky?

Why does this always happen to me?

Why are all girls/guys the same?

All people with money have screwed someone over to get there, right?

Why can't I enjoy life like others?

Why am I the only one faced with so many challenges in life?

When you change the way you think, you change the way you feel. When you change the way you feel, you change the way you act. When you change the way you act, you change your life. It starts by changing the way you . . . ?

WHO AM I?

"An unquestioned mind is the world of suffering."
—BYRON KATIE

We need to ask questions that spur growth and prevent us from feeling as if we are insignificant and worthless. It's very important to ask and reflect on the question, "Who am I?" before anything else. This may seem a daunting question at first; however, probing deeper will unravel the truth.

Not fully acknowledging the answer may cloud what you **really** want and deter you from ever experiencing greatness in life. Ask what type of person you are deep down, regardless of decisions you have made in the past. A few times in my life, I've had people ask me, "Who are you?" But it wasn't until I came to peace with the answer myself that I answered it with certainty.

Here are some questions that you can ask yourself to begin the process of self-reflection. These are questions I asked myself, but remember that everyone has moments when they fail to express their true character. For example, don't fixate on one time when you were mean and selfish if you know you're a loving person deep down. Take a few seconds to think as you go through each question.

Am I a loving person?

Am I respectful?

Am I compassionate?

Am I generous and sharing?

Am I honest?

Am I grateful?

After going through those questions, did your mind automatically begin to remind you of times that you **weren't** that person? If that was the case, it's because your mind is still conditioned to looking at experiences, and especially yourself, in the worst possible way. If you are human, then I'm sure there have been times in your life when these positive attributes haven't been displayed. I'm definitely guilty of that, but it doesn't alter the fact that you are not that person deep down. Realistically, if you were doomed by every choice you made in life, you wouldn't even be reading this right now. So don't deliberately remember the times you fell short; be intelligent and focus on the times you did display these qualities. Now, run through the questions again, but in addition ask this: **"When was a time that I did display this quality?"** After you do, come back and read on.

The more you focus on being that great person, the more invigorated and energetic you feel. Did you feel proud of yourself when you went back to that moment? How did it compare with focusing on not being that person? Reminding yourself of these essential values to gain fulfillment will give you incentive to use them more often.

If you truly don't think you are that great person, ask yourself, "How can I be?" and you will instantly be flooded with ideas. Further to that, if you don't want to be that great person, then unfortunately that's the reason you are unfulfilled in the first place, never experiencing the true essence of life. In my opinion, that is a very sad life to live, and one I wouldn't accept for all the money in the world. **The challenge isn't knowing who you are as a person, it's having the courage to act like the person you are.**

It seems that we are almost separated into two parts. One part is the "Me" and the other is the "I." The "Me" is all the social tags we adopt. For example, it is my duty to be a friend, a son, a brother, an author, and so on. It so happens that I am all these things, but weirdly enough, when I'm all alone and away from these duties, I find myself not being any of them. That's when I finally discover that the "I" is who I really am. It's those qualities within me, that diversity and ability to be everything and at times nothing. There are also times when you'll feel alienated from the world, and that's because people won't always understand the "I." But they don't have to—you do. It's not until you are aligned with who you really are as a person, not who society brands you, that you will be eternally happy and live passionately every moment.

I've experienced this personally. The outside pressure to be something in particular, to choose an identity and stick to it, created an expectation of myself that only made me feel worse. Every time I was sad, I was disappointed in myself because I thought I had to be happy. When I was weak, I thought I always had to be strong; when vulnerable, always secure. I had to finally accept that I'm human, and that it's okay to be different at different stages of my life. To feel differently, to think differently, to act differently. But the greatest thing I realized about being who I was is that I am human! And being human, I have these amazing qualities within me, at my disposal. That's what I built on—knowing that my great qualities could shape my life just as much as my "bad" ones that I used to focus so much on.

I invite you to do the next task, which is life-transforming:

1. Take five minutes and really reflect on those "Am I" questions. Make sure you don't rob yourself of this

opportunity. These are life-changing exercises. Write these down. Do not go on to Task 2 until you have completed this one.

2. Now swap the "Am" and the "I" around. It should now read "I am" followed by the quality. Write them down.

3. Next, take another few minutes and reflect on the new list you have written down. Close your eyes and repeat them in your mind or say them out loud. Just make sure all your focus is on those qualities that have the power to change your life. It's usually not being sure of who we are that causes so much confusion when it's time to make a big decision. This creates clarity.

If you're in a public place and you don't really want to scream how great you are, I suggest you do it in your mind for now. And don't forget to focus on how you feel when you read each "I am" statement: **FFF (Full Focus on Feeling).**

I don't even need to know you to know that you're a big softy deep down. By reaffirming those statements, you align yourself with who you really are. It's a very important key to finding happiness or success at any level. If completed correctly, that exercise is invigorating and fulfilling. See how easy it is to fill ourselves up once we focus all our energy on the qualities of life? That exercise can be done for any issue that you are facing to gain a clear consciousness, and I highly advise you do it on a daily basis for a while, especially when you wake up. I would never suggest something here that I don't personally do or use for others. I have used this on some of the most successful and fulfilled people I know, and it adds massive value to their life.

The qualities mentioned above are just some examples; I'm sure you can think of more. You must start with "I am," followed by a quality. Now that you covered some qualities that reflect who you really are, it allows you to properly assess decisions you make on a constant basis.

I've also come to the conclusion that all human beings have the same true essence, regardless of religious background, social status, or past decisions. I have spoken to people from all walks of life, even some hardened criminals, and never had anyone refuse, after enough probing, to finally admit that they are all those great qualities deep down. We are human and such qualities have been in us since birth. That's why babies bring so much joy to the people around them—like when you go to someone's house and everyone runs up to the baby. We nearly get into arguments over who's going to hold it first. It's amazing, and that's because babies just are who they are, pure love. They have not been restricted by social myth, and ego has yet to take control over their life. You must understand that your truth will never go away, and will always be there to correct you when you feel otherwise. It is also accessible for growth and learning; hence we can relate who we really are to any situation and any decision.

I must ask you this question: Are you really being who you know you are? Nearly everyone I've asked has become defensive and answered with, "Of course I am." In my own experience, most times we are acting how we think we have to, not the way we truly want to. We think about what others are thinking about us. What are they going to think when I do this? What are they looking at? What makes them laugh? How do I have to be to fit in? What can I do to impress them? We have thoughts like, "Oh my God, they are all looking at me, straighten up, no, don't look down, look up, look cool," and so on. We do this when we walk down the street, go for a run, visit the beach, or socialize. It's usually a subconscious reaction because we have repeated it throughout our life. If you say that you don't care about what others think or the effect they have on your life, that is an outright lie. If you didn't care what others thought, you would be walking around the streets naked. And I know I'm not alone with drifting off at some points and wondering what my funeral would be like. Come on; tell me that hasn't crossed your mind. What would people say about me? Would they cry? Would I be missed? How would they remember me?

It's human nature to care what other people think. It's obvious that people are going to remember whatever legacy we leave behind. In order to leave a legacy, we must be our legacy now. The greatest legacy we can live and leave behind is to be who we really are. Doing this allows your true destiny to be displayed. If you don't know who you are, how can you make yourself happy? So are we being who we really are, or who we feel we have to be? It's a fine line, but with a bit of thought you will be able to distinguish between the two. Finding this distinction allows progress to soar.

People will remember who you are, not what you have.

KEEP ON PROBING

> "Each man is questioned by life; and he can only
> answer to life by answering for his own life;
> to life he can only respond by being responsible."
> —VIKTOR FRANKL

Other important questions should arise about decisions you are making in life. You must be able to identify other options in order to change an old habit. Asking questions, then more probing questions, until you reach an answer that is beneficial is the key. Do not just stop at one, but ask yourself as many as you have to. In the beginning of my change, I began questioning everything about my life. I remember my friend asked me once if I was lost because I was walking around the house in a daze. I said, "I'm actually finding answers, which is the opposite of being lost." Initially you might feel a bit uncomfortable with some answers because your ego tries to stand in the way of getting the real truth out. Ask as many questions as you have to.

You must ask questions that will help you. It's easy to tell a lie, but it feels like hell to live one. You will know when you are lying to yourself because the answer will not satisfy you, and you will feel unfulfilled. This now leads us to our next set of questions, keeping in mind that you should definitely add to the list . . .

Does a loving person really judge others?

Do I respect myself enough to make change?

Do the things that I'm doing now reflect the real person I am?

Am I truthful to myself when a certain situation arises?

When things seem distorted, am I grateful to be alive and to have the opportunity to persist again?

Do I allocate some time for me, even if it's fifteen minutes a day, to really focus on how to improve my life?

Do I usually focus on the worst in life rather than the best things about it?

When I was taking drugs every day for three years, I built some distorted beliefs around the whole concept. I tried to make myself believe that drugs contributed to my happiness, and that it was a way to socialize. Obviously that's not the truth, but I would refuse to probe deeper in order to get the real answer. I did this because I thought I found comfort in doing it. In a way, I did for that brief moment; but that was only because it made me think the world, as I'd come to know it, was still intact. Along with the fear of going into the unknown, I also hadn't come to the understanding that the world only seemed the way it did because I had made it that way. I didn't allow myself to see the truth until I went through a deep process of questioning. I began to ask myself, Does taking drugs really make me happy? I would answer with, Maybe. It was still not a stable answer, so I asked again. If it makes me happy for a couple of hours, but I hate the rest of the week, is that really happiness? No.

Then another one: Is taking drugs stopping me from getting what I really want out of life? I want to achieve, I want a great relationship, and I want to be healthy, so yes, it's preventing me from ever getting those things.

Is it really socializing when *I'm* destroying my whole life in the process? No. What can I do instead? I want to build a better relationship with my family, so I could start hanging out with them.

That's what I did—I started spending more time with my family and I loved it. I applied the same process to my relationships, people I knew, situations I would put myself into, and my job. I questioned everything about my life, and I would always refer back to who I knew I really was. No area of my life weighed up, so I knew I had to start making massive changes. I was now dealing with answers that were going to benefit every step I was taking. Did I go and change everything instantly and my life was just covered with roses? Of course not. The questions kept coming, as they still do today, and as they will until the day I'm gone.

You must remain strong throughout the process, and you can do this by weighing up your answers (your new beliefs), compared with the old lies. It even reaches a point where you should be so disgusted with your old ways that it turns into good frustration.

Physically scream at yourself in the mirror if you feel the urge. I would personally repeat again and again, "That life is destroying you, you're not going back under any circumstances, do you understand? Yes." Then I would repeat, "You're living a better life, you're living a better life," and so forth. Something I highly recommend if you find yourself battling the old habit. Say it with as much **power** as you can, so it feels like you just got a baseball bat and hit those old beliefs out of the park. Also, feel free to tell people about your change. I remember the day I stopped smoking I went and told as many people as I possibly could. I made myself feel extreme pleasure and pride every time I did. I knew that if I began the habit again, everyone would consider me weak, but more important, I would consider myself weak. I reinforced the belief that if I started smoking again I would not be successful in life, and every time it came to mind I began to imagine the chemicals eating away at my body. As a result, the thought would make me nearly physically throw up. It sounds extreme, but when you think of the extreme effects smoking has on your health, it sounds like a pretty good substitute. The question is: How much do you want change?

If I told you that you could change the direction of your life so that it would be more fulfilling right now, would you? If the answer is yes, then you acknowledge that there are areas of your life that you feel you are personally destroying. No one really wants to destroy their own life. Even though they might be doing just that doesn't mean it's what they want . . .

Am I attracting what I want?

When most people question, they don't go deep enough. They deliberately ignore the answers that will serve them.

We are ready to move on to our next set of questions, which will enable us to clearly see what we want. We need to ask questions that will criticize our thinking patterns and the self-beliefs we have continually built, so we can come up with a strategic plan to implement life-changing replacements. If we don't question, we don't get answers, and hence we will not get what we want. The examples below are broad, but as we progress in further tasks they will become more specific.

Do I want to own my own business?

Do I want a girl/guy that I would like to spend my life with?

Do I want to be healthy and fit?

Do I want a better relationship with my family?

Now the next step . . .

> What would I have to do to attract that particular person?
>
> Would they want to be with someone who had unstable answers in the "keep on probing" questions we previously went through?
>
> Do people achieve when they remind themselves how lazy they are?
>
> Can I live a healthy life by flooding my liver with alcohol?
>
> Am I affecting my children or family by smoking, which could cause a terminal illness?
>
> Is the mind-set that I'm approaching life with ever going to allow me to make change in my life?
>
> Are my experiences and feelings ever going to change if I continue to think, speak, and act the same way?
>
> If my answers to some of the questions in the "keep on probing" section were unstable, how does that impact my ability to get the most out of life, and how does it affect the people I love the most?

Don't ask how life is treating you; ask how you are treating life! This shift allows you to see that you are not the victim of an unloved destiny, but equally the creator. You must think of where you are today, and say whether **who you really are** balances out with what situations you are in. Then you must take sole accountability for all your actions that have caused you to be in this situation, as no one thinks, speaks, or ultimately makes decisions for you. The more we blame our situations on others and external events, the more we remove ourselves from ever experiencing the change we so desperately desire. Once we take responsibility, we are able to determine an action plan to obtain what we really want.

Think how it feels as a passenger in a car. You may be on the highway, the car is speeding around bends, and all of a sudden you begin to feel a **lack of control.** The driver doesn't know what you're scared of, because to them they are driving normally. When you live in excuses, it seems as though everyone and everything else is in control of your life. **When you feel that you are not in control, you experience fear.**

If you are not in the cycle of self-growth, then you are taking part in self-destruction. Taking accountability means "owning" your life, and asking, "What can I do differently?"

You must question everything about your life. Massive change comes through deep questioning, so you must refuse to stop asking until an answer aligns with your truth. When you are unsure about something, or feeling stressed and worried, you should question until you get to its core. It's okay to take advice from those who clearly demonstrate an ability to have a positive effect on your life, but don't only believe what everyone else has to say. Many friends and family will feed your victimization because they love you. You ultimately know what is best for you, and you can't escape it. Once you take care of you, everyone else reaps the benefits as well.

> It takes one moment to change your course of direction, one decision that makes you step up to the greatness you deserve, and only one life to make it happen.

QUESTIONS FOR SOLUTIONS

When I tell people that a few years before this book was released, I was smoking dope in backstreets all night with no sense of direction, you could only imagine their reaction. Things can change. I'm not saying overnight, but when you commit to building something positive, it doesn't matter how long it takes. And believe me, it hasn't been a smooth ride since my awakening. That was only the beginning. I remember just as I was about to finish the main content of the book, I had to find an editor. Nearly everyone I spoke to rejected me. They wouldn't even take my money! I was told that I should pick a different career, that the only thing going for the book was its title. When I got off the phone with the last editor, I broke down. I cried. I had just been working on this book for three years, and I had had some of the best editors tell me to give up on it. I left my phone at home and went to the park near my house. I was so emotional that I literally sprinted up and down until I threw up. I didn't know what else to do.

When I got home, something changed again. A new power came over me. No one was going to change what I knew. My writing was my deepest expression, and I knew people would connect with it on that basis. My intention was pure. I didn't want to release a book so I could have some credentials to go and do talks, to say, "I'm an author," or to generate money. None of that. My book was my awakening. It was my soul's message.

I took their criticism positively and restructured the whole book in one week. A few years after they told me I should give up, the book has been a number one best seller on Amazon in the US, Australia, UK, France, Italy, Germany, Canada, and even China in the Spiritual, Motivational, and Mentoring and Coaching categories. I now get thousands of emails from people all around the world telling me their story. It was even picked up by the biggest publisher in the world, Penguin Random House, through their imprint Harmony. That's the edition you are reading right now. In no way am I saying this to toot my own horn; I am saying it in the hope that you will real-ize the enormity of human capacity, which can change your own life.

Never give up on what you truly desire

A lot of people have asked me, "What were the fundamental as-pects of your change?" My answer was that I relentlessly commit-ted to answering the following five questions. Obviously it doesn't stop there, as there is a lot more to changing your life, but these have the power to alter its direction in an instant.

As you go through each of these questions, focus on them indi-vidually for a few moments. Don't rush, but really focus on finding answers. They are life-changing.

1. What drives you every day, and what is the basis of your decisions?

2. What are you going to do today that was different from yesterday, which will ultimately shape who you are tomorrow?

3. What are the life-changing decisions you are commit-ted to making today that will produce the results you so desperately want?

4. What's at least one thing that you can change about your life right now that will prevent a lifetime of pain and generate a never-ending supply of pleasure?

If you don't think you really have a clear indication of what the answers are, think harder and implement some now. You must be specific. For the first question, examples would be: wanting to give your children the best life you possibly can, wanting to be the best person you know how to be, having that feeling of being in charge of your life, contributing to others, having that feeling of success, feeling healthy and fit, holding up that trophy, and many more.

Those **feelings must drive you, because emotion precedes action.** If you refer back to those feelings, you will soon get a whole different range of emotions on which to base your decisions.

This is the fifth question where great solutions are based:

5. How can I . . .

- be healthy and fit?

- attract that person of my dreams?

- get that **rush** in life?

- experience different emotions?

- push myself that extra mile?

- get that car?

- take control over my life?

When the question "How can I . . . ?" is asked, it allows us to broaden our options. Inspiration is noticed everywhere, even in places that would once seem to be normal daily activities, like going for a walk, shopping at the mall, or driving to work. In an amazing way, signs begin jumping out everywhere. It doesn't mean they were never there, but now **your mind is subject to taking notice of them.** You have enlarged the picture frame, so it increases the space for more pictures. The solutions may not be perfect instantly, but by asking this question, you will continue to come up with diverse answers.

All successful people dedicate their life to finding solutions. This one question allows for responses that will benefit your current situation, rather than asking, "Why can't I . . . ?"—a question that continually reaffirms to yourself that you can't create the life you desire. "How can I . . . ?" forces you to come up with answers that will drive you.

Let's now take a step into the "zone" that most of us find ourselves in, especially after a deep process of questioning. Being able to shift our mind-set in a heartbeat when in this zone is essential for creating a life worth dreaming about . . .

2

Uncomfortable in the "Comfort Zone"

"Somewhere in the archives of crudest instinct is
recorded the truth that it is better to be endangered
and free than captive and comfortable."

—TOM ROBBINS

Are you really comfortable where you are in life, or are you just settling because you don't believe you can get anything better? Most
people I have met try to display that they are comfortable, yet once
they really open up it seems there are many things that they wish
they could achieve or attain. It's then evident that they are quite
uncomfortable. Every time someone asked me how I was, I would
reply with the words "not bad" or "okay." It wasn't until I had the
feeling of being great that I realized that a "not bad" life just isn't
good enough. Life is made up of decisions we make, and accepting
a "not bad" or even "okay" life is the case for most. People rarely
admit when they aren't doing too well and believe that they can
take cover behind lying to others and themselves. There is one fact
you have to acknowledge: **You can't run and hide from yourself,
because everywhere you go, there you are.**

The harsh reality is that most people aren't truly happy with
where they are in life. They submit to beliefs that have made them
feel that whatever they are is the most they can be, and they accept

a life that never fulfills them. It's quite upsetting because I know that exact feeling, and I also know how it feels to be on the other side. This is one of the main reasons for dedicating my life to sharing this message. The first thing I would say is that facing it, rather than running, is the first step toward change. The questions we asked in the last chapter are a great start. They all lead us to a point of acknowledgment. We seem to be blind to the powerful part of that word, "acknowledgment." We can have all the knowledge in the world, have ten university degrees, have traveled the globe, or know how to speak five different languages, but if we don't have true knowledge of ourselves, we will never create the life we want.

Coming to realizations about where you are in life due to past events, decisions you are making now, and how it can affect what you create next is the greatest knowledge you can obtain. It allows you to truly come to the understanding that your life has always been controlled by you. Taking accountability for the state you find yourself in will allow you to make the changes needed to drive your life to a new level.

WHAT'S WRONG?

Does making mistakes along the way mean you are back to where you started? The intelligent answer is no, but many people fall into the trap of giving up when they've made a mistake. So why do so many people become disheartened on their journey to create an extraordinary life? They rarely look at the progress they've made, but will always notice what's wrong.

As you progress through your self-discovery, you will realize that rather than only seeing some beliefs and decisions as wrong, they actually promote massive progress. Your beliefs advance from one another and assist one another in growing. They all have purpose.

No matter how badly you think you screwed something up, you can't change it, but you can learn from it. And if you're judging yourself for doing something "wrong," then logically you're acknowledging that you can do it differently next time. You're learning to reason with yourself and becoming more self-aware. The more you ignore and disregard your ability to reason with yourself, the more energy you're putting toward a life you don't want to live. It's up to you to learn along the journey, and that's what we're all on, a journey of self-growth. No one is going to just come along and drop fulfillment into your lap. If that were the case, the great life would be a lot easier to achieve.

Setbacks are still steps forward on your journey, if you look hard enough. They have an important role to play. In order for you to see your actions as "negative," you must be able to identify the flip side. You can take action to get back on the right path and don't have to submit to the belief that it's just the way it is. This awareness will allow you to put a **strategy** in place to eliminate negative thoughts that are continually having a detrimental effect in your life. Another way of looking at negativity is that it reminds you that you are making progress. Most people surrender to negative perceptions subconsciously, but by being consciously aware that a thought is negative, you are becoming more emotionally intelligent. You are using your mind to distinguish and correct, rather than just accept! Instead of beating yourself up over thinking or acting negatively, view these experiences as a chance to learn and implement change.

THE LOGIC IN UNLOGIC

You've heard it all before: the logical and illogical sides of the brain. Becoming aware of and able to compare the two is your greatest asset to strengthen your success. You should use the logical side of your brain as your defense mechanism against those decisions that are leading you toward feelings that don't really fulfill you. It will prevent you from being in situations where you question the same thing a hundred times over, even though you are already aware of the answer that is beneficial. You will recognize in time that it will be hard not to make a decision without assessing it and finding answers that spur growth. Choosing your true side of logic will become quite natural.

I once found myself in a situation where I was helping out someone who was having a reaction to drugs that caused him to believe he had no control over himself. I went over to his apartment to talk through his feelings with him and try to calm him down the best way I knew how. He was still at the height of the drug's effects, so I knew I had to take massive action. I asked him if he needed some fresh air. He told me that he would probably do something very stupid and jump off the balcony.

Knowing that this battle of control was going on in his mind, I took a new approach. I began to explain that he just proved to me that he was much better and was making progress. Being confused and "rushing" at the same time, he was convinced he was still at his worst. I said that if he had no control over himself then he wouldn't have told me he would jump off the balcony; he would have just done it. That by being aware that he might do something "stupid," he logically understood he had a choice, and was therefore far more in control than he believed. It worked wonders, and within minutes he started to snap out of it. By being able to compare the logical side with the illogical, he had control over the way he felt and the decisions he was going to make.

He thanked me later and said that he had felt he had no control over what was happening, and just by becoming aware that he did, he started to fight that belief. His control became evident to him.

I would like to talk about how this could be relevant to everyday life, if you haven't already realized it. We make ourselves believe we have no control over the way we feel or what decisions we make, quick to throw the blame on someone or something else. We will blame it all on people around us, certain situations, or even drugs! Are they really the challenge, or is it just that you are unaware that you have always been in full control of your own emotional state? We choose to let people and situations take our happiness. We willingly submit and hand it over to them. Realistically, a situation just is, which means it's up for whatever you wish to attach to it. That's why so many people can have completely different views on exactly the same situation. We must look at it intelligently and let our initial knee-jerk reaction and common sense be good guides. We know the truth immediately, yet sometimes we are good at talking ourselves out of it. The control has always been there for your life—sometimes you just choose not to use it.

Differentiate between right and wrong, negative and positive, and the logical and illogical, and then use it to your benefit. In order to grow, you must take action based on your knowledge. If you refuse to, you are eventually forced to reach a . . .

POINT OF AWARENESS (POA)

"Don't judge each day by the harvest you reap
but by the seeds you plant."

—ROBERT LOUIS STEVENSON

We have all reached points in life where it felt as if there was nowhere to turn. Some of us have even hit points where our whole life, not just one aspect, is distorted. It then seems as if we are truly lost on this journey we call life. It's a feeling of hopelessness, of desperation, and of no sense of direction. If you are at this point in your life in one or all areas, I would like to explain that you are actually at a great spot! Yes, that's right, a great spot. I know you're probably swearing at the book and thinking I'm a madman, but just hear this out.

You are on a journey and you have been walking for days. Along the way you have felt a sense of unfamiliarity, yet you have continued to walk anyway. You're walking along singing, and all of a sudden you STOP! It hits you. You finally realize that you have been traveling a different path than you meant to this whole time. A **point of awareness** has just shown itself. Thoughts start rushing through your mind, questions begin to appear, and panic takes over your emotional state. Then you snap out of it and recognize that you'd better pull yourself together. If you don't think about your previous steps as a means to gather knowledge to get back on track, then you will sit there paralyzed by your thoughts and die of thirst.

At this point, you are actually in a good place, because **if you never had that feeling of being lost, who knows where you would have ended up.** Even when you look back at those previous steps, you stop cursing yourself for taking them, because you know it's just making things worse. You are now going to start using the information you obtained from those past steps to help yourself back on your intended path. And, more important, to arrive at that desired destination.

> "When one door closes, another opens; but we often
> look so long and so regretfully upon the closed door
> that we do not see the one which has opened for us."
>
> —ALEXANDER GRAHAM BELL

I would like to illustrate using a graph, to visually express this as much as I can.

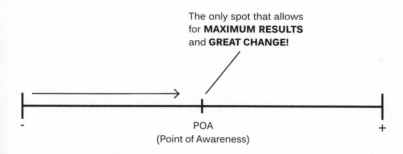

When you feel like you are declining in life, it may just be the complete opposite. You have actually advanced to a stage where you recognize how you must change in order to grow. Most people in society call a point of awareness "rock bottom." I refrain from using that metaphor because to me it is false. I believe you have actually gone up at these points, because without them you wouldn't make the crucial decisions that change your life forever. It's as if you have prevented yourself from going deeper into your confusion and pain. Often the most valuable information can be gathered from times that seem the most hopeless or distressing. I guess it's some greater force telling us that we need to wake up. A point of awareness forces you to reassess every step you took. And if you learn from this experience, it also reminds you to carefully assess future steps that are taken.

Why is it that people usually find true direction in life at a time that seems the most confusing? My opinion is that when all roads seem to be blocked, there is only one way, and that is through!

3

The Certainty of Appreciation

"There was once a man who was complaining about
only having one pair of shoes,
until he met a man with only one leg."

—MY GRANDFATHER

DON'T HATE, APPRECIATE!

In a hotel elevator in Paris, I was faced with a question that warranted an immediate answer. I was smiling from ear to ear thinking about life. I was appreciating the fact that I was in Paris, but, more important, that I had discovered my power as a human being. I was having such an overwhelming moment of appreciation that I forgot someone was in the elevator with me, a woman. She was probably in her mid-thirties and was dressed quite nicely. She turned to me and said, "Why are you so happy?" as if it was a rare sight. And I guess it is quite rare. Without hesitation, I said the first thing that came to mind: "Because I'm alive." Looking at me like I was from outer space, she stormed off when the elevator doors opened, completely irritated. I just wondered how her day, or her life, would play out with that attitude. I had sympathy for her. I doubted that she actually knew how much power she had in changing her resentment toward life. I was curious to know whether she knew how her attitude was hurting her. I didn't know anything else about her life but it still struck me as pretty sad, especially since I was reminded of a time when I felt similarly to her . . .

There was a period along my journey, definitely the point of no return, when I felt a sense of emptiness. I hadn't had that feeling in such a long time, and I must admit a fear came over me. At that point, I was teaching people about gaining fulfillment and making real positive change, yet here I was at another point of confusion. I guess I forgot to acknowledge that I was still human; yet even more important, I recognized that I had left a major hole in my daily routine. I was so caught up in getting this book finished, coaching, designing verbal programs, and helping others, that I forgot to stand still and really get into a **state of appreciation.** Anyone could have seen what was wrong with my day-to-day life, but it totally flew over my head. I even had feelings of fear before I would go and talk to someone about this stuff, like the words weren't going to come out right. I thought that I was losing my touch in writing, and everything seemed distorted. I decided that day that another would not start unless I began with reading my gratitude list, which was the first page I had ever written on my journey. That day, crying in my room, I had pulled out a piece of paper. Still crying, I rushed to write down everything that I was grateful for in my life. It has never been rewritten and I still read that rough copy today. It changed my whole life, and even now it's the only thing that can get me into a state of really embracing life's greatness. It's my true inspiration.

I then realized that this experience was just another lesson learned and a means to help me teach others about its absolute importance. I was already teaching people to appreciate and create gratitude lists, but this single event allowed me to discover the immense impact gratitude has on one's life. Getting into a state of appreciation is absolutely crucial to our happiness, regardless of how advanced we may think we are.

It doesn't matter what situation you are in, consciously summoning deep gratitude will enhance the quality of your life. We get so caught up with things that we want, experiences we have had, the hustle and bustle of working life, raising children, or getting our finances on track, that we neglect to be grateful for what we have. How can we ever be happy if we are not content with who we are and appreciative of the only thing that is ever real, right now? I mean, even if we go and make a million dollars, and then want another million, then another, we are still at that point of emptiness and unfulfillment. It's the same story with every area of our life. If we don't take a moment to really appreciate the most important things, then we are never going to be happy. It's not wrong to keep wanting—we are human, after all—but we can't forget the feeling that fulfills us: gratitude. The day I realized I had been leaving it out, I came up with an adage that I now repeat every morning: **A wise man never dwells on what he *doesn't* have. He remains in constant appreciation of what he has already, while being in pursuit of what he wants.**

It's the same with everything: If we don't use it, we lose it. The challenge is that most don't remind themselves how to love life, so they forget. Instead they continually practice how to hate it, so they get damn good at that!

> *Time is our most precious commodity. If you're not using it wisely, you're wasting it ignorantly.*

The only thing that can ever fulfill us is gratitude—acknowledging the beauty of what we have and who we really are. When I ask people what they think the most important things are in life, I usually hear the same answers. Family, friends, faith, and even being alive all make the top of the list. Would you agree? **The most important things in life deserve nothing less than constant reminders.**

Then why don't we remind ourselves? If we do not make a daily conscious effort to recognize these things, the truth is, we will search around in the dark looking for a happiness that has been with us our whole life. Ignoring what you already have is the major factor I see in unhappiness. I urge you to ask and answer this question with sincerity . . .

IN YOUR LIFE, WHAT MEANS THE MOST TO YOU?

Write a list. Whatever makes the list is a priority, so treat it that way, and make reading the list a part of your daily routine. I'll explain in greater detail how to put this list together on page 36.

> "As we express our gratitude, we must never forget
> that the highest appreciation is not to utter words,
> but to live by them."
>
> —JOHN FITZGERALD KENNEDY

Appreciation is truly the ultimate feeling, as it is the only thing that knocks down the body of ego. How many times have you wanted to tell someone whom you really love how much you appreciate everything they have ever done for you? I bet you've wanted to express your appreciation far more often than you have done it. The reason is our body of ego stands in the way. This one guy taunted me, saying he didn't have a body of ego, and I replied that he had just demonstrated it. We all have it—if we didn't, we wouldn't be human. We so often feel that great love and just wish we knew how to share it without being embarrassed. When you are in a state of appreciation, it really trains you to express that love, which means you in turn receive it. The feeling, invisible to our eyes, is euphoric. It is feeling, and feeling is power!

This simple quality of life is also crucial for success. It allows us to utilize our time efficiently and recognize every step we take. We are grateful for the time we have now, so it prevents us from just waiting around and procrastinating. We take full responsibility for our actions in the present, which allows us to really embrace our decisions as an opportunity for growth. More important, we begin to praise ourselves for who we really are, and it builds the faith and respect within us to be in pursuit of what we want. It aligns us with our friend fear, and it promotes us to work to our peak with a broadened mind. **It truly helps us enjoy the process of success** because we go in with the attitude of "nothing to lose, everything to gain." Courage soon follows.

For most, there are barriers that restrict them from discovering their slumbering power. Appreciation helps break down those psychological and emotional walls. It allows you to be more vibrant, loving, and happy—all those other qualities that are crucial for a successful life. If you begin to love life, you embrace it for the beauty and mystery it is, and that's what creates empowering energy. **Appreciation is the key to letting your spirit take over your life.** By adding such a simple ritual to your daily life, you will create a world of difference. **Success without appreciation is no success at all!**

> "Appreciation is a wonderful thing: It makes what is excellent in others belong to us as well."
>
> —VOLTAIRE

STATE OF APPRECIATION (SOA)

> "To get up each morning with the resolve to be happy . . . is to set our own conditions to the events of each day. To do this is to condition circumstances instead of being conditioned by them."
>
> —RALPH WALDO TRINE

You can only imagine what a difference it will make every day to go through a list of things that you appreciate in the morning. Most wake up in the morning complaining, feet dragging halfway across the room. They have two coffees and still seem to be tired. I used to sulk so much in the morning that at times I came to tears.

I once had someone say to me, "The reason I complain all the time is because crap keeps happening in my life." I turned to him and said, "The truth is, the reason crap keeps happening in your life is because you don't stop complaining." **When we complain, we become the victim. When we are the victim, we don't get what we want in life, we get more of what we don't want.**

The energy that you carry from that dismal beginning will surely lead to you having a miserable day. In all honesty, how do you think the day is going to turn out? What hope are you giving it to improve, and what incentive is there for life to give back if you disrespect it before you have even started your day? In order to make your day fulfilling, it is imperative that you begin by shifting your focus to the great things in life. If you do this for a few days, giving up the practice of appreciation will not be an option, because the results are just too outstanding. You should also try to maintain that mood as much as you can, but even after a week or so you will see that mood starting to become your nature. If you appreciate things, people around you will pick up that attitude as well. But to start, I'm asking you to allocate time first thing in the morning to get into a "state," because that's what conditions you.

When you appreciate something, you don't abuse it.
Learn to appreciate all that's life.

I once received an email from a woman with three children who was living overseas. She explained that she was suffering from depression. I find it amazing how people self-diagnose. People just walk around saying they are depressed as soon as something doesn't go their way for that moment. It's like, "I missed out on buying that jacket, I'm so depressed," or, "I'm so depressed, I missed going out with my friends on the weekend." People tag uncertainties in life to make something seem far worse than it actually is. How many people do you know who have taken medication for anxiety, depression, and intense nerves, but still have the same troubles? They pop those pills for years to no avail, but amazingly, what I have seen from my own experience is that as soon as people become aware of their ability to recondition their own state, they are able to heal themselves.

Branding an emotional or mental state separates you from having full control over it. And by continuing to tell people that you have "depression," you will never be able to take control over your life. I'm not saying that some people aren't suffering from mental illness, but I like to keep the faith that many of us can overcome difficult emotional or mental states with the right tools, not by taking a pill every time we feel sad. We can continue to suppress issues with a pill, but that's exactly what it does: suppress. True healing means you must get to the source, and that is within. It's all about healing, not suppression.

Anyway, I decided to coach this particular woman through Skype. When we got on our video call, I was met by a woman who was choked up from crying and basically having a meltdown. I immediately began making the weirdest noises known to mankind. I went from high-pitched to deep-voiced, then back to screeching, all in around ten seconds. It truly sounded like a language spoken by aliens with Tourette syndrome. She stopped crying, began laughing, and said, "What the hell are you doing?" I replied, "Shifting your mood. Now let's start." It was that easy!

I worked with her on an appreciation list. Three weeks later, I received another email telling me that the last week was the best one she had had in two and a half years. Lately she has told me that she is flying high again. The appreciation list has also been very effective for those who are worrying about which direction to take in life, to step up to the next level, to heal relationships and really every area of life. It's very important that you follow the steps shared in the next section to create your list. This is how I did mine, and it has been extremely effective for those that I have helped. This exercise is crucial.

Great emotions produce a great life. You have the option of generating them whenever you like. You must allocate **time to shine!**

ALLOCATE YOUR TIME TO SHINE

If you want to have an extraordinary life, you must be addicted to life.

Your **time to shine** is going to determine how your destiny is shaped. It is to be done in the morning, preferably for an hour. If you say you don't have the time, I have a great solution: Wake up earlier! An hour ritual consists of getting into an SOA (state of appreciation) as well as creating perfect scenarios in your mind of what you want your life to be (state of certainty). You must set up an attitude that will last through the whole day. If you won't spare an hour to vastly improve the quality of your life, then at least create half that time. Even fifteen minutes if you must, but I know you can create more time if you are committed to it. Here's an example of my personal ritual for getting into a state of appreciation. After that, you'll move on to creating your own.

SOA

Thank you for being a loving person; thank you for your great gifts and power that reign within me; thank you for being respectful; thank you for having a sense of humor; thank you for being kindhearted.

THEN: Thank you for the hands I have to write with; thank you for the legs I have to walk with; thank you for this beautiful world and the energy that flows through it; but above all, thank you for me still breathing and giving me the opportunity of life, to persist again and again, when so many others have gone before me.

We must always start with the basics, as that's what really fulfills us. If a woman came up and freely gave you, and another million people, $10,000 each, would you make the conscious effort to say thank you? Just because she gave it to a mass of people, does it take away the magnitude of the single act she performed for you? The generous act still warrants gratitude nonetheless, correct?

Now, how do you believe your right arm weighs up against the value of $10,000? Just because most others, although not all, have a right arm as well, does it take away the importance of such a gift? If you would say thank you for receiving $10,000 and are able to clearly recognize that your arm is worth far more than that, why don't you say thank you for it? It makes no sense! We have been given so many gifts that we should value above all else, but we deliberately ignore them on a daily basis. As long as we do not value these and we take the most important things in life for granted, we will never be fulfilled.

Next, I would be thankful for things that are outside of me. Thank you for the food I have to eat; thank you for shelter, for clothes. Thank you for my loving family and friends; thank you for the experiences I have had, as they have allowed me to grow and make everlasting change.

I personally thank God for all these things, and I say each one with as much intensity as I can. I really get myself into a state. That means using my body as well. If you do not want to say thank you to God, then say thank you to something higher than yourself, because something has given you all these gifts, the qualities of which lie within you, and that's what makes you great.

Last, I would be appreciative of . . . we will add this later in the book.

STATE OF CERTAINTY (SOC)

While taking a shower, eating breakfast, and getting dressed, I replay perfect scenarios in my mind. I imagine myself happy and having a productive day working toward my goals. While listening to upbeat music on my iPod, I walk around the house in a constant state of envisioning how I want my day to play out. At times I even dance around the kitchen while making my breakfast. Yes, in the morning! I do anything that sends my momentum through the roof.

Music has the ability to shift our state immediately, so use it to your advantage. Listen to upbeat music or anything that gets you going. Humans have a strong emotional attachment to great tunes, so music is our ticket through most times. And, yes, I do consider myself a little crazy for doing this ritual first thing in the morning, but who isn't branded crazy on the road of success? It's always impossible until someone does it, right?

I also think about how I am going to be the best person I know how to be—not just when meeting people, but to myself. This form of conditioning can be done while performing your normal morning activities. Starting off with a state of appreciation is a must if you want a great life, so let there be no exception to that.

A close friend with over a hundred retail stores under the umbrella of his franchise informed me that he would wake up in the morning doing bicycle kicks before he even got out of bed. He would then get up and sing around the house, waking his kids and wife in the process. Let's just say they weren't as enthusiastic as him when the story was being told. If you believe successful people drag their way through the morning, then dream again. While everyone else is having three coffees, two energy drinks, and sleepwalking to work, they are up and ready to go. Getting into a state of appreciation and a state of certainty at the beginning of your day is the quickest way to be inspired and create a lifetime of everlasting energy.

To recap, here are two steps to putting together your statement of appreciation for your morning ritual.

TASK

1. **Inner:** We must write down what we appreciate about ourselves. Here's a great one to get you started—the eyes that you have to read this. Also, be thankful for all the qualities you know you have access to, like love, patience, **appreciation,** respect, intelligence, trust, courage, faith, and so on.

2. **Outer:** List those things that are external but still have meaning and contribute to your life. It could be family members, a car, or shelter. Whatever it is, it's helping you live your life, so be appreciative and take nothing for granted. Also appreciate things in nature and the world, because I don't know if you have realized, but they are actually keeping you alive. You drink water, breathe air, eat fruit. It's okay, this doesn't mean you are a "greenie" or a "hippie"; you are just opening up your eyes.

3. ____?_____ : Stick to appreciating the first two now, and we will get to the third as we go along.

I advise that you write down at least five answers for each, and if you have any trouble, look at my personal list to get ideas. It could even be the same for "Inner" and "Outer." After you have written down your list in that order, you are ready to start.

Always begin by saying, **"Thank you for being alive."** Also end with repeating, **"Right now I'm alive,"** with absolute conviction until you feel pumped. This task in the morning is conditioning yourself to change your state in an instant; a must if you want an extraordinary life. In order to be abundantly happy, you must learn to ignite your own empowering emotions. It is important that you **feel the significance** of what you are appreciating and totally embrace it. Feel those qualities within you, the house that shelters you, or the hug from your loved one. **FFF (full focus on feeling)** raises hidden and fulfilling emotions, which is the key to this exercise.

This only takes around five to ten minutes to read while stationary, so if you say you don't have the time to read it, are you really being true to yourself? The rest of your time to shine can be done while getting ready. If you don't have enough time, stop watching so much TV!

By continually practicing this exercise alone and making it a ritual before starting your day, your life will be enhanced radically. Think of the difference when starting off your day with this rather than hating the world for having to wake up. **Demanding a fulfilling state also allows you to prove to yourself that you choose your own emotions.** Allocating this time to shine will condition your nervous system to experience fulfillment on a regular basis.

You now have enough information to go out on your own for **three consecutive days** and practice these tasks. It's part of the program in this book, so if you don't do it, then you should really consider passing the book on to someone else. We have all been given the keys to life; some just refuse to open the doors. I know you are reading this book to make real change in your life, so please give yourself this opportunity. Really successful people do what everyone else brands as stupid, which is why they are so different. You are to write your SOA list in the order that was given, read it for the next three mornings, and practice maintaining that mood during the day. This is it: discovering the balance between fulfillment and the drive to achieve. Remember, the change starts with you. Once that begins to happen, everything else starts to change with it. Those three days before reading on are a **must.**

And if you really want a powerful start to your day, write this on a big piece of paper or somewhere that is highly visible in the morning . . .

Whatever I do today, I will commit to doing it with love and in happiness. As challenging as it may be, I will not allow anything to overpower my great emotions, and I will get through it.

Only those few who take action get the results that everyone else dreams about.

Stop, go back. You are not to read on until this task is completed. These tasks are designed to properly train your mind and ease you into the process as everyone else who gained abundance in their life has done. Not reading on just yet is also a great test of patience—a quality that is necessary to achieve what you set out for. Take action on this, or else you learn nothing. Appreciate on a daily basis and create that **time to shine.**

4

What You Believe, You Create

The blueprint of our greatness and true calling in life is hidden under the collage of social beliefs that become self-beliefs. They include fear, doubt, hate, and all other limitations that restrict us from discovering our true passion. Unwrap the paper and you will find a gift!

WHAT ARE BELIEFS?

I came across a story a while back about two brothers who were both raised by the same abusive, alcoholic father. Years down the track, one brother had a loving family, was extremely wealthy, and enjoyed his life. The other brother turned out to be an alcoholic and was serving time in jail.

A university researcher became aware of the situation and decided to interview the two brothers. They were in different rooms, but he asked them both the same question: "With an abusive and alcoholic father, why did you turn out the way you did?" Surprisingly, they both replied with the exact same answer: "With a father like that, how else did you expect me to turn out?" Both men had the same biography, but they created different beliefs around their experiences. One brother saw it as an opportunity to inspire him into action; the other saw himself as a victim and paid the price.

Regardless of what events take place, it is always our choice what meaning we give to them. The current beliefs we choose to live by create or contribute to all of the experiences we have. Regardless of what area of life it is, they can be the basis for change or the reason we seem motionless. What exactly are beliefs? Usually they are nothing more than opinions that have been fed to us by other people, a chosen perception built from experience, and thoughts that have been repeated to you or that you have repeated to yourself.

We hear things on the radio, see them on TV, and learn through friends and family. Do we ever sit back and think about the source from which information stems? Most things are just one individual's opinion, and we know there are a lot of those flying around. It's crucial that we probe our beliefs to get to the truth. One guy I know is a great example of how other people's beliefs and opinions can affect you to the point where they become self-beliefs. He is a great, private poet and doesn't usually share his work. I've had the opportunity to read some of his poems, and I was impressed. One day, he shared a poem with a coworker only to have his poems and possible future life path ridiculed. He told me he didn't write anything else for one whole year; that person's opinion burrowed so deeply within him that he went blank every time he tried to write. He began to believe that his work wasn't good and that he would never be able to turn it into a career.

I spoke to him for a while and we dug deep until he finally realized that he could write. He had done it in the past, so there was no reasonable explanation as to why he couldn't again. All we had to do was really analyze why he was struggling to do it and direct all his energy to how he could.

He started again by writing one paragraph to prove it to himself. If everyone based their motivation on critics, there would be no such thing as success!

There are two kinds of critics. One is a coward who gains his glory by attacking things he never had the courage to do. The other is courageous enough to tell you that cowards never make it. Learn to utilize both of them.

How often do we let our limiting beliefs prevent us from taking action in our life? Funnily enough, we even let other people's limiting beliefs hold us back. We associate feelings of pleasure or pain with every belief we have, and that's what ultimately shapes our destiny. The actions we take toward life every day are also the result of our beliefs. Here are some common life-restricting beliefs that I have been guilty of having in the past:

I can't be as great as those achievers.

I can't change.

Every girl/guy is the same.

Life is a misery.

All people are rude.

I've got serious bad luck.

No one would want me.

It's too late.

I'm too young/old.

I'm useless.

And the list goes on.

I'm sure we are all aware that there are times when we have believed something that turned out to be very far from the truth. Have you ever listened to verbal abuse about another individual?

We might have a friend or work colleague who slanders another person because of an experience they have had with them. We seem to get sucked in at times and absorb a belief that this person is bad. We join the party of verbal abuse and create scenarios in our mind that aren't even real. We say things like, "Just wait and see if she does that to me, I'll fix her right up." The whole situation is quite ridiculous. How many times have you met that same individual and they turn out to be one of the nicest people you have met? Suddenly they seem fantastic. You may even go to the extent of defending them against things you once believed. The truth is that we have the power to make ourselves believe anything we want. This isn't just a figure of speech; there are scientific findings backing this up. Those beliefs become what we know as our reality.

BUILDING BELIEFS

We have found out that a belief is nothing more than an idea or chosen perception that is repeated. We create a specific idea of what we think an experience means (for example, we might create a belief that we are unlovable in the aftermath of a breakup). We then mentally, verbally, and physically act accordingly. We stick to one perception and repeat it many times, until we build our own beliefs around it. Our vocabulary and body language even align with the belief systems we have built. Imagine someone in a relationship in which their partner habitually disrespects them. While telling others about the situation, they use negative language, frown, and shake their head in disgust. By now it has tainted their trust in relationships altogether. The next time they see a happy couple smooching in the park, they follow exactly the same pattern. Realistically, it's just a loving couple, but to this person it represents heartache.

Maybe you have heard that we cannot deliberately or consciously build beliefs; that is a lie. I know there have been things in your life that you once thought you couldn't do. Once you shifted all your focus and resources to doing it, you discovered you were more than capable. You may not have believed you could run that distance, leave that person, build a relationship, make that much money, get past that fear, or break that habit. Eventually you built up enough emotional momentum to enforce a whole set of new beliefs. When you made yourself believe that you could, you did it with conviction.

All the beliefs that are currently shaping your life have been built by you. That means you have the power to create and build new beliefs that will change your life forever. The mysterious thing is that it actually doesn't take long at all. In order to speed up the process, you must become forceful and intense with your new beliefs. For example, when you say, "I can't do that" or "That's impossible," you must immediately command a physical and verbal alternative. Build up your state of mind and demand with all your power that you take control. Go through your day repeating, "I can do it, I can do it, I can do it," and "Nothing is impossible, nothing is impossible."

When I was doing tae kwon do, we had to scream during a high-intensity punch or kick to get the most out of it. Raising your voice when enforcing new beliefs puts your whole being into a different state. I have forcefully built every belief I now have about my life and success. They were not the result of one experience, nor did they magically appear strong and certain. I knew that I had to purposely build them if I wanted to take charge of my life.

I would repeat the new things I wanted to believe with so much emotional power that I gave my old self no real choice but to surrender. **The more you repeat it, the more you believe it!**

It is very important to understand that we create whatever we want to believe. It is also essential that we align our mental, verbal, and physical actions to build a new belief. The strongest way to build these beliefs is to **acknowledge what you're doing, when you're doing it.** If it is patience you are demonstrating when waiting in traffic, don't just sit there and take it for granted. Acknowledge that you are being patient right now and be proud of it. This goes for every area of our life and is an extremely strong tool in determining who we are becoming.

Reinforcement is the number one key to building and strengthening beliefs. All successful people know that **beliefs are the foreground of creating anything in their life.**

TASK

Answer the following question and come up with as many empowering beliefs as you can think of.

What would I have to believe in order to get what I want? Example: I want to be healthy and fit.

NEW BELIEF: I would have to believe that I will never get what I want in life unless I commit to living a healthy lifestyle. I would have to believe that I would never get that person I dream of. I would have to believe that my health is the most important thing in my life. Without respecting my body, I will never respect my life.

Be creative, as you are the one who picks your beliefs. These beliefs are writing your experience.

Once you write down all the beliefs that you desire, use reinforcement as much as you can. Repeat them throughout your day and in the face of experience. Overpower your old, limiting beliefs, and you will see that after a while they will diminish and the new ones will get stronger. **What you think, you believe. What you believe, you create.**

ABSOLUTE BELIEF SYSTEM (ABS)

We must also build what I call an **ABS (absolute belief system)** in order to succeed at a level that most of the world would deem unrealistic. Is there anything in the world that man has created that someone else wouldn't have called unrealistic before its existence? If you take a good look around, you will notice that most people would have perceived every creation to be impossible before it was created. Who would have ever thought that we would be able to talk to someone halfway across the world with a gadget the size of our hand? Self-taught engineer Dr. Percy Spencer invented the microwave, and you can just imagine trying to tell people three hundred years ago that we were going to cook food with no fire. We have flown to the moon and back, can see other people who are thousands of miles away as if they are right in front of us, and can check local movie times through wireless internet. I was already amazed with wired internet, and then they had to go and bamboozle me and make it wireless!

Take a look at anything around you right now and you will see that it had to have started as a mental picture in someone's mind. Do you realize how fascinating, amazing, and mysterious it is to see something in your mind, then create it to be right in front of you? How is this possible? A simple explanation would be that it began as a vision followed by a belief system around it. Those beliefs resulted in the vision becoming a reality in the mind, which then caused it to come into existence through appropriate action. Trying to ultimately explain this phenomenon is impossible. It is one of the mysteries of life. And just because we don't fully understand it, it doesn't mean that it's not our gift to put it into practice every day.

Here is a strategy and simple experiment that might help you out . . .

1. **CONCEPT:** Close your eyes and visualize holding a piece of paper in front of your face with your name written on it. Do this for ten seconds. See the letters and feel the paper, but only in your mind. This is only a mental vision, so make sure you do nothing physically.

2. **ACTION:** Did you see that paper with your name on it? Now, get out a piece of paper and a pen, and physically write your name on it.

3. **CREATION:** Hold it in front of your face. It's real; touch it. Do you now see that you actually just created that? Where was it before you were able to touch it? It was just a figment of your imagination, right? You just brought something that was only in your mind into reality. You saw the future, took action, and created it!

For a moment, comprehend the magnitude this capability can have on your life.

I want you to think back to a time when you have really felt something, visualized over it, and it has come about. It may have been a new car, an outfit, or a holiday. I was coaching this young girl who wasn't grasping just how powerful visualization actually is. I went over to her house one day to see a black BMW convertible parked in the driveway. As soon as she answered the door, she didn't hesitate to show it off. When we sat down, I asked how long she had wanted that car. After finding out it was about a year, I asked how many times she drifted off dreaming about driving it, hair in the wind, friends by her side, and music playing. I then asked how many times she searched for that car on the internet and experienced emotions as if she already had it.

She burst out laughing and said, "Yes, yes, it almost became an obsession." She explained that she made herself want that car so much and dreamed about it so much that when the thought of not getting it came to mind, she would block it out and reassure herself that she would. I then made her realize the absolute power she had in bringing something that was only ever in her mind into reality. It took the BMW example for this young girl to finally understand. I explained that she is able to do that with every part of her life, and since then she has.

Practice this strategy with anything that you want, and you will realize that you have been creating your whole life. People ask me, "How do I create things in my life like others?" I explain that they have always been doing it; the difference is that they are not aware of what they are creating. If you want to create something large, you might have to take more action. Going back to the paper experiment, if there wasn't a piece of paper right next to you, you would have had to get one. Everything comes with its challenges, but if you are committed to making your vision real, you will find a way through or around the obstacles. **This world is a place of endless possibilities,** and it's not until you acknowledge that you have always had the power to create that you finally realize anything is possible when you believe it is. You can actually create anything you desire; the only one stopping you is you.

If you think of something, see the end result, and believe it will work, then it can. Most of the time people will talk themselves out of it or convince themselves why it won't work. This is usually due to other people's opinions or letting the idea slip away before it can be reinforced. Successful people talk themselves into it and give many reasons why it will work. They focus on how they can do it and repeat it many times with so much conviction that it becomes a belief that consumes their life. They don't rely on others to build their belief; they know that when they believe it enough, others will follow.

Even when we buy a car, it's highly recommended that it be equipped with antilock brakes. Having an antilock braking system (ABS) in a car prevents the wheels from locking up or ceasing to rotate while braking. It also allows you to steer the car in the direction that you want in an emergency braking situation. When we have an ABS (absolute belief system) in life, we don't just sit there and wonder all day, we get those wheels rotating and acting. We view everything as a realistic possibility, and that's what causes us to steer our life in the direction we want. But there are particular beliefs that prevent us from creating such a system.

CONFLICTING BELIEFS

Why is it that sometimes we know exactly what we want, have a plan, but for some reason don't take the appropriate action? I couldn't count how many times I have heard someone say, "I just don't know what's holding me back." It seems that when we think of an empowering direction or something that will satisfy our wants, we automatically shift our focus to what we must sacrifice to get it. Rarely do we remain focused on what we are actually gaining, hence many fall back into the trap of procrastination.

When in pursuit of what you want, if you think of sacrifice, it makes it a lot harder to focus on the journey ahead.

When you think of the sacrifices, everything seems too hard. Do yourself a favor; focus on what you are gaining.

This topic also asks the question, "Are we really losing when in pursuit of what we want?" If you remain focused on the benefits, it becomes apparent that you actually sacrifice nothing. But on so many occasions we neglect this aspect of success and will submit to the weaker approach. We do this because it seems easier at the time to do what we have always done. We all know that produces the same results. Is it really easier to let ten years pass and realize you haven't achieved what you wanted? Now is a better time than ever, so let's go through some common conflicting beliefs:

I want a partner, but if I get one I will lose my freedom.

I want to be successful, but I still want to sleep until 1:00 p.m. and drag through my day.

I want to get fit, but that equals pain.

I want to follow my passion, but if I charge people for it, they may think I am all about the money.

I want to do what I love, but if I do, my parents will think I'm worthless.

If I become wealthy, the people around me will feel worthless and not trust me.

I want to sell my services, but I don't want to give off the impression that I am just doing it for the money.

I want a relationship, but I don't really want commitments.

I want to be healthy, but I want to continue to eat junk food on a regular basis.

I want to make massive changes in my life, but I want my friends to still like me.

I want to make a lot of money, but if I do, it may mean I am not spiritual or religious anymore.

I want to be healthy, but I still want to smoke and paralyze myself with alcohol.

I want to own my own business, but I don't want to be embarrassed if it doesn't do well.

I want to stop smoking, but I want to release stress.

I want to leave my job, start my own business, and do what I love, but if I do, people will think I'm stupid or it may be difficult.

I really want to go and chat with that homeless person, but there are people around and it may be embarrassing.

I want to start a new business, but if I do, people will think I'm a failure in my first venture.

I want to apply for a better position, but I fear rejection.

These are a few common conflicts I have come across in my time. It's like one thing is pulling us one way, while something else is tugging on the other side. With all this confusion, how can we ever get what we want? Here is an extremely effective strategy when you find yourself in one of these situations.

1. **IDENTIFY:** First, you must discover and get to the bottom of the conflict. Have a clear indication of what you want, and be aware of what other beliefs are stopping you. An example would be the list we just went through.

2. **QUESTION:** Next, you need to question what you have identified. Which one is more important to you? Which one is going to have more meaning in your life? Which one can enhance the quality of your life? Which one helps you create more energy and take action toward the bigger picture? What is going to help you grow and progress in life? Which out of the two do you value more? Will you ever ultimately be happy if you don't choose the fulfilling option? Which one can add more value to your life? How will your life look in the future if you do not face your fear? How will this decision ultimately make you feel about yourself once it's made? Could choosing the disempowering option affect future decisions you have to make? Think of more questions . . .

3. **ALIGN:** From the questions, give enough great answers for the belief that is obviously going to fulfill you. Align yourself with these beliefs and reinforce

them. Once you align yourself with the empowering beliefs associated with your real wants, you will hit your target. There is nothing pulling you on the other side anymore because you have overpowered it with enough emotion.

Seeing that we just covered how beliefs influence every area of our life, it is important to look at the scientific evidence behind these methods.

Without enjoying the process, there is no success in what you do.

5

Neuroplasticity

REWIRING YOUR BRAIN

As you continue on your journey, you will soon be amazed to see that you are attracting things that help make sense of the great changes you are making. I told people about the changes I had been through and helped them with theirs. I would tell them that it was as if I was able to rewire my mind.

I remember one day in particular when this concept played out. I was extremely busy that day, so I hadn't worked on exploring it at all until the evening hit. Just as I walked in the door, my brother called me to watch a documentary on TV that was playing. He said it looked like something I might be interested in, and it most certainly was: a program called *The Brain That Changes Itself* by Dr. Norman Doidge. This remarkable show was based on Doidge's travels to hunt down leading neuroscientists about a finding called neuroplasticity. To my surprise, we are not just figuratively rewiring our mind, we are scientifically and physically rewiring our brain.

For centuries the human brain has been thought of as incapable of fundamental change. People suffering from neurological defects, brain damage, or strokes were usually written off as hopeless cases. Recent and continuing research into the human brain is radically changing how we look at the potential for neurological recovery.

The human brain, as we are quickly learning, has a remarkable ability to change and heal itself—in fact, even to rewire itself. This has caused the old dogma to be thrown out. **In other words, you are physically changing your brain with every thought you have.**

NEUROSCIENCE EXPERIMENT—CONNECTION BETWEEN MIND AND BODY

Neuroscientist Alvaro Pascual-Leone's experiment at Harvard Medical School on this topic was quite remarkable. All the participants had to do was learn and practice a five-finger piano exercise.

He instructed the **first group** to play the piano and try to keep the same tempo as best they could. They practiced for two hours a day over five consecutive days. When they were finished, the participants were seated under a coil of wire that sent a sudden magnetic pulse into the motor cortex of the brain. There is a strip that runs from the top of the head to each ear that makes this possible. This procedure is called transcranial magnetic stimulation (TMS), and it gives information on the function of neurons. (There are billions of neurons in the human brain. Each one is designed to transmit information through the body.) They found that after just one week of this piano practice, the subject's brain had physically transformed. The TMS mapped how much of the motor cortex was needed in the finger movement for the piano exercise. Pascual-Leone then found it spread and grew over surrounding areas like the growth of ivy on a fence. It was in line with other discoveries that the constant use of one area of the brain increases the functionality of that area and physically recruits more neurons. That area is then strengthened accordingly.

The **second group** of participants were made to close their eyes and **only visually think of playing the piano.** Their hands **did not** move in the process, but they were told to totally focus on playing that same five-finger sequence in their minds. After the same amount of practice, they were taken through the TMS procedure. The findings were quite astonishing. The same area of the brain had grown, even though they had only visualized playing the piano in their minds. Neurons were still recruited and were wiring together to enhance the ability to perform that task. Even the area of the brain that was used to physically touch the piano grew in the brains of group two, even though they had not physically touched anything.

Pascual-Leone stated, "Mental practice resulted in a similar reorganization." I did this to change my whole life around and, surprisingly enough, I had no idea I was physically transforming my brain to succeed and enhance the quality of my life.

Those results were found after just one week of repetition. I definitely had a light-bulb moment when I saw that, because I had told people that a lot of their life would change drastically after one week if they did the tasks that are in this book. It also proves that full focus on visualization enriches the creativity of one's being and empowers one's passion. If these findings hold true for other physical movements (and there's no reason they shouldn't), then it means swinging a golf club, dancing, painting, or a quick block in boxing could lead to mastery. The power of the mind is everything, and any successful person will tell you that. Everything you ever do or create is a result of your thoughts.

If you are someone who doesn't believe that mind and body are one, you have obviously never had a sexual fantasy before! Further to that, you must have never felt a churning in your stomach when worried about something, never jolted when confronted with a fear, or experienced that overwhelming feeling in your chest when you see the person that you love.

OUR AMAZING BRAIN

On a visit to Melbourne, Australia, Dr. Norman Doidge stated, "Since all human activities emerge from the brain, any change in an understanding of the brain ultimately has a major impact on anything we do. I define neuroplasticity as that property of the brain that allows it to change its structure and its function. And that's in response to the actions that we commit ourselves to, in response to sensing and perceiving the world, and quite fantastically thinking and imagining."

Doidge later went on to explain how these new findings are the grounds for shaping every area of life and affect what we become. It's an amazing breakthrough, to say the least. Before we had the scientific research, many philosophers had told us that the mind shapes our destiny. Plato, the Buddha, and others in history implied that thoughts alone could restructure the brain.

Dr. Joe Dispenza also explains neuroplasticity in the hit film *What the Bleep Do We Know!? Down the Rabbit Hole:*

> The brain does not know the difference between what it sees in its environment and what it remembers, because the same specific neural nets are firing. The brain is made up of tiny nerve cells called neurons. These neurons have tiny branches that reach out and connect to other neurons to form a **neural net.** Each place where they connect is integrated into a thought or a memory. Now, the brain builds up all its concepts by the law of associative memory. For example, ideas, thoughts, and feelings are all constructed then interconnected in this neural net, and all have a possible relationship with one another. The concept in the feeling of love, for instance, is stored in the vast

neural net, but we build the concept of love from many other different ideas.

For some people, love is connected to disappointment. When they think about love they experience the memory of pain, sorrow, anger, and even rage. Rage may be linked to hurt, which may be linked to a specific person, which then is connected back to love. Who is in the driver's seat when we control our emotions or response to emotion?

We know physiologically the **nerve cells that fire together, wire together.** If you practice something over and over, those nerve cells have a long-term relationship. If you get angry on a daily basis, frustrated on a daily basis, if you suffer and give reason for the victimization in your life, you're rewiring and reintegrating that neural net on a daily basis. That net then has a long-term relationship, called an identity, with all those other nerve cells. We also know that when **nerve cells don't fire together, they no longer wire together.** They lose their long-term relationship, because every time we interrupt the thought process that produces a chemical response, those nerve cells that are connected to each other start breaking their long-term relationship.

When we start interrupting and observing, not by stimulus and response to the automatic reaction, but by observing the effects it takes, then we are no longer the emotional person who is responding to an environment on automatic.

"A life of reaction is a life of slavery,
intellectually and spiritually. One must fight
for a life of action, not reaction."

—RITA MAE BROWN

Every day, we are making neural nets stronger if we consistently repeat thoughts. Just think of it as someone tying a piece of rope together in your mind. When you repeat a thought, a word, or a physical action, another piece of rope (neuron) is attached, only to make the net larger and have more of an effect in your life.

The beliefs we have about the outside world—success, relationships, our finances, and so on—appear the way we create them to be. So how about if we broke the pattern and replaced it with an empowering alternative? If we fed those positive thoughts, which become beliefs, which turn into emotion, which then cause us to act, would they force us to make different decisions that ultimately shape our life? Of course they would, and that's exactly what we are going to do. Don't think that the tasks we are going to complete are just wishful thinking. They are creating new neural nets (NNN), so limiting beliefs are diminished and your true power is finally realized.

During a speech I gave in the summer of 2010, a gentleman wasn't grasping how the law of associative memory works. Trying not to hold up the rest of the attendees, I attempted to move on a number of times. There was a question and answer session near the end of the seminar, but this guy kept putting up his hand. I had to reward his persistence, so I invited him up to the front. I gave him the microphone and he said, "Dan, I'm really not grasping this." I started asking him simple questions such as, "What's your name? Where do you live? How would you describe the temperature? What color are zebras? **What do cows drink?**"

He immediately answered the last question with confidence

and certainty and said, "Milk." I stopped and replied, "Are you sure about that, sir?" He paused and said, "Oh my God, they drink water, don't they?" The room erupted in laughter, and I asked the audience if they had answered differently than the man. Most stood up and admitted they weren't laughing at him but at themselves.

The reason his brain came up with that answer is the law of associative memory. If I had asked him to name any drink out loud, what would have been the chances of him saying milk? You could probably agree it would have been extremely slim considering the number of drinks available. When I added cows to the question, his brain narrowed down to the one that he has associated with cows his whole life. Milk and cows go together, right? Even though the answer was wrong, it made sense to him at that moment. Our life is filled with so many undesirable associations that we have repeated. It may be in relationships, work, our finances, or excuses we come up with. The only way to break them is to be aware that they are only associations, not always the truth.

6

Breaking Old Habits

Throughout your life you have applied the notions of pleasure and pain to every decision you have made. The experiences of pleasure and pain are fundamental to humans. They are the basis of change or, on the other hand, the reason we continue to have the same experiences. Our perceptions and our belief system control what we associate pleasure and pain with. **We make drastic decisions that change our life forever as a result of massive shifts of emotion.** Just think back to life-changing decisions you have made that altered the direction you were going: Were they the result of an emotional explosion? It's similar to shaking a can of soda and then opening it. The pressure causes it to explode and forces the liquid in a completely different direction. You have always created that **pressure** within yourself, and who's to say you can't build it again with things you deliberately want to change? The truth is, you can—sometimes you just need a good shake!

We can adapt pleasure or pain to anything we desire; it all depends on how we choose to look at it. People habitually do the same thing over and over again until they have created a neural net that is similar in strength to a post stuck firmly in the ground. In order to make immediate change in your life, regardless of whether it's a habit, fear, phobia, or your perception, you must look at the effect it's having on your life and the associations of pleasure and pain you have adapted.

The following steps can be taken to break down and interrupt anything you consider a habit; for example, looking down when people talk to you, smoking cigarettes, overeating, or thinking negatively about a particular person. I used this to break habits such as smoking, not believing in myself, and, most important, my drug abuse. It got me through fears that I had and other habits that were restricting me.

I invite you to take these steps and change something in your life right now . . .

1. KNOW WHAT YOU WANT

For example, if what you want is to quit smoking cigarettes, you might say: to be healthy and fit; to be able to play at the park with my children or grandchildren one day; to discover my power; to know that I can achieve; to attend my child's wedding; to be really successful; to take control over my life. After you have written down what you ultimately want, you must pick something that is going to take the place of the old habit immediately: What do I want to do instead of smoking? What do I want to do instead of overeating? What do I want to do instead of stressing? Whatever your habit is, make sure you choose one alternative to put in its place: "Instead of smoking, I want to eat more greens."

2. KNOW WHAT'S STOPPING YOU

You have probably been making the mistake of normalizing the situation:

NORMALIZE: You say, "I have a bad relationship," as if you have nothing to do with creating the relationship. That is detachment, so you may feel better in the short term. It is like you are separate from your experience and have no control over it: "If the relationship is bad, it is out of my control and outside of my responsibility."

Instead you must:

DENORMALIZE: "I am relating poorly." Take ownership: "If it's something that I'm doing, I can do it differently."

For the smoking example, the answer to "know what's stopping you" would be "my choice to kill myself by smoking cigarettes," rather than just "cigarettes." We must take ownership so that we are able to make lasting change. If I told you to sit there and hear that voice saying, You need a cigarette right now, to really feel the sensation of picking it up and inhaling a puff, you would desire a cigarette. But the cigarette is nowhere in sight, so was it your mind that gave you the feeling, or the cigarette itself? It could not have been the physical cigarette. **It's how you think about the cigarette that gives you the sensation, not the cigarette itself.** Someone else might see the same cigarette and want to vomit, because they think differently about it, right? This applies to anything. All sensations and desires emerge from the mind.

Once you take responsibility and acknowledge that it's actually all in your mind, you can make lasting change. It would be the same if I told you to close your eyes and imagine something really hurtful that someone has said to you in the past. Take some time now and think hard about it . . . How did you feel in that moment? Did the same emotions of frustration, sadness, or anger churn within you? That person isn't actually here saying it to you, are they? But you experience the same feelings through the vast neural net you have created in your brain. This is due to your thoughts. This realization allows you to acknowledge that **you have options** rather than thinking you are stuck to one. **Our thoughts are our choice.**

TAPPING INTO YOUR MIND

Once you are aware of what you want and what's stopping you, then it's time for a small but powerful task. Nothing is going to change unless you tap into your subconscious mind. A great way of doing this is to start building your new neural net by rehearsing the reaction that you really want when faced with an old habit.

Constant repetition is what makes something a habit, so we should start breaking it right now. Close your eyes and envision the reaction you want as realistically as you possibly can when you are about to fall into an old habit. Feel the emotions of being faced with the old habit and create a perfect scenario of breaking it immediately with the new habit. This will bring forth new powerful emotions. Going back to the smoking example, you would visualize wanting a cigarette and then saying, "No." You would imagine exactly how you would feel by doing that and make it as real in your mind as you possibly can. Would you feel proud, strong, or in control?

What would your facial reaction be? Would you be smiling after you have said no? Do this around twenty-five times, which only takes around five to ten minutes. This is a great start, because it allows you to see and create the new option that is just as real as your previous automated response of giving in. **In order to reach any desired level in our life, we must mimic how we would act if we were already there.** If you want to be mentally strong, you must practice being mentally strong!

3. STANDARD AND VALUE ASSOCIATION

What do you stand for? What do you teach others? What do you pride yourself on? As you have probably already noticed throughout the book, I am extremely big on being truthful to yourself and enforcing it any way you can. We all have certain standards and values that we attempt to live by on a daily basis. We so often contradict our core beliefs due to the habits that we have put in place. Every time we do it, we seem to get weaker because we break down our emotional state. The cause of this is sometimes only that we avoid reasoning with ourselves. We will refuse to look at the truth because it seems too painful to bear. Facing those core values and standards is our ticket to an empowering life. This is the initial step in getting leverage.

Go back to your wants list and analyze it properly. It seems that the reason you wrote down all those wonderful things is they reflect who you really are as a person, rather than what you have conditioned yourself to be. Questioning is the greatest tool one can use to shift a certain mind-set and begin breaking an old pattern immediately. If you have written down on your wants list that you would like to walk your daughter down the aisle on her wedding day, but you find more pleasure in smoking, then you need to reevaluate your standards. The reason you mentioned that on your wants list is because you love her, right? But when you really love someone, are you selfish in the process? Are you demonstrating your love for her, or are you in fact stating the complete opposite with your daily decisions? If you really loved her, then you wouldn't do what you are doing. If you have written down that you want to be healthy and fit, that is because you ultimately see that you have respect for yourself. If you didn't, you wouldn't have even picked up this book.

Does someone who respects themselves and preaches to their loved ones to do the same disrespect their life by overeating? You get my drift—these are questions that we must enforce to begin the leverage process. Questioning your core beliefs and weighing what you want from your life against the current decisions you are making creates a massive shift of emotion. If you think your standards are currently low in your life, raise the bar. Only by raising our standards can we ever find the power to reach new peaks.

4. BREAK THE PATTERN—TURN UP THE HEAT, THEN COOL DOWN

How is this habit affecting me mentally, physically, emotionally, spiritually, and financially? This is the task where you are required to get massive leverage over yourself. Do you know the phrase "if you can't handle the heat, get out of the kitchen"? We are now going into the kitchen.

When you were a child and touched something that was extremely hot for the first time, it created a pain so strong that you knew you never wanted to touch it again. We need to hit the **maximum pain threshold** now. This step requires you to get into a really deep thought process and ask yourself probing questions. Basically, we are going to apply extreme emotional pain to not stopping your habit, phobia, or fear. For a brief moment, I want you to imagine the feeling you get when you see an electric appliance next to water. How have you conditioned yourself to react? In order to break the current habit, you need to condition a similar response. Go back to all those things you want out of life and think of never getting them. Referring back to the smoking example, this is how it would go: You would envision walking around with a tube stuck down your throat. You would imagine being terminally ill when your children are still young or when grandchildren are born. You would feel the extreme pain and torment you would put your family through. You would imagine inhaling a cigarette, follow the smoke into your body, and watch it physically destroy your insides. Close your eyes, and make it so real that it makes you nearly physically sick; it might even do just that and put a disgusted look on your face.

I'm sure you have heard the voice of someone who has had throat cancer and sounds like a robot. In your mind you would imagine saying, "I am choosing to destroy my life as well as the people I love the most," in that sick robotic voice. Feel the emotional and physical pain you would endure, and then transmute that inner energy into good aggression. This exercise is all about emotion, so really feel and get a great mental image of exactly what it is that you are giving up in your life and what effect it has already had. It's important to really focus on the fact that **you are choosing** to give all those things up. This requires that you close your eyes and visualize.

MAXIMIZE LEVERAGE

Humans will always move toward something that we believe is far more pleasurable than the painful option. As long as we think the old habit has more pleasure, we will continue to choose it. If you want to break the pattern, you may have to attach something that causes extreme emotional pain every time you repeat the old habit. This will ensure you condition the new habit without so much resistance.

NOW

Once you have hit that absolute pain threshold where you think you're going to get out of the chair and scream, reverse it. Begin to think of the pleasure if you stopped it **now.** The joy on your family's faces, the feeling of achievement you would attain, the strength you would display. Imagine playing with your children at the park or feeling healthy and fit. Really absorb yourself in that pleasure of being free from that choice of mental state.

Creating a completely **random scenario** in your mind that seems ridiculously stupid is also effective in the face of habits, phobias, fears, or a situation that reminds you of pain. In order for this to be successful, you must look at the scenario as if you were watching it from an outside perspective—almost like sitting at a comedy show. When you feel the sensation or begin to think of the habit, reverse the whole scenario in your mind. Have the mental image play backward, and then add some circus music to it. Replay it over and over again, and add whatever ridiculous things you want to it. This is similar to smashing a plate on the ground. Even if you try to fix it, there will still be cracks that ensure the plate is never the same. That's what we want to do with those patterns in your mind: smash them. For example, if you are scared of flying in an airplane, you would use this technique to change your state immediately. You will notice that fear disappears very quickly and may even turn into laughter. This practice is very powerful and is used by professionals around the world. **If you face it, you can break it; if you run, you're done!**

5. BUILD ON THE NNN

We live in accordance with *stimulus* and *response*. **A stimulus is something that stimulates our senses.** For the example of smoking, the stimulus would be the mere thought of a cigarette—seeing one, speaking about it, or smelling it. The automated response would be to associate pleasure with it and go get one. **A response is how we react to a stimulus.** We must break the pattern immediately in the face of the stimulus, which will reinforce the new response. In other words, the stimulus remains the same, but our response is going to be different.

If you hack at a tree (old neural net) enough times, it will eventually have to come down. By doing the last section, you have just created a NNN (new neural net). This is now an option and another route that your mind will always find to feed. We have attached more pain to the old habit and more pleasure to the new one. The more you think of that new switch in pleasure and pain, especially in the face of your habit, more neurons are recruited to respond the way you desire. You are taking rope from your previous net and making your new one stronger every time you do it. Soon enough, as the new net gets stronger, the other one will disappear. You will definitely notice it weakening as your repetition and intensity increase.

During the process of performing an undesired habit, most people think about things different from the action they are habitually doing at that time. For example, if they are smoking, they will think about what they are going to do that night. It's the same when people have a problem with overeating. They think of feeding their victimization as they eat, which may seem pleasurable. This creates an automatic reaction to think that the current habit provides benefits. But that's because you are not reminding yourself of the pain as much as you are of the pleasure, right? With the smoking example, **every time you inhale, you must think of the effects that it's having on your life and what you are potentially giving up by doing it.** By replacing your wandering thoughts with the effects of your behavior, you recondition your nervous system to associate pain with the habit. It may take one, two, or even three weeks, but it will amaze you how quickly you begin to change your reaction, thought, and feeling when faced with the old habit. This is the conditioning part of your achievement, and it must be done continuously. This works in any part of your life, and it is the key to changing anything you desire.

6. SPREAD THE WORD AND REINFORCE THE NEW HABIT

The language we use is very important. It needs to be forceful and convincing. When you are faced with your old habit, pick up strength in your voice. Going back to the example of smoking, this is how it would work. If someone offered you a cigarette, you would immediately answer, "That's disgusting" or "Yuck." Say it with meaning, confidence, and without too much deliberation. Be adamant about your speech in the face of the old habit. Get physical, verbal, and mental with your new direction. Go and tell people around you that you are over your phobia or your habit. The more you do this, the more real it becomes—and more important, it becomes far more believable to you.

The final step is to put something empowering in your habit's place and create a ritual. If you have given up cigarettes, go for a walk every day or eat a healthier breakfast. When we put something in the place of an old habit, it sets us up for **lasting change.** We must also be extremely proud of every step we take. Even if you have stopped smoking or overeating for four hours, feel the pleasurable emotion of winning. Tell yourself how great you feel and amplify the pleasure as much as you can. **Reward will always condition what we do in life, so use it to your advantage and learn to reward yourself.**

Keep the paper from step one where you have written down what you want. Fold it up and make it like an extra limb. Keep it in your pocket or somewhere where it will be visible for the next three to four weeks. This will remind you of why you are doing all of this and reinforce the new pattern.

2ND STEP
Energy—That Fundamental Force

7

The Force of Life

"A strong, successful man is not the victim of
his environment. He creates favorable conditions.
His own inherent force and energy compel things to
turn out as he desires."

—ORISON SWETT MARDEN

BOOMERANG EFFECT

It seems we have become a society that thrives on things we know are destroying us. The news is a great example, something that is displayed around the world and has enormous power in getting a message across. How often do we see positive, inspirational topics, compared with those that are filled with fear and destruction? All we are bombarded with is death, betrayal, rape, theft, and other damaging stories. Are those really the majority of things taking place in the world? Why not show stories that relate to us more, like people going to school, going down to buy the groceries, or just living a normal life? Because it doesn't sell. And the reasons the others sell, I believe, is a social and mental issue on our end that needs to be addressed. I'm not saying not to keep up with what's happening in the world, but you have to use your brain and be selective about what you think will be a benefit to yourself and society as a whole. Most people in the world aren't stabbing other people, having road rage, committing murder, etc. The news doesn't reflect the majority of the human race. Period.

A vast array of energy is being emitted to the public, who in turn go out, talk about it, and organize their lives around fear. I'm sure we are already quite aware of all those things that are happening in the world. We give them far too much attention and focus.

In some weird way, it seems we find satisfaction in discussing the things we complain about. Are we so distant from our truth that if we didn't have all these life-sucking topics to talk about, it would be difficult to hold a conversation? Are we contributing to this destruction by discussing it and giving it our attention? You bet we are.

The main thing that most of us are blind to is how much this is actually affecting our own lives. The indigenous people of Australia created the boomerang, and energy works the same way. When we throw it out there, it seems to come straight back at us. Think about how many times you discuss things that you dislike in one day. Do you think in order to reverse that dislike it would be intelligent not to soak your whole day in it?

I could just picture the different level of consciousness we would achieve if loving and inspiring stories were displayed as much as the current destructive ones. Imagine if every time we turned on the TV or opened a newspaper, we were surrounded by love and things that help us move toward uniting this world.

WHAT BENEFITS AM I GAINING FROM COMPLAINING ABOUT THIS PARTICULAR EVENT IN MY LIFE?

We complain about our work, our relationships, the world, our finances, and the people around us. There are also those who do nothing but talk about other people's lives. I know because I used to be one of them. They do that to try to place some comfort in their own lives. The things they usually find fault with in others are the same challenges they face. The things they complain about are usually the things they are guilty of themselves. Why? It's easier to blame others than ourselves. We are scared to admit the truth, so we come up with ways of dealing with that fear. It all starts with the person looking straight back at you in the mirror. We must identify and deal with our own challenges, and only then will we realize our ability to create.

> *To create the future we want, we must enjoy the present.*
> *To enjoy the present, we must make peace with our past.*

EVERLASTING ENERGY

> "Passion is energy. Feel the power that comes from focusing on what excites you."
> —OPRAH WINFREY

Why do some people always seem to be tired and dragging their way through life, yet others seem to be full of energy? The amount of sleep they get is definitely not the major challenge, as I discovered myself. I have spoken to and modeled some of the most successful people I know, and it seems nearly all of them get less sleep than recommended. Before I really started embracing life, I was getting ten hours of sleep with a minimum of eight, and I would still be tired. Now I only manage to get about six, but my energy levels are through the roof. I have realized that when energy is being used for a cause that is meaningful, beneficial, or in service of fulfilling a self-vision, it seems to be never-ending. The greatest energy is created when we set up things to look forward to. That same energy creates more energy. My point is that **it's not physical**

tiredness that makes us need as much rest as we think, but our mental state that needs more stimulation.

One of the first things to understand when it comes to energy is that you are the boss of the production line within you. As long as we are complaining about things, focusing on why our life is so bad, thinking about why we are a victim, or repeatedly reminding ourselves of things we do not want, our opportunity to produce empowering energy is nonexistent. It is, in fact, doing just the opposite, as it does nothing but drain energy straight out of our system.

We all know that when we complain about something, our energy level goes down, and that's why complaining feels like crap.

One day I decided that I would refuse to complain about anything. Even when people would tell me about their problems, I would never feed them. I would try to help them see another side, and if they didn't want to hear it, I would simply start to discuss a completely different topic. I would even go to the extent of telling them that if they ever wanted to complain about anything and were looking for someone to join the party, then don't bother calling me. If they were really going over the edge, I would tell them to stop feeling sorry for themselves or physically grab them by the shoulders and shake it out of them. It's great to show compassion, and I highly recommend it as one of a person's greatest qualities, but you also need to do what is in your own best interest and the best interest of the one you care about.

If you submit and consume yourself with everyone else's petty complaints, you leave yourself vulnerable to producing those same feelings yourself. I'm well aware that we all know someone, or maybe even a lot of people, who do nothing but whine their way through life. They are always feeling sorry for themselves, yet never seem to do anything about it. They try to place all their issues on you. They are subconsciously leaking their own energy and trying to fill themselves up with yours. So there are a few outcomes: either they just drain their own energy, or you consume yourself with theirs and go straight to their level. Speak with a powerful tone in those situations; be compassionate, but don't go along for the ride. You will notice after even one day of fending off negative vibes from others, you will feel far more productive toward the life you desire. When we focus on the great things in life, our energy levels are high.

Have you ever had three parties in one weekend that you want to attend? During that weekend you will live off four hours' sleep a night but still be energetic enough to attend all three parties, and have a great time. Your energy levels even cause you to stay up until 5:00 a.m. when you're usually tucked in and sound asleep by 11:00 p.m. Uplifting energy always creates more great energy. You are able to identify this great energy because it makes you feel good, while negative energy has the opposite effect. To be able to **command your own emotions,** a must if you want an extraordinary life, you need to imagine a group of security guards waiting at the front of your production factory. Every time you feel someone or something is trying to break in to the great energy you are now deliberately creating, overpower it in your mind. It may seem a bit challenging at the beginning for two main reasons: First, we are surrounded with so much negativity, and second, we become addicted to complaining.

Don't let people infect you with their negativity; you control the situation by displaying how much you love life.

Do not let newspapers, TV, family members, friends, work colleagues, or anyone else shift your empowering direction. If you do, you bow down to a life that is less than what you're worth, and you do nothing but manifest poor results. You will have friends and family asking what has gotten into you; just be honest and feel your truth. Some may not be able to handle it because they don't want to feel insignificant or may feel as if they are losing you. Keep at it, though; you are being much more of a friend by acting this way than by feeding emotions that are destroying their life. As well as that, you are stopping yourself from destroying your own life in the process. The funny thing is that it will eventually rub off on everyone around you, and your behavior will become infectious. People will cling to you and start asking how you do it.

I couldn't count how many people gave me a hard time about loving life more. They would say I was being fake, that life can't be that great, and all the rest of it. Their comments proved that they were vastly unaware of their own lives. Funnily enough, they were always the people who were lost and never believed they could do anything great. Knowing the effect they were having on their own lives forced me to be compassionate. Months would pass, and those same individuals would ask for guidance. Did I help them? Of course I did, or else I'd be stooping to their level. Now, we all know that we can't feel great all the time, but by practicing it, at least you will know the feeling you want. That will help you come up with ways of regaining it.

It's crucial that you always remain you and express the great person you know you are deep down. By the way, this is a journey, so you are going to make mistakes. The most important thing to remember is that you are always in control of how you feel. Use the gifts you have been given; **think and feel for yourself.**

Produce that great energy by focusing on the good things in life like your appreciation list, the things you want to achieve, and the beauty that surrounds you. Put down your phone or your laptop and go breathe the fresh air. For a brief moment, just look at the birds or up in the sky. Truly take in and focus on the beauty of this magnificent world we live in. We get so entranced by what we want, we forget about what we have. What most don't realize is it's what we have that gets us what we want.

"Life is full of beauty. Notice it. Notice the bumblebee,
the small child, and the smiling faces. Smell the rain
and feel the wind. Live your life to the fullest potential
and fight for your dreams."

—ASHLEY SMITH

Also acknowledge that practice makes perfect. As with everything in life, we have to practice loving life in order to get better at it. When faced with a disempowering experience, you must look for an alternate route immediately. That curiosity and determination will always help you find a way through.

8

Focus and Find

"Ask and you shall receive; seek and you will find;
knock and the door will be opened for you."

—JESUS CHRIST

Have you ever thought that someone was deliberately ignoring you or deceiving you behind your back? How did you feel in that moment? Were you frustrated, hurt, angry, or upset? How about when you found out that they had not done it to begin with? How did you feel then? Did you feel embarrassed, upset with yourself, or even stupid? So how were you able to feel those emotions initially, even though the deceit never happened? Before I tell you the answer, let's do one more exercise. Think of someone you really love for a moment. Really feel them next to you. Take a minute, close your eyes, and imagine their presence. Before you read on, do this. Did you just feel full of love, as if that person was actually there with you? The reason this happens is because your mind doesn't know the difference between something you are actually experiencing and something that is only in your mind. **What we focus on, we will surely feel.** By knowing you have this power, how quickly can you change the way you feel?

In order for us to fully enhance the quality of our life and achieve at our peak, we must choose wisely how our attention is being focused. Life is defined by the truth that **our mind is going to find what we focus on.** Whether that is a blessing or a curse is entirely up to you, as you're in total control of directing that energy. It becomes so frustrating when the experiences that we don't want keep showing up. The reason they show themselves so often is because we are putting so much energy toward them. When we focus on the things we don't want, we get more of them! That uneasiness then begins to consume our reality. This may create feelings of hopelessness, anger, and disappointment until other areas of our life suffer because of our inner turmoil. It's quite obvious in everyday life experience. When you are feeling angry, everything outside will seem distorted and get under your skin. When you are irritated about something, everything will seem to irritate you. When you are happy, everything seems great. It's a law of life— there is no escaping it. We must learn to enhance our emotional fitness, and that comes from what we choose to focus on. **When you continue to focus on what you want, your whole demeanor adapts to your desire. Body language, vocabulary, tone of voice, and even subconscious movements all shift to mold you into the person you need to be.**

> *Don't make things you don't want a priority in your life.*
> *If you do, they will consume your reality.*

Even in an advanced driving course, the instructor will stress that directing your focus is a crucial part of survival. It is said that if we look at a pole or a tree while losing control, we automatically get drawn to that object. The same principle applies to every area of our life. The more we focus on not having enough money, always seeming to find the wrong partner, someone not letting you live your dream, not having enough time, or always being sick, to name a few things, they become stronger. Your mind is going to find every way to attract the things you focus on.

The Bible says, "Seek and you shall find," which I think is a pretty good concept that we need to grasp. What you find depends on what you're choosing to seek. You have always gotten what you have asked for; you might just not be aware of what it is you are asking. Are you really taking notice of which doors you are knocking on? **When your mind wanders, so does what you create.** If you have ever walked a dog on a leash, you will know that sometimes it seems as if the dog is walking you. When it begins to wander off, you direct it back to position with the leash. That's exactly what you have to do with your thoughts—keep them on a leash! If you don't, you lose control.

THINK, FEEL, ACT, CREATE

When you think about what you don't want, how does it make you feel? It personally makes me feel disempowered, unmotivated, sad, and even frustrated. All these human emotions cause us to act in the same way that created and attracted those things we didn't want in the first place. As soon as we shift our focus toward things we want, our attitude changes instantly, and we begin to feel inspired—and when we feel great, we get great results. By redirecting our focus toward what we want, **our mind is more inclined to find it.**

Have you ever bought a new car and suddenly you begin to notice that same make and model everywhere? When you hear someone call out the same name as yours, it grabs your attention immediately. It might be a parent calling out to their child, but you will look around.

This power of "focus and find" truly displayed itself while my brother and I were shopping for his wedding. All we needed was a navy-blue tie, so we made a pact that our focus for the day was strictly a navy-blue tie. The amazing thing was that blue began appearing everywhere. It was like we had our own personal scanner, and as soon as blue was in sight, everything else seemed to fade away. If you have ever seen the movie *The Terminator*, you know that the closer the Terminator is to locking onto a target, the quicker his scanner beeps. That's exactly what it was like. I was noticing blue everywhere, even baby blue. I began integrating irrelevant colors into my initial focus. It even reached a point where I was looking at black ties and concentrating my hardest to see if they were navy. Even after the store clerk reminded me a number of times that they were black, I was still convinced that some were blue. Blue shoes, blue socks, blue hats, and blue suits all began to catch my attention. By the end of the day, I told my brother that I didn't want to see blue for another year. These things caught my eye because I had made it a priority in my life. **The things you prioritize, you find everywhere.**

Your emotions derive from where your focus is being directed.

As much as being able to focus and find what we are seeking among so many possibilities is an amazing human power, there is a part of the brain that makes it possible. With every thought of the mind, there is a physical action in the brain. The reticular activating system (RAS) is composed of several neuronal circuits connecting the brain stem to the cortex. This part of the brain acts like a filter between your conscious and subconscious mind. It's responsible for taking notice of new things and relating outside information that was always in existence to enhance the picture you have mentally created. There are billions of bits of information surrounding us every single moment, and if we were able to notice them all, we would definitely go crazy. The RAS helps focus on the information that is important to you. In Dr. Maxwell Maltz's 1960 self-help book, *Psycho-Cybernetics,* he describes it as being our own servomechanism.

With doing a bit of what I love—research—I discovered that auto-focus cameras contain a servomechanism. I'm not sure if you have ever used one of these, but they automatically create a sharper focus and a clearer picture once the lens is moved to the desired location. **When we make something important in our life, be it a benefit or not, it becomes a priority. The RAS in your brain is going to seek it everywhere and make the picture a whole lot clearer.** Guess who's in charge of moving that lens? You are.

SHIFTING FOCUS—MOVE YOUR LENS

"Most people have no idea of the giant capacity we can immediately command when we focus all of our resources on mastering a single area of our lives."

—ANTHONY ROBBINS

Why do some people have such a great outlook on life, while others seem to be surrounded by so much misery? Why are there some who succeed at a much greater level than others and are fulfilled? Why do those few find inspiration everywhere and are always motivated, yet others find it difficult to come up with any ideas? The answer to these questions lies in the understanding of how life actually works. People say to me, "I know how life works; you wake up, go to work, and come home. It's the same thing every day." My reply is, "No, that's how *your* life works." The truth is, the more we think about the same thing, the more we repeat the same feelings and hence the same actions. Most people believe that things must change on the outside to affect their inner self. They believe that they must have a sense of achievement in order to feel great about themselves. If you have met anyone who is really successful, rich in all areas of life, you will notice they don't attempt to live life backward. They live it the way it was intended, which is to **feel great first,** which causes them to **act great,** which results in **achieving great things.** The only way to make yourself feel great first is to be intelligent in the way you command your focus.

"Concentrate all your thoughts upon
the work at hand. The sun's rays do not burn
until brought to a focus."

—ALEXANDER GRAHAM BELL

All of our emotions arise from where our focus is being directed. Once we shift our lens over to something else, it's going to pick up detail that once went unnoticed. It's like getting a spotlight and moving it from one area to another. Once that is successfully completed, the areas of our life that once contributed to its destruction will be left in the dark. On the other hand, if we do not shift that light, these experiences and situations will keep happening, and the world as you know it will stay in check. We revolve many situations around this sense of reality, attach irrelevant things to it, and create scenarios that seem worse than they are; all to satisfy the stories we play in our mind.

Let's take someone who is paranoid. They repeatedly focus their energy on someone doing wrong by them, being unfaithful, or trying to rip them off. They have focused on that idea so hard, they believe that everyone they meet is the same. Did it ever occur to them that the reason they feel that way is because they have trained their mind to believe that is the case? Could their intentions cause a situation to actually turn out in a particular way? Or is it that they are expecting it, so they will relate anything back to that scenario? Is everyone really trying to take advantage of them, or is it just a reflection of how they are feeling internally, which causes them to perceive it that way?

I vividly remember how excited I was when I bought my first car. The last thing I thought about was that this car might have any problems. I was rapt. In my eyes it was perfect—until it started breaking down and overheating. My perception totally changed from this car being perfect to me being doomed with cars. By the time I bought my second car, I believed I would never have a reliable car. Even though the problem might have been something as simple as the window not working, I would blame it on being doomed with cars and would just wait for the next thing to go wrong. I would freak out about any unfamiliar noise, forgetting that it was a metal box and they make noises. I would tell people about my curse and stress about it every time I jumped in the car. As I would start the engine, it was as if I expected something to just blow up. It was driving me mad and took up far too much of my energy.

This paranoia of my car breaking down continued until I got in my friend's car one day and his window stopped working. I smirked, shook my head, and said, "We must be doomed with cars."

I expected him to go along with the victimization, but he turned to me and said, "Relax, it's just a window." Was it that I was doomed with cars, or was it that I personalized the innate uncertainty of life to play the victim and feel worse?

Thinking about it, I realized there are people dying of starvation in the world, and yet here I am complaining about a window not going up. Further to that, it seemed okay to spend $400 on alcohol every week, but I would whine over having to spend $100 on fixing a window that would allow me to breathe. I guess it's easier to blame external things than to take responsibility. My belief that I was doomed with cars diminished and I realized it was just a car.

This might sound like a simple scenario, but when I tell people the story, I realize I'm not alone. How often do you focus on something so hard that it begins to consume your life? How many times does something then happen, and you realize you actually had nothing to worry about in the first place? Or you eventually get over it and it has no power in your life? That surely creates different emotions.

We create our own reality, and when it has its hiccups, we think it's not living up to the high standards we have set and we start to doubt. We then shift our focus and believe that is the best life has to offer. Very far from the truth, but when we are moving our focus away from things that aren't working, we have to find something positive to focus on instead.

SUCCESSFULLY DIRECTING ENERGY

The beauty of life is just as real as the ugliness of life. It all depends on which one you choose to see.

A few years ago, while working at a call center, I noticed one of my colleagues had his head down and looked quite upset. He was never really the type to say much, so I decided to approach him. He told me that he didn't want to talk about it, so I knew I had to take action in order to help. The next day I walked past, and again his head was in his hands. I decided to clap as loudly as I could next to his ear. He jumped up, startled, and I said, "You see how quickly your mood can change." After that, we got into a conversation that quickly turned to his recent breakup. He was bereft, but our conversation allowed him to shift his perspective drastically.

Rather than beating himself up over everything he apparently did wrong, he acknowledged through reasoning with himself that it was what he had wanted for a while. He told me that he had a gut feeling it was never going to work. He also wanted to travel and experience things that he knew he couldn't do while with his ex-girlfriend. I explained that by shifting his focus toward reasons that would serve him, he would be able to pave a new direction for his life; that unless he stopped lying to himself by playing the victim and took charge of the benefits he was already aware of, he would never be able to move on. In an instant he was able to come up with a list of visions he could work toward that would allow him to be free of the emotional attachment to his former love. Challenging times would still face him, but he created empowering routes that his mind would now always find rather than the pain-enduring option. As long as he continued to reinforce the new idea of his deep truth, the other one would diminish.

When you stop focusing on things you don't want, you break the pattern of letting them consume most of your life. It also prevents you from associating irrelevant things with a situation. Sometimes a situation just is.

It's like watching a guy run across the street toward an old woman. We might perceive him to be heading in that direction to rob the lady, which causes us to become distressed. Someone else might perceive the situation as a good gesture, where the guy is going to give back the change she left at the store. But the guy runs straight past and makes no contact with her at all. Both scenarios were just as real for that moment, but only because we created them. This is the case for everything that happens or has happened in your life. That external stimulus was or is open for whatever you wish to attach to it. Analyze it properly, put things into perspective, think of something that you should be really grateful for at that time or focus on what you want, and you will experience pleasure.

Focus on how the situation could benefit your visions in life rather than distance you from them. What knowledge can you gain to take action and better your life? As long as you look hard enough, benefits can be drawn from any experience. In fact, **every situation is open for an alternative view.** Things once thought of as bad will become your greatest opportunities for self-growth and allow you to take another step toward a quality life. By practicing this strategy, even just a few times, you will soon discover that the only reason anything ever seems a particular way is due to the thoughts (and hence emotions) you **choose** to attach to it. You will relate this exercise to past and new experiences, and that's when you really take massive steps to positively shape your destiny.

When feeling down about something, you know it is actually due to your perception. These times call for full focus and not letting your mind wander. We must not settle for how things might seem in an instant, but search deeper, looking for ways to turn it around. Once you have discovered a better way of looking at an experience, even if it's only slightly better, hold on to that new thought and feed it like mad. Once that's accomplished, you have learned how to successfully direct your energy.

3RD STEP
The System of Achievement

9

Take Instant Charge

"It had long come to my attention that people of
accomplishment rarely sat back and let things happen
to them. They went out and happened to things."

—LEONARDO DA VINCI

We have all achieved something in our life, regardless of how small
we might think it is. There are times when things seem hard, almost unbearable, until we finally overcome them. Achievement is
when we accomplish something in our life, whether it is having the
courage to overcome a situation, the attainment of personal goals,
a heroic act, or putting extra effort into a task. All achievements,
from the greatest to the smallest, will play a major role in what you
set out to achieve next. Raising a child, providing the essentials
for your family, getting a relationship back on track, or overcoming one that wasn't working are all achievements. Whatever we
achieve in life, the process is quite systematic. We get a vision of
what we want, passion builds up, we align ourselves with fear, consistently think of how it can be achieved, work out our action plan,
and follow it. Regardless of whether you have taken notice of this
or not, it's usually the way it happens.

Achievement never dropped out of the sky and knocked on
your front door with a bunch of roses—you had to go and get it.

And just because you may have achieved something, it doesn't mean you are ultimately fulfilled. I couldn't count how many times I have heard of someone achieving something great, yet a month down the track they are empty because they don't know what to do next. I've met multimillionaires who are some of the unhappiest people I know. They exclusively went for the money, only to find that is not a passion but rather an attempt to find lasting happiness in a material way. That sent them to another dead end. I'm sure we have all heard stories of very wealthy people ending up as drug addicts or committing suicide, while others with very little material wealth are the happiest people alive. They are all great achievers, as that word, *achievement,* is personalized to individuals' desires. However, it is only achievement and fulfillment together that brands someone truly successful. We must learn how to gain them both, and that's what I have dedicated my life to finding. I have worked tenaciously to unravel the powers that allow us to shape our destiny on our conditions. The following knowledge and strategies steered me toward true success in no time.

THE REALITY OF COMPELLING VISIONS

"Dreaming is not enough. You have to go a step
further and use your imagination to visualize,
with intent! Forget everything you've been taught,
and believe it will happen, just as you imagined it.
That is the secret. That is the mystery of life."

—CHRISTINE ANDERSON

On October 1, 1971, just four years after the passing of Walt Disney, thousands of people gathered near Orlando, Florida, to see the grand opening of Walt Disney World. One of his closest companions said to Disney's wife, Lillian, "I wish Walt was here to see this." She turned to him and said, "If Walt didn't see this, it wouldn't be here now." She was referring to his vision. The Walt Disney Company is worth approximately $35 billion, and it all started with Mickey Mouse, who Disney said "popped out of my mind onto a drawing pad . . . on a train ride from Manhattan to Hollywood at a time when business fortunes of my brother Roy and myself were at lowest ebb and disaster seemed right around the corner." I guess that's why Disney is also known for his famous quote: "If you can dream it, you can do it."

In order for us to live to our full potential, we must embrace the dream visions that flash before us. Most people I know will use this powerful tool to feel worse in their daily lives. They envision that dream body, that nice car, or that big house and immediately begin to get angry or beat themselves up for not having it now. I think the reason is their disbelief that they are actually able to attain their dreams. It is absolutely crucial to focus on the great emotions of such visions, because that's what inspires us to action. Going on a vacation is a perfect example. We visualize being on the vacation way before most of our preparations are even organized; we build emotion around it, and that is what inspires us to action.

The reality is that if we don't create absolutely compelling visions of what we want out of life, they will never come into existence. We must understand that a dream and a vision are two different things. The word *dream* gets thrown around like a fairy tale. It's regarded as something that is not real, cannot be worked toward, and has no ground for creation. Everything that has come into existence was the result of someone's vision.

In Corey Turner's book, *Vision: The Key to Your Future,* he states:

> Living life without any clear direction for your future is like trying to drive a car blindfolded. It may

be really exciting for a few seconds but incredibly
dangerous because of the very real danger of crashing and hurting others.

I think it's also clear that we will be hurting ourselves in the
process, and I know that from personal experience.

If we don't have visions of what we want to achieve in our life,
how are we ever going to bring them about? We won't know where
to start, we'll resort to things that never fulfill us, and we'll live our
life in the desperate rage of just hoping something will change. You
might be sitting there thinking that you don't know exactly what
you want in life. I've had this discussion with many people, especially young people, but we must think deeper. Is it that we really
don't know, or is it that we don't believe we can achieve the things
we dream about? The people that never achieve much are those
who wait for things to happen on the outside to help make their
visions become clearer. What they are unaware of is that they must
create a vision first, of anything at all, and that makes everything
on the outside align and assist its accomplishment. You rarely get
it straightaway, but it will come if you hold it close to your heart
and firmly in your mind. Then there is the balance of action you
must take, but all successful people know that everything starts
with a compelling vision.

> "Good business leaders create a vision,
> articulate the vision, passionately own the vision,
> and relentlessly drive it to completion."
>
> —JACK WELCH

That vision of a special person in your life, that Ferrari, that
house by the water, that increased paycheck at the end of the
month, that good relationship with your family, being free from
drugs or an addiction—these are just a few goals. Visions don't nec-

essarily revolve around money; rather they focus on abundance in our whole life. **The more clarity you have about what you want, the more you're willing to work for it.** Most people seem to use broad terms such as "I want more money," "I want someone in my life," "I want to own my own business," or "I want to be more successful," unaware that they might get them, but only in the broad terms in which they ask. For example, you might say you want to share your life with someone and then fall in love with someone who isn't right for you. It's because you didn't have a clear indication and vision of what that person would be like. Their traits, their qualities, and the things you must have in a partner weren't clear to you at the beginning. We just end up settling for the same old things when we do this. The same goes for when we make an extra twenty dollars for two weeks' work and then we complain. You asked for more money, didn't you? In order to get exactly what you want, you need to be absolutely clear about what it is.

> "Your past is important, but it is not nearly as important to your present as the way you see your future is."
>
> —TONY CAMPOLO

Creating visions also calls for common sense, as we know things might not happen exactly the way they first appeared in our mental image. Accept the imperfections in life, because things are unstable, impermanent, and naturally subject to change. This may also be caused by our mere inability to ever see perfection. I mean, if you meet someone and they don't have the size eight foot you imagined, I would probably suggest putting down the judgment sword. It's like when you plan a trip away and you are visualizing lying on the beach. You envision how the hotel room might look and the beauty that surrounds the place. When you get there, it's not exactly what you imagined, but you still appreciate it for what it is, sometimes even more. Look at the true essence of the creation and the passion from which it stemmed. Paintings are not looked at as perfect, but those who understand them are able to see the passion of the painter within them. That's how you can bridge the gap between your dream and reality—appreciation. **Allow room for error, but never allow room for giving up on those things that you know you must have.**

YOU KNOW WHAT YOU WANT—OR DO YOU?

> "Don't ask what the world needs. Ask what makes you come alive, and go do it. Because what the world needs are people who have come alive."
>
> —HOWARD THURMAN

Sitting down in a small café one evening with a close friend, I overheard two young guys discussing how they didn't know what they wanted in their lives. I know it's not very polite to eavesdrop, but in a place where tables were almost connected, I felt as if I was meant to be there. I politely asked if I could interrupt. My friend was kicking me under the table because she was embarrassed, but I couldn't leave after hearing these guys' distress, knowing I could help. I asked them, "If I said to you that you could have the woman of your dreams right now, would you take her?" They laughed and said, "Yeah, for sure." I then asked, if I were to offer them a mansion with a Lamborghini parked out front, would they take it? Again the answer was yes. Then I asked, if they could wake up every morning feeling great with an inspiring outlook on life, contribute to the world, have a fit body, and be in a position where they were in charge of their emotions, would they embrace such a life? One guy turned to me and said, "Did you just win the lottery and now you're feeling generous?" I laughed and replied, "No, I'm proving that you know exactly what you want, you just don't think you can get it!" This is one of the major challenges I see in society today. **Most people know what they want; they just believe it's out of their reach.** It's then easier to say they don't know as an excuse to escape with some dignity.

However, if you are someone who is certain about not knowing what you want (which is the position I found myself in many times), then you might not have a deep understanding of yourself yet. How can we ever really know what we want if we don't fully know who we are? How will we know our powers? How will we ever be able to build a trusting relationship with ourselves? Most hide who they are every day until they are confused and doubt their true ability. If you know who you are, you will know what you want. You are able to identify your passion and live a life that reminds you to be conscious of every action you take. It is also imperative that what you want doesn't conflict with who you are.

Exploring yourself, nurturing your everyday life, and feeding who you really are is the basis of finding out exactly what you want. The more you stress and worry about not knowing, the cloudier your true identity. You must have faith that when you make changes in everyday life, regardless of how small the changes might seem, your truth is going to display itself.

As I mentioned, I didn't have a clear indication of what my passion in life was, I just knew I loved to help people. The last thing I thought I would become was an author. To be honest, in the beginning of my change, all I wanted to do was alter what I was doing in the present. It worked quite well, because instead of fogging my mind with what I thought I wanted, I decided to change what I was doing, which built the belief that I could achieve anything. I needed to rectify the concept of **feeling, acting,** and **creating** of my own accord. That allowed me to recognize that it could be done in any area of my life.

We must also be aware of conflicting beliefs and the influence they have on our decision making. If your appreciation list states that you are very grateful for your family, then I'm guessing they are important in your life. If you wanted to open up a brothel, that could be a conflicting belief. Ultimately, the choices you make are up to you, but it calls for some deep thinking. Go back to "Absolute Power of Questioning" (page 3) where I invited you to notice those great qualities within you. You will realize that your choices should be in line with who you really are and how they could benefit the things most important to you. This may also be the reason why you have changed your mind so many times, as you will always adapt pleasure and pain to a particular want. We are emotional creatures, so the feeling that you get from something you want is compelling. **Always go for the feeling, because that's the pinnacle of your desire.**

CREATE MASSIVE PURPOSE WITH EVERYTHING YOU DO

> "It doesn't matter what you do
> if you don't do what matters.
> If you do what matters it doesn't matter what you do."
> —UNKNOWN

There are so many people who use the excuse of having to or needing to do something in their life. I would like to point out that you never *have to* do anything. And *needing* gets thrown out most times as well. We complain about our cars, our jobs, and the people in our life. If you are continually complaining about how crappy your car is, then why don't you get a baseball bat and smash it to pieces? No one is stopping you. You don't have to keep it, and you definitely don't need it. I'm sure the bus or other transportation can take you around. If you don't like a person in your life, it's your choice to stick around. If you find yourself always complaining about your job, get up now and tell your boss how much the company stinks. Let him or her know that you are picking up your things and leaving. Come on, you only live once, so go do it. You don't want that car, that friend, that job, remember? If you are wondering whether I'm serious, you bet I am. But are you? If you are saying to yourself, "I'm not going to smash my car or say that to my boss," why not? When you answer the "why not" you will realize it's because you actually want to be there more than you don't want to be there, or else you would have already done something about it.

YOUR COMPLAINING IS
CREATING YOUR OWN DISASTER

What about doing chores around the house? Doing the dishes or mopping the floor is something that people believe they have to do or need to do. The answer again is, "No, you don't." You can quite easily walk around with grime seeping through the floor or eat off a plate that has crumbs left over from last week. If you get my point, all these things are wants. You want to keep the car because you don't want to walk everywhere you go. The reason you won't say that to your boss is because you want money. You want to wash the dishes because you don't want to get infected with bacteria. Even if someone held a gun to your head and asked you to do something, it's still a choice to obey or not, right? The solution to your complaints: Stop whining and take massive action.

A while back, I had a friend call me up to complain about helping her sister and nephew move into a new place. She had no sleep, was drained, and was acting like she was giving something up by helping. I asked her, "Do you have to do it?" She answered, "Yes, because who else is going to?" I quickly reminded her that she didn't have to do anything, and could have slept all day knowing that her sister would do it on her own. Then she replied, "No, I wouldn't let her do it on her own." Laughing to myself, I said, "Well, that means you actually want to do it, because you recognize it's a great thing to do. The fact that you're doing it means that you want to more than you don't want to. Stop complaining and be proud of yourself." She called me back an hour later and said, "You know what? I feel really good about what I just did for my sister."

When you create meaning with everything you do, it gives you the drive to go that extra mile that no one else is willing to go. **Successful people don't just do something, they acknowledge why they are doing it.**

> People ask me, "What is the purpose of life?" But I think
> the question should be, "What isn't the purpose of life?"
> Everything in life has its purpose.

When you start acknowledging that you **want** to do things, it increases purpose.

Creating purpose in your life is by far the number one way to create self-motivation. You are far more willing to do things that you want to do rather than things you feel that you have to do. **Turn your "have to" into "want to" by giving enough great reasons why you are doing something in the first place. This also increases your appreciation. If you find that it's not actually something you want to do, then also acknowledge that you never have to. Once you grasp that everything you do in life is a choice, there is no room to play the victim.** If you choose to do it, do yourself a favor and stop dwelling on what's wrong about the experience. Shift your focus to why you want to or the compelling visions that you're about to write down.

How to unleash a smothered passion and allow it to drive your life:

"Reduce your plan to writing. The moment you
complete this, you will have definitely given concrete
form to the intangible desire."

—NAPOLEON HILL

TASK

This is the third section of your appreciation list that I mentioned before. You must add this to your list to complete it.

3. WANTS: This is the part where you are to put all limitations aside and write continuously. Write down everything you have dreamed of having, and be creative. Give thanks for the things you want in life and do not hold back at all. I don't care how big or how small, you must write it. Be as specific as you can because clarity brings forth courage. If you want more money, then how much do you want? Do you want $10,000, $100,000, or $10,000,000? When your visions become too vague, you will never hit your target. **When you're not clear about the result you want, you don't result in getting anything.**

Most people aren't specific about what they want because they fear the feeling of failure if they never get it. But why worry in advance? I have discovered that in order to create an extraordinary life we must raise the bar so high that it scares us. Only by raising our standards do we give ourselves the opportunity to step up to such a level. Besides the fear aspect, most find it easier to wishfully think that what they want will just appear. What these people must realize is that the reason they will never get what they want is actually their reluctance to create more clarity in the first place.

I had a client who was going overseas at her dad's expense. Attempting to help her create more independence in her life, I asked her to set an amount of extra money she would like to have for her trip, which she would have to earn. Scared to write down a large number, she came up with $2,000. I knew that she would always cut her ability at least in half because of her dad's involvement, so I raised it to $4,000. She eventually earned $3,800. What a great achievement! If she never set $4,000 as a target, she would never have reached $3,800 and may have even saved less than her original $2,000—not to mention the massive growth and self-respect she gained in the process. If you shoot an arrow with no target set up, where do you think it's going to go? How can you hit a target if you don't have one to begin with?

"Clarity: The ability to think clearly
or understand things clearly."
—MACMILLAN DICTIONARY

When in pursuit of what you want in life, there are two things you must have in order to get it: clarity and enough emotional charge. Without either or both, you don't stand a chance. Clarity helps create that emotional charge. I hear so many people tell me that if they meet that special person, they will make changes, or if they had more money, they would then decide what they wanted to buy. I am quick to remind them that if they aren't clear on what that person is like, they won't be able to make the appropriate changes to their life that will invite in that special person. And as far as the money theory goes, it's actually the complete opposite. By having a clear indication of what you want initially, it forces you to produce more emotional charge, which will ensure you create the money you need. You must be specific with what you want first. Creating clarity is not wishful thinking; it makes what you want more real. And when something is more real, you believe it more. When you believe it more, you take action!

The only way we can accomplish beyond our known limits is by frequently raising our standards.

There is one point you should take note of. Make sure you don't drive yourself crazy filling in all the minor details, like your business having electric doors instead of manual ones. Just write down the bigger picture, and you will end up filling in the details as you progress. By staying conscious of the bigger picture, you are reminded of why you are taking all the small steps now. All exceptional achievers reached a point in their life where they stopped dwelling on not having their wants and forcefully brought forth emotions as if they already did. **You must celebrate your success now.** Imagine and create the same feelings you would have if you already had all those things you want. If you do this, it allows you to experience the powerful emotions that master your willingness to act and your goals will draw closer. Unless you build the belief by consuming yourself with what you want, you will never get it. **You can't get to a place that you don't believe exists!**

Go for it right now. Again, you must not read on until you have completed this task. Get out your appreciation list and start writing. Stay away from writing down what you don't want. Focus on what you want rather than what you don't want. An example in the financial section would be "I want to own a condo in Miami with a swimming pool on the balcony," and not "I don't want to live in the one-bedroom apartment that I am currently living in." To make it easier, create sections or a table such as:

FINANCIAL	PHYSICAL	MENTAL	EMOTIONAL

Note: This list is subject to change. It will evolve over time, but you must have a starting point initially. Think hard and dream big. Make sure you always begin with "I want ..."

At the end of reading my list, I would close my eyes, get into a state of focus, and repeat:

"Thank you for giving me everything I ever wanted—financially, physically, mentally, and emotionally. For everything I ever desired and have. Thank you, God, for being one with the qualities that reign within me and giving me the gifts to obtain and attain anything I desire."

Focus on your wants when you wake up. Carry that energy throughout your day and you will see the path begin to light up for you. Write down any progress or ideas that flow.

Do not read on until you have completed this crucial task for your personal growth.

CREATING PURPOSE AND ENOUGH EMOTIONAL CHARGE

In order to be successful, you must have purpose. In Napoleon Hill's masterpiece *Think and Grow Rich,* he presented the idea of a "definite major purpose" as a challenge to his readers to ask themselves, "In what do I truly believe?" According to Hill, 98 percent of people had few or no firm beliefs; this alone put true success firmly out of their reach. His journey also consisted of researching and interviewing five hundred of the most successful people in the world at the time. Thomas Edison, Alexander Graham Bell, Henry Ford, F. W. Woolworth, John D. Rockefeller, William Wrigley Jr., and Franklin Delano Roosevelt were only a few.

These highly successful people displayed definite patterns in their attitudes, but at that time, which was not so different from our era, most people had serious misconceptions of the qualities that brought them success. Negative emotions such as fear, selfishness, and resentment were the sources of failure. This came as a big shock to most. The opposites of these attributes were found to be some of the secrets to success, but it was said that everyone must discover this on their own and thus gain the knowledge to really influence their lives.

In my experience, achievers who think that winning means they have to be arrogant and heartless in the process actually lose more than they gain. They may have gained money, but they lost everything else, including themselves. There is a way of gaining what you want while staying true to yourself, and that's what real success consists of.

> "Your worth consists in what you are
> and not what you have."
> —THOMAS EDISON

TASK

Why do I want what I want?

Look at your wants list, and note as many reasons as you can why you want what you want. **Write down why you must have them and why you will not settle for less.** If you do not have a clear understanding of why you want what you want, then you will not enhance the emotions that create the certainty to obtain them. Passion builds up; it is not something that you just find at its peak. This exercise is crucial for assigning passion to your desires. Stay away from writing what you don't want. For example, **"I want _____ because I don't want to be poor."** *Instead you would write*, **"I want _____ because I want to feel like I have accomplished what I'm worth, or because I want to give my family great opportunities."** Go and write a list now.

These next sets of questions also create an enormous amount of emotional charge. Focus on each one individually for a few minutes and write down the answers.

- How would it make me feel if I **didn't** get what I wanted in my life?

- What would I think about myself?

- How would my body language be?

- What are the emotions I would experience on a daily basis?

- Are some of the answers to these questions things I am doing now?

If you are acting in the same way you would if you never got what you wanted, how on earth do you expect to get anything?

NOW

- How would it make me feel if I **did** get what I wanted?

- How would I hold my body? What would my body language be like? What would my shoulders, facial expressions, and attitude be like?

- Throughout my day, how can I produce the same emotions I would get when I attain what I want? How would I have to think, talk, and walk?

- Must I allocate time to really think about these accomplishments and continually embrace the emotions?

- How can I create rapid change from the answers I have obtained from these questions? What can I do differently? What are the different emotions I need to start commanding?

Only by answering these crucial questions can you bring forth the **emotional charge** needed to achieve. Take the same feelings with you all day that you imagine you would have if you gained what you wanted. Let those feelings drive your decisions. Remind yourself of why you really want what you have written down.

10

The Persistence Punch

"Nothing in the world can take the place of
persistence. Talent will not; nothing is more common
than unsuccessful people with talent. Genius will not;
unrewarded genius is almost a proverb. Education
will not; the world is full of educated derelicts.
Persistence and determination alone are omnipotent.
The slogan 'press on' has solved and always will solve
the problems of the human race."

—CALVIN COOLIDGE

Have you ever thought of an idea or something that you believe people would want, and a year or two later you see it on the shelves? It could be on TV, a new product out in supermarkets, or an invention that you once thought of. You then say things like "That was my idea," and you tell others that you had once thought of it. The difference is that the other person who had the idea decided to persist. We let so many dreams, visions, and ideas slip because we think others might find them stupid, or that it will be too hard, or we give up due to the hurdles we come across. An Olympic hurdler doesn't run off the track if he misses the first jump; he gets back up and finishes the race. **Falling doesn't mean failing.**

The concept of failing was only created by those who were too scared to succeed, and it exists in the same world as "giving up." If we never stop persevering, then failure will not be an option. There is in fact no such thing as failure; instead, everything is knowledge we can put into practice. The reason there are great achievers is because of their reluctance to see something as a failure. They stick to the belief that there is no failure, only feedback. You don't fail—you only get results. These achievers are like a bulldog with a bone clenched firmly in its teeth. The more you try to take away the bone, the harder it grips.

Even when I can't see the light at the end of the tunnel, I still believe it's there.

If you read biographies of high achievers you will notice that most of their first businesses or trials weren't the ones that took them to greatness. For some, it happened early, but other achievers used every experience as an opportunity for learning and growth.

It is easy to give up, but only in the short term. I couldn't think of anything worse than just settling, and to me that's a lot harder to live with. It's normal not to feel 100 percent motivated all the time and to have moments where you feel like you are being defeated. What you need to master is moving forward even an inch in those times, because that's how you win. Every time you win, you become stronger. Relentlessly holding on to your visions is winning in essence.

One of the most inspirational stories of persistence I have ever seen was of an Australian man stuck in a Southeast Asian jungle for eleven days. The documentary is called *Miracle in the Jungle,* and it was based on Hayden Adcock's amazing story of survival. On a trek that was only supposed to last a few hours, he got lost in some of the roughest terrain known to mankind. With no food and faced with every challenge possible during a national storm alert, he thought his life was over. His wounds were so deep and so moist that his body became a feeding ground for disease. Parasites entered and hallucination started to kick in. Halfway through his ordeal, Hayden found himself at a waterfall, where he considered jumping off. He said that just as he was about to jump and end his own life, he thought about his parents and all his loved ones. He thought if he were to give up now he would be leaving absolutely no hope, so he didn't jump because of his strong love for his family. Hayden survived another six days in the jungle after that before being rescued, and he faced challenges that most would consider insurmountable. It just goes to show one man's persistence can defy all the odds against him. It is a documentary I highly recommend.

> "Permanence, perseverance, and persistence in spite of all obstacles, discouragement, and impossibilities: It is this that in all things distinguishes the strong soul from the weak."
>
> —THOMAS CARLYLE

In order to stay persistent, you must cut off every avenue of retreat. Succeeding needs to be the only way in your mind, because that's when you will go that extra mile and push past the limit that you once thought was impassable. There needs to be no other way than that to which your passion directs you. If you believe something can work, then it can, because you have been there in your mind. Every creation began from a vision and a belief, even when most people called that idea nuts. When you really believe in yourself, it will eventually rub off on everyone around you, and you will notice your persistence is desirable. **Don't forget that we build our own beliefs.** It is said that Colonel Sanders went to nine hundred chicken shops with his recipe and had the door closed in his face. They said his recipe would never work and that his idea was crazy. Yes, nine hundred times! Ask yourself how many people would have given up after five refusals. He believed in his idea and finally got his first break. His sheer persistence and determination transformed his recipe into the franchise we all know as KFC.

Tommy Hilfiger started by selling his jeans out of the trunk of his car. Not many would have the guts to do that. If he hadn't persisted, do you think he would have one of the greatest clothing companies of all time? Even those who have won a medal, passed a test, owned a local business, or dedicated their life to contribution have remained persistent to see it through. **There are certain breaks that successful people have, but in order for those opportunities to arise in the first place, they had to persist—and they knew it.** The problem with most people is that they give up, unaware that their big break might have been just around the corner. That's why it is imperative to continue pushing on, because these breaks do happen, and when they hit, they hit big. If you are finding it hard to believe in yourself, then prove it to yourself.

I'm sure there has been a time in your life when you had to do a new task. Let's take a new job as an example. The first day you walked in, how nervous and excited were you? That job may have been really difficult to comprehend and do. It may have even gotten to a point where you thought you would never get the hang of it. A few weeks went by, and you wondered why you ever stressed because it now seems so easy. If you look for it hard enough, your ability in life will astound you—but most people don't take the time to notice it. The truth is, we have the ability to do anything in our life. People throughout history, with all different biographies, have proved that time and time again.

There will be times when you feel as if your head is underwater, and you will question what you are doing, doubt your ability, and have others call you stupid. What will bring you to greatness is acting the way the great do. **Everyone on the road of achievement has experienced self-doubt. Those who win, though, always overpower that doubt with self-assurance.** If you have ever bought a new car, you will be familiar with that uncomfortable feeling when you sit behind the wheel the first few times. Then you might sort of miss your old car because of its comfort, but there is no way you would go back, because you know the new one is better. We will persist in driving until it becomes second nature.

> "By perseverance the snail reached the ark."
>
> —CHARLES H. SPURGEON

I have had some people confuse the notion of "letting go" with that of "giving up." Letting go of something you don't want anymore is not the same as giving up on something that you truly do want. For example, if you are in a relationship that is not working, and you don't want to be in it anymore, then following a new path is imperative to your happiness. Letting go of something you do not want anymore displays strength; that's why it is not called "giving up." Your mind tries to play tricks on you sometimes and tells you that you may want something when you know deep down you don't. Your truth will always ask, "Is this something I really want, or am I just scared to let go and push past my known limits?"

It's just like when we want to grow a particular muscle in our body. We work out, and we have to strain and stretch to the point of discomfort, and then as time goes on the muscle grows. If we only ever stop at our limit, we see no improvement. This goes for any part of our life. You will know in your heart whether it's a sign of weakness for hanging around in a situation that you don't want to be in anymore.

In saying that, you will also know when you are using excuses not to go and get what you deserve. We all face challenges when we go after what we want, but not many persist in the face of them. **Challenges are also there to help you eliminate what you don't want, so what you do want becomes clearer.**

Sheer determination is crucial for manifesting our visions into reality. Your idea or vision is probably just as good as the last great achiever's—you just need to let your passion drive you. Stay strong, keep the faith, believe in yourself, and never give up or accept less than what you know you must have. Most importantly, make sure you enjoy the process. **As soon as you stop adding pleasure to what you are doing, you are certain to experience pain.** Living the dream isn't just when you get what you want; it's actually the process of getting it. Things may seem hard at times, but remember, they are never so hard that you can't get through them!

PEOPLE WE KNOW—IN THE FACE OF OBSTACLES

> "Adversity has the effect of eliciting talents,
> which in prosperous circumstances
> would have lain dormant."
>
> —HORACE

The vice president of Columbia Pictures told Harrison Ford that he was never going to make it in the business.

John Grisham's first book was rejected by twelve publishing houses and sixteen agents.

A recording company said about the Beatles: "We don't like their sound and guitar music is on the way out."

Charles Darwin's father told him that he would amount to nothing and be a disgrace to himself and his family.

A music teacher said about Beethoven: "As a composer he is hopeless."

Enrico Caruso was told that he couldn't sing at all.

Walt Disney was fired from a newspaper because he "lacked imagination and had no original ideas."

The author of *Chicken Soup for the Soul* was told by publishers that "anthologies didn't sell" and the book was "too positive." It was rejected a total of 140 times. It now has sixty-five different titles and has sold over 80 million copies all over the world.

Thomas Edison was told by a teacher he was "too stupid to learn anything."

Winston Churchill failed the sixth grade.

Albert Einstein wasn't able to speak until he was almost four years old, and his teachers said he would "never amount to much."

Isaac Newton did poorly in school and failed at running the family farm.

F. W. Woolworth was not allowed to wait on customers in the store he worked in because "he didn't have enough sense."

Michael Jordan was cut from the high school basketball team, went home, locked himself in his room, and cried.

A producer told Marilyn Monroe she was "unattractive" and could not act.

Jonathan Livingston Seagull by Richard Bach was rejected eighteen times before it was published. It then sold over one million copies the first year.

Julia Roberts auditioned for *All My Children* and got rejected.

Abraham Lincoln's fiancée died, and he failed in business twice, had a nervous breakdown, and was defeated in eight elections.

We all fall down, but not everyone picks themselves up. Never give up!

> "All the adversity I've had in my life, all my troubles and obstacles, have strengthened me. . . . You may not realize it when it happens, but a good kick in the teeth may be the best thing in the world for you."
>
> —WALT DISNEY

ACHIEVEMENT ADVERSITIES— BE SWIFT AND BOLD ON YOUR ROAD

> "Adversity exasperates fools, rejects cowards, draws out the faculties of the wise and industrious, puts the modest to the necessity of trying their skill, awes the opulent, and makes the idle industrious."
>
> —UNKNOWN

A very good friend of mine who began importing stock from China hit a massive rut after his launch. He had seen a "success mentor" who told him that if he put it out there to the universe, it would come back at him. This "expert" forgot to mention the massive action taken by people who actually achieve. Is it that easy that you can just think wishfully? Throw it out there to the universe and it will bounce back at you? I'm not even going to tell you the answer to that because you already know it. We all know that we can't sit there and think, *My car is going to be in the driveway, my car is going to be in the driveway,* then open our eyes and our car is in the driveway. If you think that sounds ridiculous, it's because it is. Unless we get up and move the car, it's going to remain on the street. But people still buy the concept. There will be a lot of people, and many books, documentaries, and seminars that try to sugarcoat achievement. I even heard one speaker and author say that we can "manifest effortlessly" when it comes to what we want. If you ever hear anything like this and believe it, realize you are setting yourself up for a big disappointment. There never has been, and never will be, an easy way of achieving something great.

The positive side, however, is that even though sometimes in life there is no way out, **there is always a way through.** You will always hear from others that someone out there is worse off, although that's not really inspiring, is it? Inspiration comes from acknowledging that there was someone worse off that actually got through it! There is always a way. You must accept and make peace with a challenging situation, and look for every way to push forward or move swiftly around it. Don't resist; instead embrace how your experience can change your life for the better. We so often focus all our energy on the obstacles and not on the desired outcome. It's just like when there is a car in front of us that has its turn signal on, we automatically look for a way around, right? The last thing we want to do is stop the flow of where we are heading. **We must focus on the outcome, not the obstacles.**

I think we are all very aware that if we want something in life, we must go and get it. If you wait around and just bliss out all day, it will never come about. There is never an easy road to success, so put down the books and skip the seminars that tell you that. Most people also want the easier option because we like to believe we can do less and gain more. Definitely not the truth, and that's why most people never get what they want. It's a great selling tool for liars, though, because they're not telling the real story. Notice that only a few tell you about their adversities. Wonder why? It's a shame for those who, ten years down the track, are still sitting in their bedroom waiting for their Ferrari or their dream partner to drop out of the sky. Life is about learning, and the only way to grow is through challenges.

> "Adversity is a fact of life. It can't be controlled.
> What we can control is how we react to it."
> —ENGLISH PROVERB

This particular friend of mine did so much in the lead-up to his launch and expected such a great outcome that he neglected the "after" plan. When the phone wasn't ringing off the hook and the stock wasn't flying out the door, he assessed this outcome as a failure. What he wasn't aware of is that most business launches don't actually go according to plan.

It is absolutely crucial that your road of success is not based on one particular event. If it is, you leave yourself open to great disappointment. If you prepare for one big event, build up momentum and take massive action, then end up disheartened, that's worse than never going for it in the first place. This usually happens to people who have defined one set way to achieve something. Don't ever change your ultimate want if you truly believe in it, but be able to move around. You must diversify your efforts.

Bruce Lee summed it up beautifully when he said, "When you put water in a teacup, it becomes the teacup; when you put water in a bowl, it becomes the bowl. It can also crash or flow. Be water, my friends." What he was referring to is how water is able to mold its shape into anything it is put into. We must be able to mold ourselves into any situation we find ourselves in, as there is never one set way to be. There are many different avenues to be taken at all times. When you do find yourself at points of challenge, be aware that they are actually for your benefit. Any successful person will tell you that it was times of challenge that made them push harder and think broader. Adversities and challenges are actually **learning opportunities.**

117

Regarding my friend's business launch, I'd like to add that twelve months later, a businessman walked into his showroom and bought $60,000 worth of stock in one day. The ball rolled from there. He was quick to remind me that he had nights when he felt like his head was underwater and would run to his toilet to throw up, but he refused to put a time limit on what he believed in. He kept the faith, persisted, and finally got his break.

Life is a gift, my friends. You may only be one step away from unwrapping the paper.

If happiness is looking forward to something, and great emotions inspire us to act, then we must continue to set up new challenges, yes? Never lose sight of your passion, and always set up new visions and challenges far before the completion of the imminent one. The most important thing to recognize when setting out to achieve is that every step you take is one step closer. You must have your eyes fixed on this notion so it builds massive incentive, and you must never lose sight of your goals. Continue to take action and walk those steps that light up in front of you every day. Keep the faith if you believe in what you are doing, and there you have the ingredient to great achievement. Here's a strategy to ensure the strength of your success . . .

"Adversity precedes growth."

—ROSEMARIE ROSSETTI

STEP 1: CREATE MANY PLANS

If you have a plan, that's absolutely great. Create another one! Create five more if you can. Always have many options for improvement. If you don't have a plan, then make one. If you're thinking you don't know where to start, then my advice is to keep your eyes fixed on the prize. Feel it, be it, breathe it, meditate over it, talk about it, pray for it—I don't care what it is, just consume yourself with it. This will allow for inspiration to appear everywhere, and then write stuff down. Even if it seems extremely small at the time, make sure you catch it on paper, and things will flow from there. Create the after-after-after-plan. **If there are roadblocks, this will allow you to change direction.**

STEP 2: TAKE APPROPRIATE ACTION

You must take action every single day. Do two, three, five, or ten things a day; just make sure you are doing something. This will create momentum. Small steps equal massive progress. If you beat at a piñata enough times, the candy will eventually fall out. Use that concept with your visions.

STEP 3: ACKNOWLEDGE CHALLENGES/ADVERSITIES CORRECTLY

Don't just accept how things seem in an instant; that's narrow-minded. You must have an open mind on the road of achievement. Every time a challenge or adversity appears in your life, it doesn't matter how small, see it as a **learning point.** If you commit to making this simple adjustment, you will be inundated with great opportunities for growth.

STEP 4: NEVER LOSE SIGHT

Never ever take your eyes off the prize. Always remain focused on what you believe in. If it makes your heart sing, then don't stop. Holding your ultimate visions close to your heart and mind will continue to light up the path for you. It's our true inspiration.

"Boldness be my friend."

—WILLIAM SHAKESPEARE

GETTING DOWN TO BUSINESS

"Take up one idea. Make that one idea your life—
think of it, dream of it, live on that idea. Let the brain,
muscles, nerves, every part of your body, be full on
that idea, and just leave every other idea alone. This
is the way to success, that is the way great spiritual
giants are produced."

—SWAMI VIVEKANANDA

Wishful thinking doesn't work without action, so now it's time to see how action might not always work without some sort of plan. They say hard work always pays off. Well, I know people who have worked hard for thirty years and still don't have the things they wanted twenty years ago. I'm the first to admit that achievement doesn't come easy, but when you enjoy the process it doesn't seem that hard either. You enjoy the process when you have created so much emotional attachment to its result that you wouldn't live any other way.

We must learn to work smart and with a strategy. In the beginning of my change, I made a promise to myself that I would only model the elite of whatever industry I wanted to learn about. What would be the point of finding patterns from those who weren't as successful as others? Why not just go straight to the top and find their patterns? When I wanted to learn how to play tennis, I researched Roger Federer's style. The way he held the racquet, his motion, and his game mind-set became the groundwork for my practice. When I wanted to learn about business, I looked at the

Chinese and Japanese. I was always fascinated with the way they did business. It always seemed secretive and mysterious to me. It was as if they knew things that the West had not yet grasped. Through my quest to find answers, I stumbled across a book called *The Art of War,* written by an ancient Chinese military general, strategist, and philosopher, Sun-tzu. I discovered that the Chinese and Japanese use this book, and similar war books, as a basis for their business ventures. They view business like going into battle, and I guess in most cases it is. Courage, honor, strategy, preparation, when to attack or defend, and when to retreat are all important aspects for these people's success.

In order to make money from your passion, or even increase your wealth, you must think business. Does that mean your work isn't coming from your heart? If you are selfish and have no intention of sharing your success, then I guess it's not. If your work improves the lives of others and your business lifts your community, then of course it's still from your heart. It depends on the belief system you choose to build around monetizing your passion. When looking to build beliefs about money, think of a knife. If a knife was given to a humble man on an island, he could use it to cut fruit, which would make his life a little easier. If you gave the knife to a serial killer, you could probably bet what he would use it for. The knife can be two different tools; it all depends on how you look at it.

Most of the people I have heard say "money is evil" or slander those who have a lot are usually the same ones I hear complaining about not having enough. That's a contradiction, if you ask me, but it's because the majority don't think they have the capability to increase their wealth. It's much easier to attack people who do have that capacity in order to gain some quick satisfaction. How many of those people do you think would refuse a $10 million check? How many of them would refuse a double income bonus for the year? So is it money that is evil, or is it that some people do evil things with money? It's easier to blame a piece of paper than humans.

While I was in Thailand learning about the power of the mind, I had the pleasure of staying with some monks for three days. Even they were reliant on financial donations from the laypeople. In order for them to survive and keep the temples running in Bangkok, they needed money. Love it or lump it, it's a major part of our society. You might not want millions of dollars, and that's fine. I know people who have money that will last them a lifetime and they are unhappy, while some who are just comfortable are the happiest people alive. I also know people with no money who are the biggest haters, and those who have a lot and are doing great things for the world. How you deal with your financial situation is your choice. If you want to turn your passion into a lifelong career or create massive amounts of wealth, the reality is you must be prepared. Business is not for the fainthearted, so it means we must set ourselves up and build strength. If history has taught us anything, it's that everyone is capable of achieving. You could buy a business, start your own, or you alone could be your business. Whatever it is, here are some questions to get your mind going . . .

- How can I make my idea feasible and profitable?

- Do I have a marketing plan? How can I market? What can I do to reach a large amount of people without taking the edge from the image I want to portray?

- Do I have some sort of business plan?

- Do I want investors? If so, when do they break even? At what point do they see profit?

- Are my visions still too vague? Do I need to create more clarity about what I want?

- Are there operational skills in the business I need to learn? Do I need six to twelve months' practice in that type of business first?

- Are there people in the industry I can talk to and gain ideas from?

- Do I want a loan? If so, how much capital versus loan do I want?

- Am I likely to make profits instantly? If not, do I need another job to survive and continue to invest?

- What are the **principles** and **culture** I want to promote in my business? (Examples: honor, integrity, loyalty, fun, trust, etc. All successful businesses have these two areas cemented. They pass through to customers, staff, advertising, and marketing. It's also crucial that the owner practices what he preaches.)

- Do I need to lengthen my days to get more done? Is it beneficial to condition myself to six hours of sleep rather than eight or ten?

Why do you want to achieve in business? Are you going to treat it like your own mission? Is it because you want to be your own boss or like being in charge of your life? Are you passionate about what you do? If you are only doing it for the money, not the feeling, you will never be happy. **The cause must always override the materials. If it doesn't, you're in trouble.** It's fine to want the big toys, but never let them be the basis of crucial decision making. Instead, let your passion be the sole decider. People do things that destroy their life when driven by material concerns. Make sure you keep on top of it.

> "A business that makes nothing but money
> is a poor kind of business."
>
> —HENRY FORD

Don't be scared off by the questions on pages 122–23. Sometimes we ignore these things, but I guess that's why so many businesses crumble or people give up. I never went to university to learn how to answer them, and most successful businesspeople I know didn't either. All you have to do is get the ball rolling. Even taking notice of some of these questions will help you fill in the gaps as you go along. For example, my marketing plan began on a notepad with a pencil. I started by listing a few ideas of how I could market the book. After about a month, it turned into about ten pages. I would even pull over when driving so I could write a new idea in my phone. Then I began structuring it into sections and time frames. If you have yet to browse the internet for things you think will improve your business, do so immediately. You can find practically anything on the internet, and it's a free source. I'm not saying you will base your success on it, but it's a great reference. I typed in "ways to market a book," and was instantly bombarded with thousands of ideas.

ONLY BUILD ON PROGRESS

"Correction does much,
but encouragement does more."
—JOHANN WOLFGANG VON GOETHE

When we are working toward our visions, it is crucial that we acknowledge every step we take. It seems we go around reminding ourselves about when we make mistakes, but how often do we pat ourselves on the back for doing something great? Even if it's having the courage to tell someone how much you love them, sending one email toward your vision, or finding growth from self-criticism—they are all things to be really proud of.

Any great achiever has used this critical tool in reaching their peak. If you take a minute, you will actually realize that it's impossible to gain growth from something that you see as a negative. We have to shift our mind-sets to reward ourselves with every step. The way we train police dogs is a great example. These dogs are the elite of the elite, and they are very disciplined and trustworthy. The officers know that when it's time to deliver, these canines step up to the plate with accuracy and certainty. They are not beaten or screamed at in their training. They are conditioned by being rewarded every time they make progress. When this is repeated, it gives them the incentive to do it again and again, until they are like machines. The only way to really enjoy our life and achieve our goals is to condition ourselves to the great feeling we attain when we are rewarded.

When you were a child and your parents screamed at you to do something, even though you might have done it, you didn't want to do it again. On the other hand, when you did something and they mentioned how proud they were and how well you did, you felt happy enough to repeat it. We live in a society where punishment for doing the wrong thing is seen as the solution. It seems that misbehaving gets far more attention, so it becomes quite appealing to those in search of a spotlight. But how often do we praise people for doing great things for the world? How often are they recognized? Is it any wonder why there are so many people who are lost and confused? The only way to change is by building on positive progress.

Our true motivation lies in repeatedly being proud of yourself. If you ever wonder how some people seem to stay so motivated in life, this is why. They don't wait for other people to come and praise them for their efforts, they do it themselves. This influences others to do it, because they feel your passion. Even if it's something that you think you might have done poorly, always look for the growth in it.

I was coaching an aspiring singer who would really beat herself up over not hitting the correct notes. All she focused on was how poorly she had done, and she forgot to recognize the great aspects of her performance. Instead of looking at her mistakes and saying, "How can I improve these areas and work on them?" she would view them as a failure. We are our own biggest critics, but once you recognize that your criticism is the best life coach you will ever have, you will excel. You need to get physically excited with every step you take, regardless of how small it might seem at the time. This allows you to realize that accomplishment feels great on all levels. Get physical, get vocal, jump up and down, dance around your house, look like a crazy person—it doesn't matter; just build incentive. **Your feelings of today shape tomorrow.**

> "Most of us, swimming against the tides of trouble the world knows nothing about, need only a bit of praise or encouragement—and we will make the goal."
>
> —ROBERT COLLIER

11

Times of Crisis—Let's Be Honest

"Every crisis offers you extra desired power."

—WILLIAM MOULTON MARSTON

Nothing in the world stands still—it either depletes or grows. We are no exception to that rule, so if you're not appreciating, you're depreciating. At times, it even seems as though we are proud of being worse off than others and will brag about it, saying, "Oh, I've got bigger problems to worry about." Attempting to prove you are worse off than others is like competing for the most miserable life, and I don't see that as something to boast or brag about. If you don't like your job, then leave; if you didn't have enough sleep, then go to bed earlier.

Going back to the common social complaint about work, is it really the actual job one doesn't like, or is it the belief systems one has around work itself? I used to be someone who would complain about the job I had, yet every other job seemed just as bad. We will find every excuse not to like our new job, continually saying the same things. I have discovered that it's usually the attitude one takes toward the word *work*. If we have no vision for ourselves, we will never be happy with feeling as though we are making someone else wealthy while we are missing out in the process.

A great friend who is like a brother to me said, "The system I was brought up to believe would grant me success was a lie." He completed a university degree and then worked for multiple companies over ten years. Even the thought that his approach to life would be a safe one failed him. Two separate companies, who had no mercy at the time of the cull, laid him off. The last company he worked for gave him a role where his target revenue was $17 million a year. He made the target, but only made a salary of $80,000 himself. He contacted the owner of the company to ask for a raise, only to receive a response saying his boss was "too busy" to discuss it because he was on vacation on his yacht.

He made a conscious decision to take his knowledge and start his own marketing business. If you are an employee of a company, make sure you are doing it for your own cause. Build the belief that work is the stepping-stone and foundation for your own endeavors. I think having a solid known income is a great thing, but if you are looking to expand yourself, then use it for your own benefit. Look at it as working for yourself, rather than working for somebody else. It may even be something you have on the side, like investing in property or shares. At one stage I had two jobs and partnership of my own business. I would finish work at 6:00 p.m., go deliver pizza until 10:00 p.m., then go and work on my business. You will always find the time if you are committed, and excuses won't get in the way.

You may call it work; I call it building a dream.

People become addicted to their victimization and start believing that it's an escape for feeling better, but we all know that isn't true, because we are likely to break down and give up not long after. People make things out to be worse than they are so they don't have to do anything about them. In every area of life, it seems like a pretty good escape, but we are in fact cornering ourselves. Those same people don't want to be disappointed, or feel rejection or failure, so they say things like "I'm skeptical" or "I'm pessimistic" when faced with an empowering alternative. I believe it's just being too weak to face the truth and admit they see a better way. It doesn't take courage to be a pessimist. What's wrong is always accessible, but leaders and those who take control over their own lives decide to look at what's right in the same situation.

The answer in any time of crisis or victimization is not "positive thinking" in the bubbly, saccharine way it's often portrayed. It is great to be upbeat, but we are not going to be like that all the time, period. We can never be just one way in life; different situations call for different reactions. If your house is on fire, I'm sure you are not going to be skipping down the street singing nursery rhymes. At that time you won't even be conscious of positive thinking, but you can be **intelligent.** And by thinking intelligently, you can quickly get yourself together and say, "Okay, what am I going to do here? How can I make this better? I should start by calling the firefighters." Intelligent thinking helps you to assess a situation properly and create a strategy. That's how positive thinking should be portrayed, especially with any crossroad you find yourself at. The challenge is that most people I come across attempt to think positively, but very few ever get to the core of what they are feeling or experiencing. It's always about intelligent thinking. **When you decide to see things for what they really are, not worse than they are, you will always find another avenue for growth.**

I once had an overweight client who told me that he had a slow metabolism and was big boned. He victimized himself in every way possible and made it sound worse than it was so that he didn't have to face the short-term pain of hearing the bald truth. I looked him dead in the eye and said, "No, you are obese, and you need to get off your ass and run like you have never run before." Call me the bully, or call me someone who cares. A few months later I received an email from him. It was a picture of him by a hotel pool in China, where he was then working, and I must say even I was shocked at his achievement. He thanked me dearly because all he needed was to hear someone spit out the truth, and that was enough to shoot him off into an empowering direction. For his whole life, his family members and friends had covered the truth because they didn't want to feel bad by telling him. That was obviously selfish and contributed to his health problems. I've trained many clients with supposed "slow metabolisms" or who are "big boned," and they get fit just like anyone else.

> They say the truth hurts, but don't they also say the truth sets you free? The things that usually hurt us the most are the same things that set us free.

I came from a family that didn't have a lot of money, and I always had to think of my own way to make it. My parents didn't buy me my first car, pay for my vacations, or invest in my business. I never asked them for it, because I knew if they had it, they would have already given it to me. For a long time, while seeing people around me getting all those things handed to them, I told myself I was the victim of an unloved destiny. I had decided to look at it in the worst possible way rather than to look at it how it actually was. Here I was in a country where I was surrounded by so many resources and opportunities. My parents provided me with food, education, shelter, and love, when so many others never have this experience. I finally realized I had a compelling future, if only I decided to look at it that way, and then the situation seemed like a pretty good one. **Most times we complain about things that we have full control over.** We need to stop lying to ourselves and be completely honest, or else we will never make a change. Others will say they are being realistic when looking at a situation in the worst possible way, but is that the truth, or are they just exaggerating? Being real requires you to be honest with yourself.

TAKE OWNERSHIP. OBSERVE THE SITUATION AS IT REALLY IS, NOT WORSE THAN IT IS.

Now that we have stopped seeing our situation as worse than it is, we can take the next step. If it's true that we can look at things as worse than they are and that view can be real to our minds, who's to say we can't look at things as better than they are? This would have just as much impact on our reaction to a situation, but for the better. It would actually change everything about the situation and, more important, change the outcome of our total approach. You must look at the situation as being **better** than it is. Even if something seems to be a massive challenge, if you have something great to look forward to, you will find a way to get there. Set up a compelling vision, put things into perspective, and draw out what you can learn from this. Make the vision as real as possible, and you have automatically set up another path to go on.

VISION. SEE IT BETTER THAN IT IS.

Now that you have created something beneficial to work toward, it's time to shape your vision. This calls for an action plan, or a strategy that is aligned with your new outcome. Take action in order to bring that very vision into reality. Focus your decision making around it, remind yourself of the desired outcome, and become it. What would you have to believe? How would you have to stand? What would you have to remain focused on? Who could you talk to? What other action can you take to create it to be that way?

NEW STRATEGY. ACTION THE WAY YOU NOW SEE IT.

12

The Action Trilogy

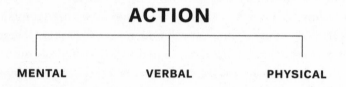

Something I've noticed after speaking to many people about life is that most see their physical actions as having more effect than their mental and verbal ones. I'm here to smash that belief and tell you that every thought you have and word you speak has just as much power in shaping your destiny. Most do not acknowledge that everything is outsourced from their thoughts. Thoughts cause words to come out of their mouths, and thoughts are the basis of all decision making. The balance is symmetrical, but our greatest downfall is not being aware of this. We are continually shaping our destiny through these three types of action—and we are continually shaping our nature and beliefs. If you got offered the mind of Bill Gates, would you take it? How about the dancing ability of Michael Jackson? Or the golf swing of Tiger Woods? If the answer is yes, then why don't people set out to learn the traits and skills they desire? These professionals must have learned to become that great, right? Surely it wasn't easy.

The reason most people refuse to believe they can be great is that they condition themselves to believe they are stuck with the actions they have always chosen. Furthermore, they create an illusion that their previous choices and experiences sum up who they are and what they are becoming.

> "It doesn't matter where you came from,
> it matters only where you're going."
> —CONDOLEEZZA RICE

Take a look at those individuals who seem to have had everything given to them on a silver platter and then end up in rehab, while others who have been through the most horrific experiences set out to make the biggest impact on the world. **We are not stuck with our experiences, and they do not determine who we are.** What's happened doesn't dictate what's going to happen. A wise man once said, "Tomorrow doesn't equal yesterday." That said, we are the sum of our thoughts and what we choose to do right now. We have an addiction to things that are worlds away from common sense, and that's why common sense doesn't seem all that common. Surprisingly, those people who use common sense are actually branded as uncommon these days. They are usually seen as crazy until they prove they are a cut above the rest. Are they special? No, they just used common sense. There are patterns that we think we must continue to be slaves to because we always have. That's a lie, as the choices we make right now ultimately shape who we are becoming.

It seems that most of us have a clear indication of what we should do, but don't actually do it. This is why obtaining knowledge in life is not the same as learning. If you gain knowledge but don't put it into practice, it leads to nothing being learned. I've had so many people say to me, "I know this stuff"; my response is that knowing doesn't seem to be making a difference, you **have to do it.** They continue to act the same way, have the same experiences and the same emotions, and they are never fulfilled.

A man twice my age once confronted me and said, "What have you learned about life? You're half my age." The reason this friend of a friend was so angry was that he had just found out his girlfriend cheated on him for the third time. I explained to him that it only took one similar experience for me to make my decision. It seems he knows a lot about what he should do, but what has he learned by going back to a relationship that causes him so much pain? He has learned nothing. It doesn't matter whether you have had ten experiences or one, the only time you can learn is by taking action.

We must shift from thinking, change is painful, to thinking, change is pleasurable. Basic methods of discipline might not seem to last long, but what does work is becoming addicted to something positive and new. You must exchange a disempowering addiction for an empowering alternative. Embracing this concept allows for a conscious shift and enforces real growth. It's not until we turn our knowledge into action that we achieve growth in our life. Only by this formula can you experience the never-ending cycle of self-growth.

PERSONAL GROWTH FORMULA:

L = K + A

LEARNING, KNOWLEDGE, ACTION

THE BATTLE

The battle has only ever been you against you!

Most great things in life lie in simplicity; the trouble is, we have made things so complicated that being simple itself is a challenge. We race around trying to figure out all these complex ways to gain fulfillment and success, but we have always had the qualities within us. The challenge is putting your knowledge into practice. As long as there is life, there will be challenges. Our character is not based on the absence of challenges but on how well we handle ourselves in the face of them.

I once had a conversation about life and change with a lady who inspired me to add this section, "The Battle," to the book. It's an essential section to take note of. As we were discussing all this stuff, I was full of energy, and she said, "You make it sound so easy, just like other motivational speakers." I had to remind her that I was not a motivational speaker. It's one thing to be pumped up for an hour by hearing some inspiring words, but it's another thing to be pumped up for life, and that takes strategy. I educate, not just motivate, and there's a major difference. I educate people on how to motivate themselves, because that's what I have done for myself. However, I thought about what she said for a second, and it reminded me how hard it was at times and how strong I had to remain. It was a battle in its truest form, but by being equipped with the appropriate strategies and solutions, I wasn't setting myself up to be defeated anymore.

Change is a challenge. It's not a mere walk in the park. The great thing is that it's a simple equation. **If you want change, you have to make change, or else nothing is going to change.** We seem to be oblivious to it, or in some cases we do realize this, but we are scared to embrace it. We are scared that it might have the power to actually change our life forever. Even if it's in a positive way, we still seem to fear the unknown.

> In order to win any battle, you must be equipped with the most powerful arsenal. The battle of the mind is no exception.

Life is about learning and growing, and it's not easy at times. Who you were is more than ready to battle who you're trying to become. That self is not just going to give up without a fight. You have trained that self to fall into guilt or depression, along with the fear that you can't achieve—I'm sure you can help me out with the list. But you have the power to rewire yourself. The way you physically, mentally, and verbally act must change if you want change; there is no other way through. I can only show you ways to get there and make your walk as comfortable as I possibly can. You have to go on the journey and walk your own path. I just want you to know that it's not all a bed of roses, so you can be prepared. When a mental, verbal, or physical battle does come up, don't think you're alone and submit to being the victim.

Everyone who has been on this journey, achieved great things, or made massive change in their life has acknowledged that giving up would have been easier. Anyone who says that it was easy must be a superman or woman. If someone makes you believe that suddenly their whole life turned around completely, and everything they knew or thought changed instantly, they're taking you for a long ride. You may never get to your destination, and you may even crash pretty hard along the way. I've seen too many people left in the dark by misguided motivational speakers or authors who are out on their own selfish agenda. We must use our intelligence on this journey. **Nothing in life that is great is easy. If it was easy, then it wouldn't be great.** We wouldn't be able to tell the difference between living an ordinary life and an amazing life. Given that it's not going to be a breeze, it's important to acknowledge that it's not that hard either. I've come to realize that human beings do not like problems, but we thrive when challenged, and that's what reconditioning yourself to find your truth is.

> "The gate to life is narrow and the way that leads to it
> is hard, and there are few people who find it."
> —MATTHEW 7:14

In order to overcome these challenges, especially the mental ones, we need to have an army always waiting at the entrance of our mind, not so much anticipating a challenge as always ready.

Every time you take down thoughts or emotions that are preventing you from excelling in that moment, more recruits jump on board. Before you know it, the army within is far more powerful than anything else.

> "Your worst enemy cannot harm you
> as much as your own unguarded thoughts."
> —THE BUDDHA

Think of this reconditioning process like that of a right-handed boxer who is preparing to lead with his left. The trainer's instructions are that he has to learn to lead with his left hand to win the fight. The boxer will get confused during sparring and will swap to his right numerous times, but **now** he knows what he has to do to win the fight. He stays conscious of it and quickly corrects himself until it becomes a part of his nature.

Whenever your limiting side seems to be winning a mental battle, here is a quick strategy to gain control again:

- **Stop resisting.** When you feel you are resisting your mind too much, just stop! Make peace with the situation and tell your limiting side, "Okay, you're here and I know what you're trying to do, but you will never win." Say it in a relaxed tone and nod your head as if you are certain about your comment. Think of a time when someone has tried to upset you, but you have assured them that their efforts are pointless. It's the same when you try to upset yourself. Your limiting thoughts will eventually pass by doing this.

- **Write.** You must write down how you feel. When you feel great, write it down. When you feel upset, write down how you can turn it around. You can always go back to when you felt great and read that again. As you are probably aware, the times that we have resistance building up within ourselves are the same times that everything seems to irritate us. It could be an issue we have with a friend, a partner, or a job. It's not until we get it off our chest that we feel free again. The same goes with resisting our thoughts. Get them out and write them down.

MENTAL ACTION—ALL IN THE MIND

"Men get rich by doing things in a Certain Way; and in order to do so, men must become able to think in a Certain Way. A man's way of doing things is the direct result of the way he thinks about things."

—WALLACE D. WATTLES

Once you become aware that every thought you have is shaping your destiny and re-creating your reality, you have won half the battle. The best way to come to terms with this is to take a good look at the thoughts you are having. Notice the pattern with experiences you have had and continue to have. Check whether your thoughts are making you act in a certain way and attracting certain kinds of experiences. Once this is done, you will almost always see a pattern that can be broken. We are usually just reacting to our environment on automatic. We feel as though we have no real control over our experiences or how to think when a challenge arises. The truth is, we have always been in control of which direction we take, and until we take full accountability for where we are in our life, we cannot make change. Obviously there are experiences and people we cannot control, but we can always decide what significance they have for our life, our perception, and how we react to them. **Most people believe our thoughts are at the mercy of our eyes. I disagree. Our eyes are at the mercy of our thoughts, and hence our feelings.** As long as we let our mind wander all day, we get set up for having many unexpected experiences. We are not in control of what we are creating. The only time your life is really affected by the world outside is when you lose control of your mind.

When we monitor our thoughts, we are able to shift their direction to where we want to go. In order to live an outstanding life, we must capture the great thoughts and let the other ones pass. Everyone has the same thoughts flowing through them; certain people just choose to capture certain ones. It is your choice to hold on to a thought that is disempowering, and it will also be up to you whether you let it flow out of you the same way it came in. You don't need to hold on to them.

Relate every experience you have to benefit the bigger picture you have set for your life.

Human beings have approximately 60,000 thoughts a day. How many of those are you using to create the life you want? As you would probably agree, it seems difficult to change the thoughts that you normally have subconsciously. We have repeated these thoughts so many times that we have them with no real conscious thought process. The only way to truly rewire your subconscious mind, which is crucial for success, is to **look at the effect that every one of your thoughts is having on your life.**

The reason why humans like analogies and stories so much is that we love looking at things from an outside perspective, then relating that to our own experiences. When you look at your thoughts from an outside perspective, you find a clearer way to relate to them. In order to have an extraordinary life, you must stay conscious of everything you do. Breaking the unconscious pattern of disempowering thoughts and getting off that wheel that brings you unhappiness requires you to look at the cause and effect of every thought you have. If you need a refresher on how every thought physically changes your state, go back to the discussion of neuroplasticity in our 1st Step (page 52). Also, use this question for your thoughts:

*Is what I am choosing to tzhink about now productive
toward what I want?*

I've explained this throughout the book, but I'll give you another detailed example. Let's say someone cuts you off while driving and you react with anger, as most do. It is going to affect what you create next in your life, as the energy of that anger will flow on to whatever activity follows. More important, it builds the belief that when a challenge comes up, the option is to get angry and not be productive toward your growth. On the other hand, you could react, but instantly correct yourself, because you now see the detrimental effect your thoughts are having on your life. I'm not saying you won't react at all, but by being aware of your thoughts, you are ready to turn them around if a challenging situation arises. This allows you to take a different approach and build on productive thoughts. Monitor your thoughts throughout your day, and correct yourself or counter-think. Sometimes it's a battle because you have been used to looking at something in a particular way, but you must look for another avenue that will benefit you. It's not hard to see that every day your thoughts create your life.

"A man is but the product of his thoughts;
what he thinks, he becomes."

—MAHATMA GANDHI

The commitment to do this is one that is made by every successful person. If their thoughts are not monitored and continually corrected toward what they want, they know they will never get it. It comes naturally to some, so a lot of the time they might not even realize they are doing it until questioned deeply on the topic. For others, like me, it is something we learn to do. I just knew I was sick of feeling the way I did, so I decided to take mental action. It wasn't until I discovered that my thought patterns created my emotions that I was able to take control of my life. I did this to turn my whole life around and, surprisingly, it didn't take long at all. It's actually quite amazing how much you learn and grow by monitoring your thoughts for one week.

You should also challenge yourself to think big during the day. To reach our peak we must think about the bigger picture. If all you think about is small achievements, then that's all you will ever get. When you stay open to thinking big, the rest in between doesn't seem overwhelming because you are keeping your eyes on that prize. I remember sitting down in my bedroom only a year and a half before my book was finished; I had written one page and I had no clients at the time, but I knew what I wanted. I asked myself, "Daniel, how on earth are you going to write a whole book?" Every time I would begin to stress over the number of pages, or begin to think about not being able to put my ideas on paper, I would fight it. I mean, I had never written anything in my life besides a few literature projects at school that I had completely forgotten about. I would block out the negative thoughts with as much power as I had. I continued to reassure myself that it was going to happen. I would envision myself opening up the finished product, and only a few months later I created it. The ideas and words of the book just flowed. I would meet people who were in search of coaching, and I began attracting all the things I had remained focused on.

Realistically, there is only one way to change your life: Change the way you think.

Thinking about the end result also has a funny way of cutting time. Even the smaller steps are achieved at a much faster pace. After a week or two of staying focused on the bigger picture, you will notice the massive growth spurt that was available to you your whole life. **When you think on a large scale, ideas will flow to and from that direction.** Even if you learn something that you think is small about the new direction you are heading, write down that progress. Turn the imaginary thought into concrete form by making it as real as you can. Any growth or idea, big or small, don't miss it or let it slip, and soon enough they will be flowing on a regular basis.

To strengthen and expand our mind, we must invest in it. You must read books, listen to audiotapes or CDs, go to seminars, and, most important, guide your thoughts successfully. Individuals who have had an influence on my growth and to whom I pay homage are Ralph Waldo Emerson, Napoleon Hill, Kahlil Gibran, Wallace D. Wattles, Maya Angelou, Deepak Chopra, and Mahatma Gandhi. These people are just some of the giants who have made the world better. Learning from extraordinary people is a great way to invest in your development. **Investing in yourself is like investing in the greatest shares—the more you invest, the greater the dividends.** By feeding your mind the right information, you strengthen its ability to create a great life.

"I am no longer cursed by poverty because
I took possession of my own mind,
and that mind has yielded me every material thing
I want, and much more than I need.
But this power of mind is a universal one,
available to the humblest person
as it is to the greatest."

—ANDREW CARNEGIE

VERBAL ACTION—WHAT YOU SAY IS WHAT YOU ARE

> "Great people talk about ideas. Average people talk
> about things. Small people talk about other people."
>
> —TOBIAS S. GIBSON

Kids say the darnedest things, don't they? When I was a child there was a particular retort we would fling at other kids after they said a judgmental slur: "What you say is what you are." I didn't realize how much truth that held until recently. People have no idea of the giant impact their choice of vocabulary has on their lives. **The words we commit to shape and condition who we are just as much as our thoughts and physical actions.** It does not matter in what context or subject; as long as you use words that have limitations, you are limiting your state and hence your success. A quick example is when we use the word *can't* in everyday conversation. Take a second to ponder this, and you will realize that nearly every time you say the word *can't,* it is untrue. You do have a choice. It's not so much that you can't do something; it's that you don't want to. The more you say you can't do things, the more your mind conditions that notion, and it will appear every time a challenge comes up.

By replacing our current vocabulary with new empowering substitutions, we will influence the emotions we experience throughout our day. That emotional experience determines how we act and the results we get. We are linguistically programming our subconscious mind with every word, which turns into ritual and becomes our nature. We say things unaware of the massive effect they have on our lives. I cannot overstate the importance of this; it will be the be-all and end-all of your success. Here are some examples of words and sayings that we must stay away from in everyday speech, and some **great ones to put in their place:**

- I could never do that—**I can do that**

- I'm not smart enough—**I am infinitely intelligent, have the resources, and will learn**

- I'll never be wealthy—**I must be wealthy**

- I'm always sick—**I feel great**

- I'm too fat—**I want to be fit and healthy**

- I'm unattractive—**I'm beautiful**

- If I start my own business, I'll fail—**I'll do whatever it takes to succeed**

- I can't earn more than my parents—**I can earn more than my parents**

- I'm a loser—**I will win**

- I can't be bothered—**My existence is energy**

- I'm too tired—**I must demand an energetic state now**

- That's really bad—**What's great about this?**

- That's impossible—**Anything is possible**

- I feel drained—**I'm a powerhouse**

- I can't—**I can**

- What a coincidence, or What luck—**Cause and effect**

- Maybe one day—**I'll make the day**

- Hopefully—**I'm certain**

- That's too hard—**I love a challenge**

- I'll do it later—**I must do it now**

- I'm over it—**I'm just getting started**

- What if . . . —**It's not happening now, so don't worry in advance**

- I should have—**I didn't, but I'm in control of myself now, which means I can**

- I'll try—**Do or don't do**

- I hate my life—**Love is life**

- I wish I was happy—**I choose to be happy or not**

- He's lucky—**He's successful**

- I hate him/her—**I love myself enough not to hate**

- I hope something bad happens to them—**I wish the best for them, which means I will be blessed**

- I hope I get there—**I know I will get there**

- I won't find that person—**I have faith and I'll make sure I do**

- I need that—**I want that**

- I'm okay/not bad—**I'm great**

- I don't know—**I'll find out**

- There is nothing I can do about it—**Is there really nothing I can do about it?**

The first sets of words are all limiting. By habitually repeating them, they are causing you to never get past those views. The second words, in bold, are empowering and will benefit your life. It doesn't matter how hard it may seem at times, you must replace words that have no benefit for your life with empowering substitutes. When an athlete is playing poorly for his team, does the coach leave him in the whole game? If he is a good coach, he will take him out and put someone in that will enhance the team's success. You must coach the words you commit to strategically.

Another myth I would like to clear up is the concept of being jinxed. We are taught to believe that if we say things that will benefit our life, we will jinx ourselves. I'm sure you have heard this outright lie throughout your life. The power of it really occurred to me when I heard my friend repeating how well he was going to do on a written test that was going to ultimately determine the grades he received for his last year at university. His father overheard him and said, "I wouldn't be talking like that, son, you don't want to jinx yourself." That sounds absurd, doesn't it? But just think how many times you have heard that and, more important, submitted to that belief. Some people see it as a way of being less disappointed if the worst happens. Exactly: **if!** Why on earth would you predict the worst possible outcome? Why would you worry in advance over something that isn't even real? Where is the intelligence in that? Realistically, does it lessen the disappointment? The reason that some people never achieve what they want is that they lack self-belief. What hope do you give yourself if you are too scared to have faith and believe in your own ability to begin with?

It doesn't matter if you are using restrictive words in a joking manner or in a serious or destructive manner, they all have equal effect. Only use words that have power to help you grow: I can, I will, I am, and I must. These words make you feel great about yourself. For a brief moment, think about how many conversations a day you are involved in. Now count how many contribute to creating what you want in life, compared with how many contribute to things you don't want. How many of the conversations make you feel empowered and inspired, compared with the number that make you feel the opposite? How many are you complaining in?

Stay away from negative notations and words.

You might feel a bit funny walking around and only spitting out words that you think are positive, but the notion of "positive" isn't the only factor here. It's all about using the common sense we are built with. **Is there any sense in using vocabulary that restricts**

us from excelling in life? What you decide to say on a daily basis becomes your reality, so it's just as real in conditioning you. If you say it's too hard, then it always will be. If you say it's impossible or you can't, then that's how you will perceive reality. Whatever you decide to say is in fact real, because it will force you to act that way. I ask people how they are and they reply "not bad" or "okay." If you want to be great, then say it, and you will start believing it. I would be focusing on why I said "not bad" in the first place and immediately do something to turn it around. We must train ourselves to speak with powerful, inspiring, and productive language.

By being aware of how powerful language is in shaping our destiny, you can now watch the pattern with those who use limiting words. Look at their whole demeanor. Notice how miserable their day is and how unproductive they usually are in moving toward any real visions. Next time you hear people talking at work or at a café, listen and notice how much their conversation contributes to the very feeling and situation they are complaining about. Observe how much energy they are giving it. Most important, use it as an eye-opener to observe and correct yourself. You will condition and reprogram your state in no time.

> "Death and life are in the power of the tongue, and
> those who love its use will eat its fruit."
> —PROVERBS 18:21

Do you think the most successful people or those who add value to the world waste their day discussing irrelevant things? You bet they don't. If you want to add value, talk like it; if you want to achieve at your peak, speak like it; and if you want real success, surround your conversations with it. Hype it up so much to yourself and those around you that you know you have to deliver. People say, "talk is cheap," but what I think they mean is "Talk is cheap on its own." Talking big is actually quite valuable when you know you are going to follow through. **If you don't speak it, you won't get it; if you don't talk like it, you will never be it.**

PHYSICAL ACTION—SMALL STEPS ARE MASSIVE PROGRESS

"A journey of a thousand miles
begins with one small step."

—LAO-TZU

I truly believe that most people know exactly what they must do to get what they want, but their biggest downfall is never taking action. They will listen to other people's opinions on the secrets of success, but they never put them into action. What they don't realize is that the secret is in doing! Only then will they understand how the concepts they have learned actually work. The strategies in this book create extraordinary lives, but even they are useless if they are not practiced. It's those who act that get rewards instantly.

Even if you get just an inkling that something will be beneficial in the shaping of your life, you must act. Those inklings usually turn into great satisfaction. Even if you commit to doing five different activities that are only 10 percent a week better than what you normally do, that increase in performance will vastly improve your life.

"You don't have to be great to get started,
but you have to get started to be great."

—LES BROWN

It's obviously one thing telling yourself to get up and take action toward your growth, but as we all know, it's another thing actually doing it. Do you ever have those times where you really want to do something, but your mind gets so bogged down with ideas and things to do that you just seem to stand still? It was happening to me while I was writing this book, and I knew other people would have gone through the same thing. All these ideas seem to flow, but it's a lot easier to just think about them rather than actually doing them. We have all these great ideas for our business, sorting out our finances, schooling, and our relationships, but we never seem to act. Why is that? It's because most of the time we are collecting so much information that it almost feels unrealistic to see them all through. The amount that we have piled up scares us, so it's much easier to run rather than face them. We say things like "I'll do it later" or "It can wait until tomorrow." Do you really get it done later or tomorrow? By the time you have piled up all these things to do later or tomorrow, you're going to need a day to transform into a year. Then you will find absolutely anything and everything to do except for the task that you have set yourself. If there were rankings for that, I would have been a champion in the game. **Stop weighing too many options. You are most likely weighing yourself down in the process. Just do it!**

> "A life that does not go into action is a failure."
> —ARNOLD TOYNBEE

The great solution is that small steps equal massive progress. Nothing in the world starts itself, so it means we have to get the ball rolling. Think of a snowball going down a mountain and picking up mass and speed as it takes each new turn. We still have to begin by pushing it, right? In David J. Schwartz's self-help book *The Magic of Thinking Big,* he states: "Action must precede action. That's a law of nature. Nothing starts itself, not even the dozens of mechanical gadgets we use daily." He goes on to explain that even an automatic heater that regulates temperature in our house requires us to set the temperature. I don't care how small or insignificant it may seem to the bigger picture at the time, I promise you that every step counts. Without those small steps first, you will never gain the strength and momentum to get to those bigger steps.

We don't enter this world running. Life requires us to grow, just like anything else that exists in the world. All successful people know it's about getting into gear and kick-starting without too much deliberation. Others who don't achieve are those who focus on why they can't do it, why it's too hard, and why they shouldn't, instead of doing what they know they must do. Successful people convince themselves of the opposite of those limiting questions. They give reasons **why they must do it, how it can be done, and reaffirm that it's the only way.** Most decisions we make are due to a strong level of self-convincing, and that requires a buildup. We must use our convincing tool to direct our energy toward what will ultimately benefit us. People can become overwhelmed because they see all the small steps as an alliance with pain. They will evaluate a million different things to do instead of focusing on the massive value of the end result. Imagine a lazy person thinking about washing his own car. He will think of all the undesirable activities he has do to get the job done before he even gets there. He thinks about getting off the couch, getting a bucket of water, grabbing the soap and sponge, and changing his clothes. Then he must wash the car, dry it, undress, and take a shower. All this overwhelming thought helps him to talk himself out of it. He wiggles his backside farther into the deep grooves of his favorite couch and dozes off for his sixth nap of the day. His partner then walks in the door and tells him there is a car wash up the road that has a special discount of $10 just for today. He gets up and shoots out the door. Ten dollars is more than he would have paid for washing it himself, yet he put more value on the end result and attached more pain to the other scenario. He neglected to consider that he would still have to get up off the couch, change his clothes, get in the car, drive there, and so on. He left out all the small steps because it was easier to think of the pleasurable outcome. In order to get things done in life, we must remain focused on the pleasure of the end result. If we do, most of the steps in between switch from pain to pleasure.

When you don't set up something to look forward to, the little things frequently get to you.

All great achievers know that their accomplishments begin with taking an initial step. Once you get started by doing the small steps first, your interest in doing more skyrockets. The results and how much you grow in such a short amount of time are actually quite amazing. After persisting in doing a few small tasks, you will notice that you willingly take time to do more. Those ten minutes will turn into thirty, which will turn into an hour. It becomes exciting working toward something that you actually want, and soon enough it will consume your whole life. It doesn't feel like a boring process because you have vision.

Throughout our lives we have heard that if we believe in ourselves, then we can achieve anything. There is no greater truth, but how do we do that? Once you spark yourself into action, you build faith in your ability to create the life you desire. You acknowledge the mass of energy you have within you that can be accessed in an instant, which helps build your self-belief. A sense of pride soon follows every step forward, and that's when you become a very powerful being. I urge you to spark your life **right now** and take action toward something on your wants list. When I say do anything, I actually mean it. Send an email, make a phone call, go and get a brochure, speak to someone, inquire on the internet, go and get the materials, book a dance lesson, write down an idea that you thought of—absolutely anything.

"A superior man is modest in his speech,
but exceeds in his actions."

—CONFUCIUS

The main message I am trying to get across is that if you think something as small as making a phone call is insignificant to the bigger picture, then you have automatically gone back into the majority. Seriously, how do you think these great achievers did it? Where do you think they started? You must take action every single day toward what you want, no matter how small it may seem at the time. **Do at least one thing each day, make sure you recognize the progress, and be proud of yourself for doing it.** Each day's progress means you are one step closer than you were the day before, and then after a week, that's a great improvement. The small steps you take now determine exactly what your outcome will be. Sometimes you're only a little bit off, and directing those steps intelligently in everyday life will make a world of difference.

There was a day when I was faced with a mental battle. I was considering whether I should continue fighting for my dreams. To reassure myself, I kept repeating, "It's all going to happen," referring to the bigger picture I had set for my life. But then I stopped! It was as if someone said to me in a loud voice, "It's not all going to happen—it's already happening." I'm in the process of creating my visions with every step I take. There is no real end or destination. The growth is consistent and never-ending. Where do we stop? Our visions don't just come one day; we contribute to creating them every day with the actions we commit to. Success is the journey.

Everyone is too concerned with what they are going to do instead of what they are doing.

152

TASK

Go and take action right now—anything at all, just get it started and push that snowball down the mountain. Do not read on until you have completed at least one thing, it doesn't matter how small, then come back and write it here:

_____

_____

_____

_____

_____

_____

It's also great to set short-term goals, but keep your eyes on the bigger prize. The small steps will light up for you as you keep your eyes fixed. You will be far more empowered to take them when emotions around the bigger picture are produced.

Have you ever been driving on the highway when the speed limit reduces to almost half because of construction? It goes from 100 kph (60 mph) to 60 kph (37 mph). How slow does it feel? It almost feels like you are crawling, doesn't it? You then wait in anticipation for the end of the construction so you can zoom off again. On a suburban road, however, that reduced speed is the normal speed, and hence feels quite normal. So why does it feel so slow on the highway? Once you have been driving at 100 kph, there is no way you want to go back to feeling like a snail! Once you speed up your life, you will never want to go back to the way you were. Every time your action starts to slow down toward things you want, your awareness will immediately remind you to speed it back up.

And don't be disheartened if you don't hit a target in the time you set—it's happened to the greatest. It will come if you continue to persist. Funnily enough, it usually comes when you are ready for it. Whoever warrants these gifts to us is very intelligent, and most times I have been thankful for them coming after I would have initially liked them to. I noticed that if certain things had come my way when I really wanted them, I might not have been mentally or emotionally ready. Does that mean I didn't do everything I could to bring them about? No, of course not, I took action every day. You have to build and stick to the belief that **"no matter how long it takes, or what it takes, I am going to get there."**

> "You don't have to see the whole staircase,
> just take the first step."
> —MARTIN LUTHER KING JR.

STATE OF PEAK PHYSIOLOGY— BODY LANGUAGE

Are you aware of the enormous impact your body language has on your life? In order to build confidence and get into a state of certainty, your body must align with your new thoughts and vocabulary. When you complain about something, you will notice the shift in your face or your shoulders. You may even be someone who has a permanent frown on your face. Some people I have met would actually strain muscles in their face if the thought of smiling came to mind. It's as if there is a single gray cloud hovering over their head, raining, while the sun is shining all around. Okay, let's do a little exercise. Right now, I want you to push your shoulders back and sit upright. Come on, straighten that back. Now put on the biggest smile you possibly can. Don't read on until you do. How did you feel when you just did that? Ridiculously stupid? Did you feel more in control? An increase in confidence? More enthusiastic? A state of happiness? Or are you laughing because you can't believe how quickly your mood and physiology can change from a sudden shift in the way you hold your body? **Your body language assists in creating your emotions.** By acknowledging this, how quickly are you able to change your state from lazy to energetic, sad to happy, or nervous to confident?

CHANGING STATE FORMULA:
BODY + FOCUS = CONTROL

Our body must be used when getting into a state of certainty. In any form of negotiation, the person who is more certain usually gets the best part of the deal. While the other person is trying to build a state of certainty when you walk in the door, you have already hit your peak far before your entry. Most people attempt to build certainty by succeeding more. They subconsciously think that succeeding more guarantees more certainty in their life. But they neglect the fact that it's certainty that actually brings success in the first place. All successful people live by this, and unfortunately for others who don't, their dreams will go untouched. Our body language is also crucial in the way we communicate with others.

It is estimated that **it takes the average person three to seven seconds to unconsciously judge someone they meet for the first time.** It could be someone we are interested in romantically, someone we are making a business deal with, or someone we meet casually. Our initial response decides how comfortable we are with that person. We either get a perception of pain and danger from that person or a sense of comfort. Once we have that initial perception we adapt our feelings, language, posture, and tone. The most crucial signal in this initial response is—you got it—the **smile!** The mouth area is the first impression we get, and a smile signifies a happy, friendly demeanor. There are two types of smile: the genuine smile and the fake smile. I know you know what I'm talking about when I say "the fake one," because you notice when others are doing it. Well, guess what? They see you, too. A genuine smile consists of using the upper muscles of your face as well as your mouth. A fake one usually consists of using just the mouth and excluding the eyes and upper face. A fake smile usually hides your teeth as well. Do not fake a smile when meeting someone! Research shows that a large majority of people unconsciously recognize the sincerity of your smile by simply looking at the top half of your face. That means using your whole face when smiling could make a huge difference in the initial contact.

The physiology of a smile is also remarkable. When you smile, your body releases endorphins, which send a message to your brain. That message is to feel good, confident, and satisfied. If you genuinely smile right now and try to bring forth sad emotions at the same time, you will notice it's extremely difficult. As babies we learned to smile when someone else smiles at us, so that is programmed with nearly everyone you come in contact with. This means when you smile at someone, they smile back, which then releases endorphins in their body. Voilà! The unconscious message they receive is "this person makes me feel great." That also means when we smile to ourselves, it makes us say, "Hey, this person makes me feel great." You will notice the power you have in creating and controlling your own emotions, even in times that could also be distressing. This is what abundant people do to shift their outlook immediately and create a clearer mind to find a more beneficial avenue to focus on.

I spoke to a guy one day whom I hadn't seen in a while. I asked him how work was, and before I knew it, I was bombarded with complaints. It was like he had been waiting for years for someone to ask that question. His tone dropped, he sounded drained, his shoulders slouched, he frowned, and he was in a state of hating life. I knew he had planned a vacation with a few of my friends, so I decided to shift the subject and ask him about that. It was as if the sky had just opened up and the sun shone right on him. His whole mood shifted within a second. He sat upright, his tone was stronger and more confident, he began to smile, and his whole demeanor changed. It was as if I was talking to a completely different person. I decided to point out to him what I had just done, and he was pretty surprised. It's so simple, yet it usually flies right under our radar. I told him to take that same body language to work or use it when someone asked him about work, and it would enforce a different mood. He called me two days later and said he had the best day at work in six months. He finally realized it was the attitude he was bringing to life every day that was affecting how his day was panning out. He was always in control of how he perceived his day, he just needed someone to make him aware of it.

I'm sure you have met someone who is successful in life, so I want you to think back for a second. I don't mean successful in just achieving, I mean in all areas of life. I bet they didn't talk in a voice that sounded depressed, have their shoulders forward, their head down, or their feet dragging. They were energetic, confident, shoulders back, head up, strong tone of voice, and certain. Don't be a fool and think you should only hold yourself like that when you are successful; holding yourself like that initially is what creates success. That's what makes a leader in life, and the way you carry yourself every day is crucial to success. **The petty thinkers mope around and only live because they were born. True winners acknowledge they were born to LIVE!**

THE BALANCE

As with anything in the world, life requires balance. Without balance, things seem out of their nature and don't function properly. Doing too much of one thing without doing other things to balance it out usually results in burnout. If you have ever really gotten into gym training, you will have noticed that it doesn't seem to last too long unless you have a balanced life. If all your focus is on your body, then other areas start to falter. You may have a great body for the next two years, but then the other areas of life seem to weigh it down, and you can find yourself back where you started. That is the same for every area of our life. It is also crucial to have balance when it comes to your actions.

I know we all cross paths with individuals who go around talking themselves up and say they are going to do great things in their life, yet five years down the track we see no progress. We must attain a balance between how we think, the words we say, and the physical actions we take. If we say something but we think otherwise, we will never be able to create the way we say it. If we physically act a certain way but we do not speak like it, then we cannot create it. If we think in a particular way but we don't act or speak like it, then, again, we cannot create. You must think success, speak success, and act success, and then your gift to create will absolutely astound you. Once this balance is accomplished, your growth amplifies immediately.

If it's just positive thinking that you believe will change your life, think again. If you don't act accordingly, you're never going to get what you want, are you? We get a concept in our mind first, but we create with the balance. The "mega-state challenge" further in the book is crucial to gaining this balance. It also helps in mastering our emotions, which are the basis of all decisions we make. **When we align our mental, verbal, and physical actions toward what we want, we create the way we intend.**

13

Fear—Friend or Foe?

"Too many people are thinking of security
instead of opportunity. They seem to be
more afraid of life than death."

—JAMES F. BYRNES

As a child, if you woke up facing the wrong side of the bed, you would feel scared for that moment. Nothing looks the same. The place where you sleep every night suddenly seems out of the ordinary, everything's out of place, and panic begins to set in. But the more you start to focus and take a closer look, the more your surroundings begin to make sense. Relief takes over your emotional state, and you realize you had nothing to panic about in the first place. In order to make peace with fear, we need to take a closer look.

Throughout our life we have been bombarded with the notion that fear is a foe that should be avoided at all costs. I'm here to tell you that fear is actually the best friend some have never had. Fear has a tendency to send us unconscious messages that will benefit our life. Just like any best friend, it is telling you to step up and pick up your game. It might be an area of your life that you are lacking in, and all fear is there to do is remind you that you shouldn't forget about it and walk off. Think of it as your own success alarm clock that says, "If you don't listen to me carefully in this instance, you can't get the most out of life." If we never get scared, it means we aren't taking any chances. Being scared also tells us that something important is happening, right? We must search deeper into the feeling and listen carefully to what it's telling us. Once we've achieved that, we will be able to see a new way in which to take action against fear.

The more we attempt to eliminate fear instead of using it to our benefit, the more it feels like trying to put out fire with gasoline. This creates more fire and more fear. As I was writing this book I was scared that my writing wasn't up to scratch. There was a period when I thought I was losing my touch and it began to worry me. Knowing that I had to quickly question this feeling, I began probing. I discovered that I was feeling fear of not knowing whether this would resonate with people from all different walks of life. I wanted it to be adaptable to everyone, regardless of financial, religious, and social position. I knew that I had to align myself with fear and, just as any good friend does, it reminded me when it was time to raise my standards. I went to people from all walks of life and gave them the same section to read. It was the chapter on questioning, and it seemed they were all fascinated. That was the power of getting to the heart of my feeling. **Fear is looking at something with the worst possible outcome.** Is someone really scared of snakes, or are they scared of getting bitten by a snake? Do they fear the tall building, or do they fear falling off the tall building? Are they really afraid of venturing into business, or are they afraid of failing? People are only scared of an outcome that is imaginary! The three initial questions I would ask are:

1. "What am I really scared of here?" rather than thinking, "I'm scared."

2. "How can I view this differently, and what new beliefs would I have to implement in order for it to benefit

my life? Would I have to believe that overcoming this fear is the only way to get the most out of life?"

3. "How can I use this to take action and help myself grow?"

Again, it is a process of deep questioning rather than just accepting. This is how we grow and exceed our expectations. Let's say you have made an important appointment to be somewhere at 3:00 p.m. on Monday. When the day comes, you hop out of the shower and realize it's already 2:40 p.m. Fear starts to kick in because you just missed the bus. All the positive thinking in the world isn't going to help you if the next bus comes at 2:55 p.m., so you now use the knee-jerk feeling of fear to support your action. You call the local taxi service and off you go. Your fear has taught you that next time you should plan better. This is a basic example, but one that seems to be very common in our society. In essence, if we don't align ourselves with fear in everyday life, we will never learn, and we all know that learning equals growth. **Don't resist fear; embrace it!**

> "You gain strength, courage, and confidence by every experience in which you really stop to look fear in the face. You must do the thing which you think you cannot do."
> —ELEANOR ROOSEVELT

You must give strong reasons as to why you want to overcome a particular fear. This will add purpose to its accomplishment. Replay these new reasons with intensity every time the fear comes to mind. If we have a fear of snakes, but common sense tells us that there are none around, does it mean we won't be scared from the thought of them? We definitely will be, because it's only ever in our mind. A particular client of mine would almost be in tears when her friends would say, "Howsssssss your day been, Jesssss?" Seems pretty funny, but hearing a noise similar to that a snake would make caused her to shake in her boots. **By enforcing new reasons why you want to overcome the fear, you break your neurological pattern and get into a different state.** Surprisingly, it doesn't take long to condition a new one. It can happen so quickly that I've seen people's habits, phobias, and fears literally disappear in one week. It sounds simple enough, but how many people do you think take the time to do it? Not many, I can tell you. Or they will repeat, "This stuff doesn't work," because they don't believe how quickly they can turn their life around.

IN THE FACE OF FEAR

Confidence is self-trust. The only way to build trust in your ability is to face and overcome your fears.

I've always said there are two sides to ourselves: the scared guy and the inspirational guy. The scared guy is the weak one, and in the face of a fear he will tremble, think his life is about to end, and look for the closest exit. The inspirational guy is trying to help you and will say, "You're not going anywhere, you're coming with me." He will drag you if he has to and make you stare at the fear straight in the face. The question is, how do you empower and grow your inspirational side and weaken the other one? **We must counteract fear in any way possible.**

We all know that when we are feeding a baby we don't shove two steaks down its throat to ensure nourishment. The aim is to build your strength, so act as soon as fear shows itself, but don't kill yourself in the process. Let's look at a treadmill, for example: Most would initially see running on a treadmill as being painful, too hard, embarrassing, or a waste of time. In order for us to shift our mind-set, we must first sort out our belief system. We would begin to see the treadmill as being very pleasurable. It would represent a healthy life, a fit-looking body, confidence, strength, a must in order to be successful, and a step toward achieving a lot of things on your wants list. The major tip is to feed this little by little, so you could start by walking. Now isn't that a different approach? Most would look at that equipment and automatically think running, which equals embarrassment and more pain, but start off by walking, and then suddenly it doesn't seem that hard. If you hit it really hard the first time, it could come as a big shock and cause even more pain. It will be more fun this way, and more desirable the next time that scared voice tells you to run away. You will eventually want to push yourself to the limits and be much stronger when faced with your limiting side.

> "Courage is not the absence of fear,
> but rather the judgment that something else is
> more important than fear."
> —JAMES NEIL HOLLINGWORTH, A.K.A. AMBROSE REDMOON

Fear is also a physical emotion, so it means we have to counteract it with our body and get into a state of certainty. We know it's physical as much as mental and emotional because we feel fear throughout our whole body. You must get really physical and loud with yourself when encountering it. This rule can be applied to any fear we face, as we must learn to drag out the strength that lies within us. It's never a question of whether your strength is there, but rather what you do to drag it out. As time goes on and you begin to feed your strength, you will notice that you become fearful when you think of settling for the life that once made you unhappy. Just the thought of it pushes you to act even harder, because there is nothing scarier than living an undesired life once you have created a compelling vision of what you really want.

1. Ask yourself how you have overcome fears in the past. What did you do? Whom did you talk to? Who else has been in a similar situation and gotten through it?

2. Shift beliefs around the certain experience or object— add value to its accomplishment and make it pleasurable.

3. Stay focused on the desired outcome. This will **turn your fear into excitement.**

4. Counteract your fear immediately. Use your body to get into a different state to overpower it.

Write down all the great things you can attain from overcoming this fear. Keep your eye fixed firmly on these benefits. Your fears will soon turn into challenges, and those will turn into excitement!

FEAR OF ACHIEVEMENT

> "At Microsoft, there are lots of brilliant ideas
> but the image is that they all come from the top—
> I'm afraid that's not quite right."
>
> —BILL GATES

I have heard so many people talk about top athletes, people who are worth massive amounts of money, or those who are in a great relationship. They say things like, "He was born to be a golfer," or "She has always been a smart businesswoman." I know because I used to join in those conversations. We say it as if these people had no real choice in the matter. In some way we try to believe that it was planned out for them, and no matter which way they went in life, that's how they would have ended up. I don't see how any view could be so ignorant after witnessing the passion these people put into their success. If you are one of the people who have this thought, instead of lying to yourself and believing successful people are vastly different from you, I urge you to look fear in the face and prove yourself otherwise.

Underachievers always pick out the few stories where people got everything on a silver platter, and use that excuse when they hear of anyone achieving. For example, they will say things like, "He has a rich dad," "They were lucky," or "She did that in an era when new ideas were available to create." We all know that's only an attempt to shade the lack of action they are taking in their own lives. It's nothing short of garbage! There are more young, innovative, self-made millionaires now than ever before. There is even a saying in the financial world that "billionaire is the new millionaire." It takes someone to be courageous and wise to recognize the hard work and determination of those who have achieved. By acknowledging that truth, it helps you respect the game a whole lot more. It even promotes the understanding that you're not the only one who has experienced or will experience hardship on your road, and that's inspiring.

> "That some achieve great success,
> is proof to all that others can achieve it as well."
> —ABRAHAM LINCOLN

Being guilty of undermining achievers myself in the past, I have now come to realize that my limiting thoughts were just me being afraid of achievement. I never believed I could be great, so it was easier to escape in fear than to face the truth. What I came to acknowledge is that the major difference with these great achievers is that they conquered that restrictive view of success. Were they born programmed with that powerful mind-set? Was their journey a perfect walk? Some of the greatest achievers have been through experiences we would never trade for. We live in the same world, with the same capabilities.

Look at Tiger Woods. Regardless of his off-field antics, the guy is the best at what he does. Playing golf, of course! At the age of five, he went on the show *That's Incredible!* and declared that by the age of twenty he would beat the best golfers in history. Do you believe he ever lost sight of that vision? No matter what challenges came up, that vision stayed cemented. He continued to create his reality around that concept. This is a man who worked extremely hard for his achievements. Woods even asked his dad to give him military-style coaching. His dad would be in his face or use loud and annoying noises every time he went to swing. He would do anything to distract Woods in a moment of concentration. Toward the end of the intense program, Woods did not budge when faced with these challenges, and his dad then told him that his training was complete. His father also mentioned that he now had the strongest golf mind on the planet. He wasn't wrong! Woods knew the importance of mental training so much that he even hired a mind coach. Dr. Jay Brunza would make him sit down and visualize hitting perfect shots over and over—the same technique of visualization we are learning in this book. Woods built an **absolute belief system** around his success. And who's to say there aren't fifty or a thousand other potential better golfers than Tiger Woods? There may just be, but will they fight for their vision, or will they let their fear get in the way of achieving?

> *Life is not to be feared or resisted. It is to be embraced, to be the best you can possibly be, and to live the life you dare to dream.*

We see the effects of great achievers' success, like the money they spend and the way they live, yet we rarely take the time to find out how they did it. We ignore that these achievers are just normal men and women who decided to pursue their true potential. We neglect everything that came before: their persistence, their compelling visions, their passion, or the strength they had to build. All these things needed to be conditioned. Albert Einstein once said, "I'm not particularly intelligent or particularly talented. I'm just very, very curious."

Oprah Winfrey is a woman who was sexually abused and who lived in poverty as a child, but her passion for life became so overwhelming that she had to live it the best way she knew how. The guys from Google are another example of defying the odds and starting off small, in their garage, competing against Yahoo!, the larger company at the time. It almost seems impossible to think that someone could actually achieve so much in one lifetime, let alone a few years. They all came to a point in their life where they decided they would never settle, but rather go on a quest for their dreams no matter what challenges came their way.

When you surrender to this commitment, the world smiles with you, and you get breaks you never believed possible. You don't have to want to make billions or even millions of dollars; it is entirely up to you. It's whatever makes you happy; just understand that taking a chapter out of the book of some of the greatest is the best start to obtaining what you want. I have researched and met some of the greatest succeeders I know, and there are patterns. This book is based on those very patterns. They all stopped thinking, speaking, acting, and believing that they had no purpose in this world, and began learning how to add value. They learned to use fear to grow, researched what successful people did before them, and lived by the exact strategies and values you are reading, rather than escape in their fear.

Appreciating other people's success is vastly important when enhancing our own. Being jealous or in disbelief will distance you from ever understanding the qualities you have within you. We must look at them and find out what they did differently from everyone else. As soon as you start doubting them, or believe that it was luck or coincidence, you fall back into the mass of under-achievers. When you start to question and get intrigued by others' success, that's when you enter the minority of the greatest achievers in the world.

> "Every person who wins in any undertaking
> must be willing to cut all sources of retreat.
> Only by doing so can one be sure of maintaining that
> state of mind known as a burning desire to win—
> essential to success."
>
> —NAPOLEON HILL

14

Shaping Your Destiny: Mega-State Seven-Day Challenge

MEGA-STATE = MENTAL + VERBAL + PHYSICAL

Having the ability to quickly and intelligently change the way you feel in times of emotional challenges is critical on the road to achievement. It's time for us to raise the bar and take enormous action. The following tasks are things you are going to apply to your daily lives, so saying you don't have the time is unacceptable. Remember, you signed the contract at the beginning of the book and said you were ready for change. If you do not want to act, then close the book and pack it up. You cannot be helped unless you are willing to help yourself. If you want to excel, then make it happen.

Look at yourself in the mirror and **repeat this ten times before you start each day for the next seven days.** Make sure you get very vocal, emotional, physical, and forceful until it gets you into a complete mega-state of certainty:

"I am in control of shaping my whole life through my state of mind, the emotions I choose, and the actions I take every day. No matter what challenges I am faced with in these next seven days, my spirit will display and direct my strength to my success. It will empower me to do it forever. I can do anything I want in my life."

By doing this every morning for the next seven days, you will prove your commitment to yourself. It makes what you are doing concrete and helps condition your state immediately. All people with extraordinary lives are able to change their state in an instant. That is the advantage they have over the masses. What is worth more than your life? What are you willing to do to enhance it? Are you really committed to changing your course of direction forever? Is your truth telling that you are doing enough as it is? It doesn't matter how much you are doing toward empowering your life, it's still not enough. **The moment you think you have done enough is the moment you stop growing.**

TASK 1

COMMANDING FOCUS

> "Since belief is all-important, it behooves you
> to guard your thoughts; and as your beliefs will be
> shaped to a very great extent by the things you
> observe and think about, it is important that you
> should command your attention."
>
> —WALLACE D. WATTLES

REQUIREMENT: Monitor your thoughts and redirect them intelligently

DURATION: Days 1, 2, and 3

DESCRIPTION: You have already been implementing great changes with the previous tasks, but now we are stepping it up. When you start thinking of something that makes you feel down, worried, or stressed, you know that it's only because of your choice of focus and it must be corrected immediately. You must look at the effect that every thought is having on your success. Once you look at the effects of your thoughts rather than just thinking them, you jump off the "automatic wheel" and you are able to enhance your life. Being aware of the power of your thoughts is absolutely crucial for attaining happiness and gaining what you set out for. Only by doing this are you able to begin forming the mind-set of the most successful people in history.

Don't deliberate about the disempowering thoughts too much, just block them out with as much power as you possibly can and replace them with something that you love, something that makes you happy, or something that would put you in a state of excitement or fulfillment. **A projection of a desired vision you have put in place for yourself or something that you really appreciate is a great way to shift your focus and emotion immediately.** Even if you feel that you shouldn't, it doesn't matter, you must! If there is a secret to true fulfillment and achievement, it's being able to take control of your mind.

I don't care what you have to do to get that thought out of your head, you must do it. Scream at yourself, or forcefully let yourself know that thought is not going to take control over your life anymore and repeat the new thought over and over. One day my auntie thought I was crazy because she heard me screaming from outside my house. She said it sounded like a lion that hadn't eaten in a week. Quite a funny comparison, I thought, because that's how hungry I felt for my success. Good aggression is different from anger, don't be mistaken. It's fine to get forceful with yourself, and is necessary in some challenging situations. No matter what it is or how challenging it may seem, you have to fight. Keep repeating that it's going to be okay, that it's all in your mind, and that you have full control of yourself at all times. There is always another way of looking at something. **You choose the way you feel through your choice of thoughts.** Tell your mind that you are now in control and you are not going to let it wander.

To determine if a thought is having a detrimental effect on your life, you must examine the feeling you get from it. You must have that army always ready at the entrance of your mind. For example, if you are thinking, *I can't make it,* you will quickly repeat, "I can make it, I can make it," over and over with more force. This is training your mind, and what goes on in your mind determines the outcomes you get in life. You must maintain focus on your new direction. Even after a week you will notice that disempowering thoughts diminish just by being aware of them. **Proper attention doesn't just miraculously appear, it needs to be directed and deliberately commanded with intensity.**

TASK 2

SHIFT VOCABULARY AND BODY

> "A helping word to one in trouble is often
> like a switch on a railroad track ... an inch between
> wreck and smooth, rolling prosperity."
>
> —HENRY WARD BEECHER

REQUIREMENT: Take control over the words you say and your body language

DURATION: Days 4, 5, and 6

DESCRIPTION: We previously covered the importance that your language has on your life. Now it's time to monitor and course-correct for the empowering options. Go back to the list of options in the "Verbal Action" section (page 143) and use that as a guide. For these three days, there are to be no negative connotations or limiting words whatsoever. Speak with confidence and enthusiasm. Every time you say *can't, impossible, I'm drained,* or *too hard,* you are to correct yourself immediately. Even by staying conscious of this, you will break your old patterns and the emotions you experience throughout your day. You will make your day surprisingly better just by doing this exercise. When people complain to you, do not join in. The results you see from this are actually going to make you laugh after the week is over. You will be wondering why you ever chose to shape your life with your previous discussions. Avoid the news on TV, in newspapers, or anything else that can implant negative thoughts in your mind during this exercise. This way you will not be able to talk to others about these emotionally draining topics **unless you are using it to benefit yourself or others.** It will force you to come up with intelligent things to discuss—an important aspect to living a happy life.

This also goes for the way in which you are going to hold your body in the next three days. When you are humble yet confident, you become a powerhouse. Don't be egotistical or walk around like you have a stick up your backside, because it may just have the opposite effect on what you want to achieve. It's not brain surgery to figure out how to stand confidently. Unless you are aware of your actions, you will never achieve or be fulfilled. Take as much physical action as you can toward one of your wants on your list. Emails, phone calls, browsing the internet for information, and speaking to people are all taking action. It will build up.

TASK 3

HAVE FUN WITH FAITH

Don't wait for experience, create your experience!

REQUIREMENT: Take the leap of faith and do something that you have never done before

DURATION: Day 7

DESCRIPTION: Are you ready to explore? This is the task where you turn your fear into excitement and explore your ability to enrich your life experience. This exercise is so important to every part of your life that it absolutely must be completed. Do something that you have always wanted to do, or think of something new. Bungee jump, skydive, ice-skate, go to an improv or cooking class, drive a go-kart, paint, talk to that person at the office or your coffee shop who seems cool, submit a short story to a publication, go to the gym, rock climb, or do whatever you can think of. If you're sixty-five years old and you think you're too old to go paintball shooting, then think again. I was up against one such player the last time I went. Let's just say I got my butt kicked. That senior could shoot—not to mention the team of girls digging into me as well. My point is that there are no excuses, only fear. Put that fear on the shelf for one day and do something that electrifies your spirit. **No matter what it is, if it's pushing the boundaries for you, then do it.** We get so caught up in routine that we forget to live. We experience the same emotions day in and day out. In order to create happiness in your life, you must stay excited and have something to look forward to. Set this challenge up, but most important, enjoy it!

15

Quality-Driven Success

"Educating the mind without educating
the heart is no education at all."

—ARISTOTLE

Too many people have become misled by the concept of achievement and the word *success*. We have proved many times throughout history that the view of success that so many people take on board is a myth. It was February 2010 when a close friend rang me up to tell me that famous fashion designer Alexander McQueen had hanged himself in his apartment. But he had all this money, and all this fame, so why would he commit suicide? He is just one of many great achievers who have taken their life. Edwin Armstrong, inventor of FM radio, in 1954; Pierre Bérégovoy, former French prime minister, in 1993; Kurt Cobain, singer/songwriter and Nirvana cofounder, in 1994; and Robin Williams, actor and comedian, in 2014, all ended their own lives. The list goes on, not to mention how many top actors, athletes, and artists suffer from drug abuse and emotional torment. On the other hand, there are many who have it all in life: fulfillment and great achievements. What's the difference between the two? Some searched for a feeling of success only through their achievements; the others acknowledge that success is in who they are and how they live their life, not in what they have!

The truth is, we can continue to achieve in our life and still be unfulfilled.

You might want to be successful in raising a child, in fitness, in your finances, in your relationships with others, in one particular area of your life, or in all of them. I just want you to understand that success does not exist in anything outside of you and should never be looked at as a thing you must chase. Success does not lie in a Ferrari, a mansion, or any of the achievements mentioned above. Just like any purchase or singular desire you have wanted in your life, the feeling doesn't last. All people who base their definition of success on external desires eventually ask themselves, "Is that it . . . What now?" I know that's happened to you in the past with something, and you should understand that it will never change. It may have been the new watch, the handbag, the vacation, or the new car. Regardless of what it was, there came a time when you were once again at a standstill. **You need depth and meaning in your life.** True success is to discover the enormous power you have within, who you are, and the attitude you take out to life every day. Once you have grasped this, everything else will flow. Success must come well before obtaining those external wants. Once you attain real success first and begin to live a great life, the rest becomes the cherries on top of a beautifully made cake. If the cherries are taken away for whatever reason, it won't really make much difference, because the cake is already complete. It's extremely important to realize that it's success that actually gets what you want, not the other way around.

When one isn't at peace, nothing makes sense.

People have based success on money for many years. In recent times, success has taken on a whole new meaning as more people are striving to be genuinely successful and focusing on abundance. Surrounded by so much external pressure and demand by fast-moving societies, we are now striving for quality success. This is a balance between an inner peace and the constant self-growth that leads to achievement in all areas of life. Obviously, the degree of achievement is based on an individual's particular wants.

Time doesn't stand still, so we always aspire to grow to the next level in our lives. Anchoring our success to important qualities will prevent going around in circles, just waiting to achieve fulfillment. Don't be mistaken—just because someone is a great achiever doesn't mean they are successful. **In essence, success equals fulfillment,** that deep understanding of ourselves. We all seek different dreams, but everyone strives for a balance. This is why I have worked to discover and find the qualities that must drive success— QDS.

QDS is the process of eliminating negativity from within and hence from your surroundings right now, so you are able to attract and create more intelligently. If we allow the term *success* to drive the quality of our life, then we may become misled along the way and continue to work against what will really fulfill us. **Never let it be the notion of success that enhances the quality of your life; rather let it be the qualities of your life that enhance success.** It's like trying to build a state-of-the-art house on a poor foundation. It will never be stable but, more important, it will never be state of the art. Those qualities are the great foundation. When challenges arise on your journey, your strong foundation will prove that you can resist the pressure.

I used these qualities to attract the most marvelous experiences, discover hidden knowledge, strengthen persistence, and achieve at a greater level. This stuff is powerful. What's great about these qualities is that all of us have them now, accessible and ready to use. Don't be someone who blindly walks around life believing they have to get patience, love, strength, or the truth. **The sudden reality is that you have all the qualities you have been searching**

for; they have always been within you. Whether you choose to use them or not is up to you.

1. LOVE—THE ULTIMATE QUALITY

> "A coward is incapable of exhibiting love;
> it is the prerogative of the brave."
> —MAHATMA GANDHI

They say love comes in many forms. They also say that love can drive us crazy. Is it really love that does those things, or are we tarnishing the reputation of the divine emotion? Are we undermining love and giving it unnecessary associations? I believe love comes in only one form, in the purest state. I had someone refer to love as "coming in many different forms" when they told a story of a man who became so obsessed with his ex-girlfriend, that he stalked her for three years. Love doesn't drive these actions—jealousy, greed, hatred, or vengefulness should never be mistaken for the almighty love, for true love opposes such things. Love doesn't drive us crazy; our inner demons battling it do.

Love is the primary quality that can set us free from that feeling of emptiness. I am speaking of a love so pure it is not restricted by what we see with our eyes, but is the feeling we attain from within—like the love some have for their mother, pet, child, husband, or life itself. That love is far beyond our eyes. Your dog may be the ugliest mutt to some, but the love you have for it is not restricted by its outward appearance. True love asks nothing but to fulfill itself. **You alone can fulfill yourself with that love that lies eagerly within you.** It will appear, but we ignore it on so many occasions. Love is the true guide in life and the only one to be served. If we do things out of pure intent, love will surely answer. Through love your dreams become real, and everyday life will show itself in the most beautiful way it knows how. It takes the cloth from your eyes and allows you to see the world in its truest essence. You align yourself with the world and everything in it, which is the basis of your dreams coming true.

One man who had much controversy surrounding him, but who I believe demonstrated much love that went unnoticed, was Michael Jackson. A particular statement of his that I thought was truth in essence was, "Let us dream of tomorrow, where we can truly love from the soul, and know love as the ultimate truth at the heart of all creation." Regardless of perception or judgment of this man, that saying is undeniably true. The great know that greatness is love.

Once you experience true love in your heart, you dedicate your life to showing the earth what you have discovered.

All the important aspects for achieving fulfillment stem from love. My plan is to cover some of the main ones that have a direct impact on obtaining that goal. Love is like the seed of a plant. The seed is already planted within us. It is then fed by water and sunlight, which are your experiences and time to act. The two must correlate; in order to be fed, the seed must be ready for it, correct? The root then shoots out to the world and is exposed. It begins to blossom with all the effects of love—inner peace, patience, respect, and appreciation, to name a few. Its roots grow far and wide until they eventually intertwine with other plants. We all have that seed, and it's just waiting to be fed. Love by its very nature creates, and we are no exception. All men in history who have accomplished great things have used love as their driving force. It's the true essence of your being that will make you go well past your previous limitations and achieve things you once thought impossible. When love takes over your life, buckle up and get ready for a ride beyond your wildest dreams. This love is so great that it is reflected in everyone and everything. With love, your intention is to be the best person you know how and treat everyone and everything with that same respect and love. That's the secret to fulfillment.

> "Life without love is like a tree
> without blossoms or fruit."
> —KAHLIL GIBRAN

Greatness also stems from love. In fact, everyone is great right now, but most are unaware of it. Loving yourself is an essential part of success—if you don't love yourself, you can never trust yourself to gain success. Would you really trust someone with your life that you didn't love? Well, if you don't love yourself deep down and embrace it on a daily basis, how can you trust yourself to get what you want? **There is a difference between loving who you really are and loving who you pretend to be.** Loving yourself is not about putting yourself above anyone else; rather, a true self-love equalizes you with the world. You are able to understand yourself more, and it allows you to better understand others. We have been conditioned to believe that loving ourselves is egotistical, but it's not loving ourselves that actually displays EGO, because we Edge God Out of our life. If you truly love yourself, you won't allow yourself to go against your claimed morals.

You would acknowledge that others' growth is your growth and vice versa. In saying this, you can't really help anyone until you help yourself first. While helping yourself, you will be helping them. Contributing your true self is far greater than materialistic help. We must not judge people on their appearance, religious status, or environment; we are all human and have an equally important role to play. If you commit to those limiting actions, you are only tarnishing a relationship with yourself, and it will never be the means to gain true success. When you treat others with respect, the respect you have for yourself grows. It's like when we meet someone who backs the same sports team or has the same cultural background; there is an instant bond and respect. We gain a sense of belonging from that person and will immediately get into conversation, maybe share a laugh or two. There's a feeling of camaraderie that seems to arise. Imagine considering mankind as being on the same team. Picture the sense of belonging now, and the rapport you will be able to build with others. Picture the difference in attitude and your approach toward those you come into contact with.

> *Everything you do to others, you are equally doing to yourself. That is the law of life; no one escapes.*

My way of dealing with others is quite simple. I always take notice that they have the potential to love, were created by love, and I am convinced they are great people deep down. I choose not to see what others see, and it greatly affects my experience with people. By doing this they will feel your genuine approach and lack of ego. This method unconsciously forces others to react in a similar way. That's truly acting out of love and it is reflected in everything and everyone around you.

We are in this together; it's called networking. But remember, no one wants to help those who aren't willing to help themselves, so do things out of love and good intentions and there will always be people willing to lend a hand. *We* is greater than *me,* but the change must start with you. Look in the mirror and tell yourself how much you love the person you see, regardless of what you have been through. It might seem stupid at the beginning, but that's only because social norms and other unfulfilled people have influenced your beliefs. Look at what this person in the mirror has been through, yet they are still here to face the music. That's something to love and respect, because it shows strength and the determination to never give up. If you want to give love and be loved, you must love yourself first. **When you feel love on the inside, you will see love on the outside. You are love!**

It is better to start loving yourself than to wait around for someone else to do it for you.

PURE LOVE IS FREEDOM

"Eventually you will come to understand that love heals everything, and love is all there is."
—GARY ZUKAV

Freedom begins with the power that comes from understanding that you control your life. It is the absolute knowledge that you choose the way you feel, and hence the way you live is structured by freedom of choice. We have been socially programmed to believe that our freedom is based on outside events—in other words, we must wait for things to make us happy on the outside to complete our inner self.

In order to experience true freedom in your life, you must realize that your perception of the outside world is nothing more than a mirror reflection of the internal self that you create. **How you feel is what you see!** The inside must change first, in order for the outside to be seen in happiness. At a deeper level, when we change our perception of the outside, it really does change what happens on the outside. We choose to create our physical, mental, and verbal actions every day. Without realizing it we make them stronger by repetition. Mostly we are oblivious to the fact that we are creating our lives under such slavery.

Our freedom is not dependent on a job, a vacation, or any other person. We may change a job or decide to go on a trip, but essentially it is the freedom that was discovered first that allows us to do those things. Attaining freedom by choice is the only way to discover fulfillment. If you are looking for the material world to free you, then you will never find it. Eternal freedom stems from pure love of oneself—a love so strong that it trusts you to feed your intuition, all the while projecting that same love out to the world. Cold and wet nights seem to be appreciated just as much as warm ones, challenges are seen as life's growth, faith in yourself blossoms, and you finally witness the beauty that surrounds you. You choose to be free, or not, every day.

What is it about love that makes it so fascinating? Could it be its ability to transcend the earthly concept of time, its power to defy all odds, its infiniteness, its courage to conquer all things, its dwelling in all creation, or just its very existence?

2. THE QUALITY OF KNOWING YOUR TRUTH

Since love and not understanding is the starting point for the journey of self-truth, all who wish to walk it can take the first step.

As I was cleaning the mirrors at a boxing gym I once worked at, something dawned on me. Looking at them from a distance, I wasn't able to tell whether they were dirty or not. The closer I looked, the more unclean they became. The only way I was able to clean the mirror was by taking a closer look. With my reflection staring back at me, I wondered how I could use this principle in my life. We don't notice our truth or the uncleanliness we surround ourselves with unless we decide to take a closer look. From a distance we can be fooled into thinking that we are following our heart and need no improvement, but dare to take a closer look and the real answers begin to appear. **In order to be truly happy and obtain what we desire, we must be honest with ourselves.**

Why do we undermine our ability to achieve happiness? So

often we ignore what we know will ultimately benefit our life. I believe that we all have a sound understanding of our truthful side when it's time to make a decision, but it may be the easier option to lie to ourselves. Initially this might seem like the case, but the truth has an uncanny way of catching up to us, doesn't it? Someone named Chris asked me a challenging question on this topic. He said, "If the ultimate truth is love, that inner voice, and we are all able to recognize it, what about a terrorist's truth? Their truth is to kill people." This was how the conversation went on:

> **ME:** Does a terrorist love something? It could be his mother, sister, pet, or anything.
>
> **CHRIS:** Well, I guess he would, yeah.
>
> **ME:** Okay, so he knows that love feels good, right?
>
> **CHRIS:** Yes.
>
> **ME:** So what would happen if someone came up and killed that something that he loved, how would that make him feel?
>
> **CHRIS:** Being human, I'd say it would feel like hell.
>
> **ME:** Okay, so the terrorist is able to distinguish that love feels good, and having something killed feels rotten?
>
> **CHRIS:** I see where you're going with this.
>
> **ME:** Yes or no?
>
> **CHRIS:** Yes.

Well, that's the truth right there, isn't it? When a terrorist kills someone who he knows is loved by somebody else, it's for greed, ill power, or selfish satisfaction. It's not the truth; he is feeding his lies and he knows it. He will never find fulfillment during such an act because he is separating himself from his true essence. Humans have a fundamental tendency toward truth. Call it common sense, conscious ability, reasoning, it doesn't matter; we are all able to distinguish between a loving act and a hateful one. We are built with love, that ultimate truth, and love will question every decision we make. Lying to yourself doesn't hide the truth, so you can bet your life that it will always come and display itself.

We don't have a very high tolerance for psychological dissonance of any kind. Self-deception can have terrible consequences for a person's experience of their conscience, even in a person with a not so advanced conscience.

> "A man may imagine things that are false,
> but he can only understand things that are true,
> for if the things be false, the apprehension
> of them is not understanding."
> —ISAAC NEWTON

The greatest indication of knowing our truth is listening to that deep voice within that tells us what is correct. It's that same voice that tells you one way will make you ultimately happy, while the other path will only bring you short-term satisfaction. Some call it the heart, and science is proving now more than ever the connection between emotional and physiological changes in our body. Dr. Deepak Chopra has a deep understanding of how these two correlate and the vast impact they have on our lives. I never realized how crucial the saying "Follow your heart" is in shaping our destiny. The problem is we rarely listen to it. Realistically, **we can ask as many questions as we want, to as many people as we need, until we get the answer we desire. Surprisingly enough, we always know the truth is different; we just occasionally think that feeding a lie will fulfill us. But it doesn't.**

"A lie stands on one leg, truth on two."

—BENJAMIN FRANKLIN

We also judge ourselves on those decisions we choose to make. We are our own judge and decider on where we go in life—another God-given gift we all have. We are able to distinguish between a lie and the truth, but instead of taking action, we submit again to what we know is creating suffering. This continues to create a life we don't want to live. Don't we judge ourselves? We lie to ourselves and are forced to visit that inner courtroom a thousand times over, with the same faults.

Most people will play both parts and won't fight for their truth every time, even though they are able to acknowledge it. They aren't just in their judging. They do things that they know are against their moral laws or who they really are. The more they lose in their courtroom, the harder it is to believe they can win the next trial. They live a life of losing their truth to lies and are never happy. We must be fair and just judges.

If you have a belief that causes you to act in a certain way toward yourself, life, the environment, or others, I urge you to ask this one question: **Does this belief or decision ultimately help me demonstrate more love to myself, and everyone and everything around me?** If the answer is no, then it is not worthy to hold up in the courtroom of truth. No one escapes this law of life. It's supremely important to refer back to love in your beliefs, and I'd even suggest questioning it against the teachings in this book. I don't want you to just believe this because I have said so; I want you to reason with your own truth. Acknowledge that your truth has always and will always hold love as the pinnacle of your fulfillment. If you make decisions that don't display love, especially for yourself, then life will force you to. And at times, it has no mercy in the lengths it will go to to wake you up. I'm sure we can all relate to that at one stage in our life.

All the answers you seek are within; they have never ceased to exist.

You must be willing to reason with yourself in order to bring out the truth. As the famous poet Kahlil Gibran says so superbly in his masterpiece *The Prophet,* "God rests in reason . . . God moves in passion. And since you are a breath in God's sphere, and a leaf in God's forest, you, too, should rest in reason and move in passion." **I must say, I truly find peace not just in knowing I have the ability to reason with myself but in putting it into practice.** The only way to know a wise person, a great teacher of the truth, or an enlightened soul is if they speak of a love for all as the ultimate truth. If they don't teach you this, you are sadly being lied to.

It's one thing being able to distinguish between your truth and your lie, yet it's vastly different when it's time to act. Mastering this next quality is the key to experiencing a joy most people only dream about having.

3. FEEDING YOUR TRUTH IS THE QUALITY FOR EVERLASTING HAPPINESS

"There are only two mistakes one can
make along the Way to Truth: 1. not going all the way;
and 2. not starting."

—THE BUDDHA

When we feed something, it grows. For some, fear, sadness, lack of direction, and unhappiness have become daily indulgences. Every time you make a decision or commit an act that is against your truth (love, kindness, happiness, giving, patience), it sabotages the relationship you have with yourself. Is it any wonder that so many people don't know what they want or which direction to take? On the other hand, when you feed your truth it will grow to a size you never imagined possible. In your truth also lies fulfillment. When we begin to feed that truth, our happiness gets fuller, and in it is found inner peace. There is no limit to the growth; it's a never- ending supply, because you are supplying it. You are the hand that feeds you, so you can always rely on yourself! However, if your hand is always reaching out to be fed by an external supply, that growth can stop at any time. Those people, money, and situations may not last forever. The more you grow, the more your supply of truth grows.

I'm so glad I trained myself to feed my truth because it's definitely the reason you are reading this. If I hadn't, I would never have been able to discover what I'm great at. I've spoken to excellent achievers, but more important, those who are successful, and they all have the same thing to say. They began listening to and acting on that voice deep inside—not only for major decisions that had to be made but also for the smallest acts of everyday life. There is a distinguishable truth in every moment, opportunity, or experience. If you are willing to reason with yourself, you will be able to clearly identify it, and more important, act on it.

We must really start listening to that intelligent and wise voice within. If brushing it off has become a way of life, you must change immediately. Here is one example of how I conditioned myself to feed my truth: We all know what a garbage bin is used for, so we are able to distinguish that the bin is there to serve that purpose and throw garbage in. (Common sense reminded me of this my whole life, but I chose to ignore it on so many occasions.) The difference now was that I began to amplify my truth (common sense), which clearly told me to throw my trash in the bin. Throwing something on the ground when I knew there was a better alternative was disrespectful. And I guess **if we want respect, we must give respect.** By taking my truth into consideration and actually listening to it, I was able see the important role it played in my own life. This change in action taught me a few other things. One of them was that I was able to commit to doing something that I actually wanted to do. I fed that deep voice, and it instantly created new emotions.

"Follow your heart, but be quiet for a while first.
Ask questions, then feel the answer.
Learn to trust your heart."
—UNKNOWN

This simple change in behavior will train you to have patience. When something (like a garbage bin) isn't accessible right away, you don't do something that is against what you really know you should do just to obtain some short-term satisfaction. Can you see how this could benefit us in reaching our greater visions? It might seem very insignificant, but this is what allows you to acknowledge that you have the power to think, act, and create for yourself. It allows you to **create your own happiness,** which in turn helps you to respect more of your decisions. More important, it proves that the feeling of fulfillment does exist. Even when you make a decision that is extremely hard at the time, you will never regret it if it's aligned with your truth. When you believe something enough, you live by it. **We always force ourselves to feel down when we do something that is against our truth, but how often do we recognize or acknowledge when we do something great?** To condition a great and rewarding feeling when acting on that conscious voice is the ultimate advantage in life. Remember, it starts with the small things, because that's what gets the ball rolling. If you don't have the energy to do the small tasks, how are you ever going to reach your peak in performance or get the most out of life? When you make the decision to feed your truth, don't dither about it. Make sure you create the energy if you must and do it with great intention.

A smoker is a perfect example. When I ask people about their smoking habit, they say, "But I want to smoke." Nearly every time I ask if they were in an ideal world and could be free from smoking, would they, I get the answer, "Yes, of course." The truth is the voice that tells them to give it up, and they know it.

That voice is always speaking, and you know when it does. Are you going to mess up along the way? Of course, you're human. In life we may not make all the best decisions, but we are not meant to. If we did, we would never know growth.

> "The seeker after Truth should be humbler than the dust. Only then, and not till then, will he have a glimpse of Truth . . . In the march toward Truth, anger, selfishness, hatred, etc., naturally give way, for otherwise Truth would be impossible to attain."
>
> —MAHATMA GANDHI

A social term for acting on our truth is **integrity.** In Western ethics, integrity is regarded as the quality of having an intuitive sense of honesty and truthfulness in regard to the motivations for one's actions, and it can be regarded as the opposite of hypocrisy. The word *integrity* stems from the Latin adjective *integer* (whole, complete). In this context, integrity is the inner sense of wholeness deriving from qualities such as honesty and consistency of character. As such, one may judge that others have integrity to the extent that one judges whether they behave according to the values, beliefs, and principles they claim to hold. Just really listen to yourself, then act on it. That's all it takes.

Mahatma Gandhi summed up our inner voice best:

> There come to us moments in life when about some things we need no proof from without. A little voice within us tells us, "You are on the right track, move

neither to your left nor right, but keep to the straight and narrow way."

There are moments in your life when you must act, even though you cannot carry your best friends with you. The "still small voice" within you must always be the final arbiter when there is a conflict of duty.

Having made a ceaseless effort to attain self-purification, I have developed some little capacity to hear correctly and clearly the "still small voice within."

I shall lose my usefulness the moment I stifle the "still small voice within."

. . . Penances with me are no mechanical acts. They are done in obedience to the inner voice.

—Excerpt from *Mahatma: A Golden Treasury of Wisdom–Thoughts & Glimpses of Life*

4. QUALITY OF FORGIVENESS— DON'T LIVE IN REGRET

"You think you look strong because you can hold on, but strength lies in letting go."

—ALAN MANDELL

You can spend your whole life hanging on to what could or should have been, but you can't go back in time. When we read a novel we turn the pages forward, not backward. If we did read it backward, the story would make no sense and confuse us. Having regrets is taking away the essence of life, because at the moment when the decision was made, it was exactly what you wanted. The decision was made for a particular reason. The great thing is that you may now see a different path of greater benefit. Using this knowledge for new experiences is the advantage successful people have over the masses. It is absolutely crucial to obtain knowledge from our experiences, but we should never be remorseful over past decisions that helped shape our destiny. Residing in regret is like being stuck in a dark hole, where your mind is telling you there is no hope or means to get out. If you switch on a light bulb, but cover it with a thick piece of material that makes the room dark, does that mean there is no light? No, the light is still there, it's just covered.

We have the ability to take off that material at any time. Just think of that material as being your regretful mind-set and the illusions that come along with it. Previous experiences that so many people allow to control their life are nothing more than a mental image. It is a story that we replay over and over again, tormenting ourselves, but it is gone in reality. Take a look around. You're not physically in that moment that hurt you anymore, are you? Your memory of that experience is a figment of your imagination, so it means you have the power to change the way you think about it. It is now only in your mind. It is never the experience that is making you feel like you can't move on; it's your perception of the experience. No experience needs to be looked at in one set way.

> "When you change the way you look at things,
> the things you look at change."
>
> —MAX PLANCK

I can't think of anything worse than living in regret. It's true that we shaped our life around those decisions, but in the same sense we have the ability to shape our life around our current decisions. **As long as you regret the decisions you have already made, the ones you must make will be sabotaged.**

In the process of eliminating regret, we must use forgiveness to conquer it. Forgiveness is one of the greatest gifts we have. It grants us permission to break free of burdens that restrict us from being at peace with ourselves. Resentment and remorse leave no room for growth. If we do not forgive ourselves we will remain stagnant and hateful, and that will definitely affect what we create next in our lives. We must be at peace with our past in order to gain a full view of opportunities, to stop being restricted by a narrow mind, and to allow for different decisions to be made in the future. There is no future in the past.

> "Accept the pain, cherish the joys, resolve the regrets;
> then can come the best of benedictions: 'If I had my
> life to live over again, I'd do it all the same.'"
>
> —UNKNOWN

It is essential that we accept our previous actions and those of others as an opportunity for growth. You may say sorry to someone, but don't expect their acceptance. Such an expectation could lead to constant disappointment. You must accept that you did your part. Apologizing to someone is not admitting that you did something wrong, it's allowing the other person, and yourself, to acknowledge that you now see a better way. The most important thing you can do is forgive yourself. This will allow you to move on and make progress toward visions that you never trusted yourself to entertain. And if you think about a time when you have forgiven someone, wasn't it the case that you only truly came to forgive them once you forgave yourself for being in that situation? What someone does to you cannot change, but how you see it can. So in order to forgive yourself and others, you must accept inwardly that it was your choice to be in that situation, to feel the way you did about it, to observe it the way you did, and to learn what you did from it. You can't grab the future if you are still holding on to the past.

I once spoke to a woman who was raped as a young teen. The

hatred she felt toward her attacker stopped her from excelling in life, especially in her relationships with other men. It wasn't until she found peace within herself that she was able to forgive him. She explained to me that through such an evil act, she found liberation within herself and began viewing the experience as one she could gain self-knowledge and strength from.

> "Forgiveness is letting go
> of the hope that the past can be changed."
> —OPRAH WINFREY

Self-forgiveness allows us to rebuild the faith in ourselves and those around us. It helps us realize that we are free from emotional restrictions, so we can once again portray real love. Forgiveness is truly a courageous act and helps liberate the soul. Without forgiveness and acceptance of the past, we remain crippled and unable to run. Failing to forgive will prevent us from ever gaining true happiness or fully respecting the great qualities that reign within us; two major keys to real success. **The deeper your scars, the more room there is to fill them up with love. Don't hate your scars, appreciate their depth.** Free your mind, body, and soul.

TASK

Write down the answers to these questions:

> What are the benefits of living in regret?
>
> Does it really make me feel better about myself to have resentment? What are the benefits of accepting my past decisions as an opportunity for growth?
>
> Can I gain knowledge from my past that will help shape my current decisions?

What momentum can I build in my life if I make the decision to move forward and never look back?

Using the empowering information and wisdom gained from my old experience, what can I now achieve in my future endeavors?

5. PATIENCE—A MASTER QUALITY

"As you put into practice the qualities of patience, punctuality, sincerity, and solitude, you will have a better opinion of the world around you."
—GRENVILLE KLEISER

Anyone who has created an extraordinary life will agree that patience is definitely at the top of the list. Without the constant use of this quality, it is impossible to create. If you follow a great achiever, someone who has a great relationship, or an individual who would be regarded as a wise mentor, you will see that patience is what keeps the fine line between sane and insane. It enhances the ability to clearly see what is around and make sense of a situation that we would otherwise get angry about or not properly assess. Without using this master quality, we will make irrational decisions that could have a detrimental effect on our life. In business, a lack of patience could influence us to make decisions that will adversely affect our goals. In relationships, it may cause unnecessary difficulties such as stress, lack of trust, or paranoia, which would then also result in the deterioration of our health. Impatience will attack every part of your life, especially when in pursuit of your visions. Some people get confused by the whole concept and think that taking action every day toward a vision is being impatient. I would just like to clear up that it's precisely the opposite.

Lack of patience especially takes its toll when on the road to achievement. Most people go for the quick dollar when impatience starts to take over, or settle for less than the bigger picture they have set up. You will notice that most really successful people struggled drastically at the beginning of their journey, yet they refused to stop pursuing their goal. It wasn't about wealth right away; it was about getting themselves right first. We must build that inner strength initially. I can't tell you how many people have told me they attempted to do something they love, but said after a little while they went back to working a full-time job that they didn't enjoy, just for the short-term satisfaction of having income. They get that money but are even more unproductive with it because they aren't enjoying their life. A regular income can really benefit you, but not if it takes over your desired passion in life and is just an excuse to settle or give up. You will never be fulfilled that way. Some powerful achievers have had debts through the roof and been ejected from their houses because they couldn't pay the rent, but they never lost sight of their vision. That persistence always pays off.

> *Stop comparing your journey with somebody else's . . .*
> *Not all flowers blossom at the same time.*

In my experience and through speaking to many about this topic, I have discovered that impatience is the main factor in what we call "quitting." What we want seems so far away that it appears easier to stay where we are and just settle. This important question must then follow: **Is it really easier living a life that is less than what you know you deserve?** We will find everything and anything to do besides what we need to do in order to get what we want. We will call multiple friends, think of ten different movies to see, or go for another coffee; anything to escape the fear that "it's just too much to handle."

Patience is a quality that should be put into practice every day, with every situation. Every time I get impatient, I think back to the life I don't want to submit to, and it nearly makes me physically sick. I then visualize my dream life and I am instantly powered with motivation to push forward.

> "He that can have Patience, can have as he will."
> —BENJAMIN FRANKLIN

I determined that no matter what life threw at me, I was going to do what I had to do. Training yourself to be patient is a great test of strength and something that needs to be done if you want success in any area. It starts in traffic, at work, and in your relationships with others. Don't forget, even holding on to trash until you find a bin is a great strategy!

We must make changes that will empower our life with patience, even in the simplest of scenarios. Change really can happen in an instant. We all know there have been some defining moments in our lives that have shaped our destiny. Regardless of being a benefit or not, the decision to change can happen quickly and the results are acutely evident. At times we are not satisfied until we see the end result of our decision. The same goes for when we make the decision to practice patience in our daily lives. In business, for example, most will neglect to feed the quality of patience. They will wait to base their happiness on the end result; for example, the next monthly profits. What they don't realize is that it's a buildup of little decisions that cause the end result they desire to become reality. Look at nature: from the growth of a plant, which is the result of a seed, to a collision of clouds, which results in a storm. There is a buildup, and many small things that must take place before a massive result is seen. **The calm before the storm!** If we don't plant the seed and water it, how will it ever blossom? In one moment you can decide that you want change and gather the inner motivation to do it. It is motivation in that instant that gets you started, but it is routine that makes it habit. Think back to the first time you went to the gym, for instance. Because there was too much pain associated with not doing it, and more pleasure in doing it, something switched inside of you. As time went on, you kept up the routine and it became a way of life. So, yes, change does happen in an instant, but true results come from repetition, and that takes patience.

> "Have patience with all things,
> but chiefly have patience with yourself."
>
> —ST. FRANCIS DE SALES

To master patience is to also have faith in yourself and your creator. I used to fall back on the idea that "I know why this has all happened." That was my favorite saying to myself, reassurance of the greater plan I set for my life. You must build the belief that you know—as surely as you know the back of your hand—that it's going to happen. We have all visualized the great life we aspire to, although impatience plays a major role in stopping us from ever experiencing it. Self-control and remaining strong in the face of impatience are the keys to winning. You are still going to get angry or impatient at times, but battle your hardest not to vent it. **Letting out anger is like facing a strong gust of wind and spitting directly in it: You affect yourself the most.** Use all the power you have and focus on making an internal shift. Fight it, overpower your limiting thoughts, and you will win. When faced with a challenging situation, use it to practice the art of patience. Once mastered, it will help you beat the next one with a little more ease.

Before you know it, patience will be your subconscious reaction, and impatience will quickly result in correcting yourself. Another great tool is to put things into perspective. If you're waiting in traffic, just sit back and think about all those who don't even have food to eat, let alone a car to drive, and you will soon realize that your complaints are very petty. To cut above the rest, you must also use situations like these to your advantage. I've had so many people tell me that they don't have time to themselves to think about bettering their lives, and then I always refer back to the "stuck in traffic" situation. I'm not sure about you, but I see a lot of time in the day when you can really think. **Finding the balance between persistence and patience is the pinnacle when creating something great.** This can only be achieved by constant practice. Without patience, you are likely to give up.

> "Patience can't be acquired overnight.
> It is just like building up a muscle.
> Every day you need to work on it."
> —EKNATH EASWARAN

6. THE QUALITY OF GIVING—WHAT A GIFT!

Take a lit candle and light many others with it. Has the flame suffered any loss? What happens to the flame when you put all those flames together? It gets bigger.

It is the same principle in life. We should always seek to light that flame with an inner peace and self-love from within. Once that has been attained you will be like a light in the world, ready to ignite anyone who crosses your path. People will feel your warmth. There is no greater gift than giving itself.

> "It is one of the most beautiful compensations of life,
> that no man can sincerely try to help another
> without helping himself."
> —RALPH WALDO EMERSON

In the car one afternoon with a friend, another realization dawned on me. He let someone go in front of him and was waiting for a thank-you wave. When he didn't get it, he cursed himself for letting the guy in. It hit me: Why expect a wave to determine how you feel about your great action?

When you recognize that your feeling should be determined by your own action, not someone else's reaction, your decision to give will not be for any selfish desire of recognition or praise. It will be purely out of good intention, and that's giving. Things that are done out of pure intent are an amazing gift to all. It is evident that some people only give to obtain something in return. Is that really giving? Even if it is just a thank-you that you expect, it takes away the true essence of the act.

You should be proud of yourself, not proud of what others think and feel about you. If you can be really happy in giving, then it's already complete. If you want to be happy for anyone outside of you, be happy for them. Also take note that others' growth is your growth, and vice versa. Contribution is one of only three ways to ever be truly fulfilled.

I have heard people say, "Oh, so I have to give money to charity?" First, you don't have to do anything in life; everything is a choice. Second, is that what this world has made us believe, that the only gifts come in a box or a check? I know most people wouldn't lose even a minute of sleep over kids halfway across the world. I don't expect them to yet. We must rediscover and feed our true qualities first. Start with the people around you and begin with things that are basic. What about the gift of love, change, or generosity in everyday life? How about the gifts of appreciation, acceptance, gratitude, and communication? Why don't we give ourselves back the gift of life, which so many seem to forget? They are all free and help you and the people around you. They are far more important than a few checks a year. In saying that, helping a fellow human in need is the most fulfilling act we could ever perform. As we become more self-aware and the heart opens, we will notice the power we have to change someone's life. It will become like an addiction, something you'll feel you cannot live without.

> "It is more blessed to give than to receive."
> —JESUS CHRIST

A story that really inspired me and brought me to tears was one that I heard on the radio. It was about a wealthy man who went to Africa to visit a poor village. He met a young boy there who was seven years old and dying of malnutrition. He said the boy's stomach was bloated, his hair was discolored, and he could hardly stand up. He knelt down and gave the boy an open coconut. He expected the child to eat it immediately, but to his amazement the boy left the fruit by his side. The man walked off, puzzled. A few minutes later, out of the corner of his eye, he saw the boy pick up the coconut and walk to a tent. Without hesitation he secretly followed. Pulling back the entrance to the tent, he saw the boy kneeling down, holding in one hand a baby, and in the other the coconut.

Tour guides later informed this wealthy man that the baby was the boy's dying brother. The young boy loved his baby brother so much that any bit of food he got, he fed the baby, going hungry himself. What a moving, touching, and inspiring story of the human bond. A boy so young, faced with death, is still able to surrender for human love. That really penetrated my soul. Just think of how many of us are blessed with so much, yet we give nothing. **One man can save another man's life. That's what one man can do.** There is no greater act than that.

> "Happiness . . . consists in giving,
> and in serving others."
> —HENRY DRUMMOND

We all have an amazing gift that was given to us. How many times have you had a gift, wrapped up with your name on it, and you didn't open it? I'm guessing your answer will probably be "never." Well, I have a rude awakening for some: The answer is "every day." There is a God-given gift, all wrapped up by the hate, despair, fear, complaining, and other limitations we let consume our lives. We have the power to perceive things in a different light, and even more important, the power to change the way we act.

Sadly, the vast majority of people believe that when they give they are emptying themselves, or they are giving something up in the process. In order for them to feel significant, they unconsciously attempt to fill that gap with someone else's approval or praise. When it doesn't happen, they seem to be disappointed. In order to be happy in life, we must recognize that every time we give, we automatically receive. The feeling of giving is the gift! If you focus your energy on the great acts you commit to every day, you will experience fulfillment.

Real success also thrives on the idea of giving. It helps you to create a stronger passion to not just follow achievement for yourself but to better everyone around you. I could just imagine how lonely and unfulfilling life would be if I were to celebrate success on my own. That doesn't merely mean money but keeping the great qualities you know you have all to yourself. Share them, **allow people to see you for who you really are,** give of yourself, and it will come back tenfold. The energy we express with our thoughts, words, and actions is the real contribution to the world. It becomes contagious to those around you, because every soul is striving for that fulfillment. Before you know it, it will feel not like a process but rather like a way of life. Then the universe will be happy to welcome you to the never-ending cycle of self-growth.

GOLD WITH GRAHAM . . .

It takes a simpleminded man to linger around those who are praised, yet a courageous man to pick up those who have fallen.

Walking in the heart of Melbourne, I passed a distressed-looking man sitting against a storefront. Near him lay a beanie, a cup, and a dirty backpack. Knees up and head bent, he appeared to have given up all hope. I put some coins in his cup and continued on to do some shopping. As I walked back from the store, I decided to sit down on a chair across from him. Watching people walk past, deliberately staying clear and acting as if he were an alien, I couldn't help but enter a state of compassion. Thinking about what others would think if I sat next to him, I hesitated. I mean, this was the main street in the city, Bourke Street Mall. If you have ever been to Melbourne, Australia, you would understand what I'm talking about.

My love for this human was far too great to be held back by what others thought, though, so I left my fear behind and walked up. I finally realized that it was only when I cared that it seemed others did as well. When I stopped caring what they thought, it seemed they stopped caring, too. I guess our mind really does create our reality! I knelt down, gave him ten dollars, and said, "Do you mind if I have a chat with you, sir?" He looked up and said no. I sat right next to him in the same position he was in. It was an eye-opener to watch people walk past from down there. I then recognized that this man, named Graham, was disabled. His hands were deformed and he could hardly get the words out to speak. He mumbled that the government had shut down his hospital. He had a volunteer who used to look after him, but they had also left. I might add this gentleman was one of the nicest individuals I have ever met. He told me that the previous day he had been spat on and kicked in the face by someone who called him a retard.

What amazed me was his attitude toward life. He said he would help those people if they needed his help, regardless of what they did to him. He even thanked God that he was shown manners as a child. He prays to God every morning and says thank you for being alive. He said that he knows God will watch over him and provide. He hasn't been let down yet and has taken his challenge as a way of life that he must deal with the best way he can. He understands that these people who ridicule him are only affecting themselves and battling their inner turmoil.

As we continued to chat I noticed he sat up and created more energy. I seemed to forget everyone else around while talking until something wonderful happened. People began walking up and dropping money in his cup. Another man brought over food and people were smiling in our direction. I told him to smile back, and he did. This one moment touched my heart and I will never forget it. Graham taught me the power of what one person can do. People will follow your great act.

This man has had so many challenges in his life yet has such a positive outlook. He loves the people who beat him, and has such strong faith. He assured me that he does not beg people but has faith God will provide. He said whenever he starts to complain he thinks of all the people who were kicked out of the hospital who were far worse off than him. He is compassionate toward the human race and said his dream is for equality. What a golden moment in my life.

> "If you can't feed a hundred people, just feed one."
>
> —MOTHER TERESA

7. UNDERSTANDING OUR BODY OF EGO

Appreciation, contribution, and self-growth are the only ways to true fulfillment. To embrace any one of these, we are required to put down our body of ego. Don't be ashamed of having an ego; it's human nature. But some people feed theirs so much that it gets in the way of really getting the most out of life.

Ego is a great indicator of whether someone is genuine or not. An ego is like a shield that protects us from feeling embarrassed and prevents us from displaying who we really are. We believe if we put it down, others might think we are weird, which would alienate us. Someone with a big ego is generally hiding much deeper issues, and they are the people who are unfulfilled. They wear a mask their whole life, and when they feel they are about to be exposed, they lash out and attack your actions, rarely looking at their own. They fear meeting the stranger underneath the mask. They are the same people who usually look at how much they can take rather than what they can give. They are commonly self-centered, their intentions are frequently ill, and their desires are far from contributing. The sad thing is that even though most people are aware of this fact, but they still display their ego. We must learn to direct our ego in a way that actually benefits the world and ourselves. Being human, I still find myself being caught up in ego at times, yet my self-awareness pulls me back into line almost instantly. So if you think you are too cool for school, think again. **No one escapes the classroom of life; humbly embrace its knowledge or feel its punishment.**

Putting down our ego is crucial not just for lasting happiness but also for achievement. Self-growth requires us to listen and obtain knowledge from people, which requires that our ego be put aside. Ego is the number one factor that prevents us from listening, with its attitude that we don't need help and we can do it on our own.

I was out for coffee with a property investor one afternoon, and he told me a story that Sir Bob Geldof had shared at a seminar. Geldof was telling them about this chubby little kid who would always be hanging around and asking for advice. He later mentioned that he never knew that same kid would grow up to be Bono from U2. Another great story is that of Michael Dell, the creator of Dell computers. He had his first job working in a Chinese restaurant for $2.30 an hour. He would go in early and humbled himself by listening to the wise owner speak about his passion and love for the business.

Taking the advice of others and always being willing to take in new information is vital to success. Your ego must be down in order for you to listen to the advice your spirit gives you every day. If you have a stubborn mind-set that is stuck in one position, you will never be fulfilled. Your spirit is by far your best teacher and guide, as it knows all the answers to your questions. That deep voice inside knows what's best and will bump you initially if something doesn't feel right. How many times has your gut feeling been right? How many times have you convinced yourself otherwise and been unhappy? It's usually our mind that gets in the way of listening to our spirit. The key to aligning them both is separating yourself from your ego. When you unify the power of your thoughts with that wise inner voice, your success is self-evident.

If you still feel empty in your life, it is because you have yet to surrender your ego to humbleness.

People will cross our path to help us grow in life, but it's our ego that stops us from noticing this and allows them to slip away. We don't like the way they look, we are judgmental, or we aren't willing to hear what we know is the truth. Being humble throughout your experiences is a true indicator of whether you are fulfilled or not. If you are not humble, you'd better start being so, or you will never find fulfillment, period. Confidence plays a major role in having an outstanding life, but make sure you find the line between confident and cocky. It's a thin line, but you will be aware of which one you are showing.

TASK

Do not read on until tomorrow. The qualities we just went through are extremely important to your growth and success. I want you to take them with you for now. The next section is on a different topic, so until tomorrow, focus on the qualities that drive success.

16

Life's Ultimate Duo—
The Spirit and Its Visions

PASSION—THE VOICE OF YOUR SPIRIT

"If there is no passion in your life, then have you
really lived? Find your passion, whatever it may be.
Become it, and let it become you and you will find great
things happen for you, to you, and because of you."

—ALAN ARMSTRONG

During a chat with a friend of mine, I was shocked to hear that
he wasn't happy after achieving something massive on his wants
list. He was an international DJ and radio show host. His songs
were making the top of charts and he was playing in the biggest
nightclubs in the world. One of his dreams was to play in Europe,
which he had just achieved before I saw him. As he walked into the
room to greet me, he said, "It wasn't what I expected." He told me
that he went back to his hotel room after the show and wondered
whether he even wanted to pursue a music career. The show went
well, the people were great, and everything was in place. So what

was happening? After a long conversation, we got to the bottom of it and he walked out with a breakthrough. Throughout his career he had focused on what he thought was his passion: to play music. I asked him this question: "If I gave you all your equipment on a deserted island, how long do you think you would last playing music all alone?" He replied, "Probably a few hours." Then I asked another question: "But your passion is to play music, isn't it?" He replied, "Yes, so I don't know why I would only last that long, and I don't know what is making me unhappy." I turned to him and said, "Your passion isn't just to play music. **Your true passion is to inspire others with your music.**" When he focused on other people's emotions when they listened to his music, rather than just his own desire, he experienced a key turning point in his career.

We all want to know how to add value to this world, the people around us, and ourselves. Doing things for others will always create more meaning in your life. The people who have been the most influential and successful were those who were committed to doing this. A passion is far deeper than material satisfaction; it's that drive within us that sparks the feeling that is far too great to be restricted by words. Once you put a lot of energy toward a passionate life you enter the realm of the elite. The thought of it fills you with emotions you have never experienced, keeps you up at night, and wakes you up in the morning. It is enforced and embedded so deep within you that it surely becomes the basis of your decisions. It will guide you over hurdles, find inspiration once gone unnoticed, pick you up when you fall, and be the air you breathe.

You can definitely feel the difference when you enter a room with someone who has passion and someone who doesn't. In whatever area of life, you will notice the ones with a strong passion are those who are running far beyond what others think is the finish line. When everyone else says it's too hard or impossible, they are the ones that prove them wrong.

"If you can imagine it, you can achieve it.
If you dream it, you can become it."
—WILLIAM ARTHUR WARD

I hear people tell me they have a vision, so I ask what it is and they say things like "to buy that house." Now that's great, but what after that? See, a **passion is an invisible force that consumes your whole life and creates vision after vision.** A true passion sees no end, but only everlasting growth. A passion would be to provide for your children, to inspire people to be the best they can be, to add value to the world, to help others, to provide a service like no one else, or to do something that you love. Being the best you can be is another great one. If there's any passion that is at the heart of every person, it is to exude that greatness that lies deep within them. We must prove our greatness to ourselves, because if we don't, we are the one who has to answer the question "Why?"

We all know that we have a lot more to give, but we just need to let that inner person speak. A great way to drag that spirit out and begin to steer it is to give as many reasons as you can why you want to do something.

We put all these material wants in front of us and call them visions, yet sometimes we struggle to achieve them. The reason is that we forget to build the foundation that is going to hold everything up. We must search deeper and ask why we want what we do. Whatever it is, you need to build as many reasons as possible why you are doing what you are doing, and let them really align themselves with who you are deep down. That's how you remain at full strength. I personally do not let material things drive me because I know they will flow through my passion. I have a clear indication of what I want, but then I let my spirit guide me. If we don't do it this way, we get caught up in greed and we will never be fulfilled. You will notice that you continue to come back to that point of emptiness and then wonder why you even bothered in the first place.

A true passion doesn't just appear bright and strong one day, it evolves over time.

I can't tell you what your passion in life is—no one but you can do that. This is one of the biggest challenges I see today. It seems when the thought of trying to discover our true passion or calling comes up, it causes us to worry and become stressed. All that does is cloud and suffocate your spirit. As we all know, stress is a major contributor to our despair, so it is definitely not the road to finding your passion. In order to discover the blueprint of our greatness hidden under the collage of social beliefs that become self-beliefs, we must unwrap the paper and then the gift will be displayed. That collage is all the limitations such as hate, fear, self-doubt, judgment, lack of self-love, and many more that restrict us from seeing our true path.

Lack of passion in life is truly a grave issue in society. I have coached people searching for their passion in life more than any other challenge. What I am about to tell you will probably change your perception of your passion forever—our whole life we seem to be in search of this one passion that we think will win us fulfillment, and the concept is usually based around a career. We believe that without finding what it is, we are hopeless. Well, guess what: No one who is passionate is only passionate about one thing! I would consider myself a passionate person now, but I didn't wait to find out what career I wanted to do in order to decide that. In all honesty, I don't even consider educating and inspiring people a career; rather, it is a passion that flowed from first being passionate in many other areas of life. I am passionate about being a great person, treating everyone as equals, sustaining the quality of nature, my body, my family, people in general, and so on. I have many passions in life. I didn't just wake up one day knowing what my career was and begin being a passionate person, nor did any of the vastly successful people I have met on my journey. If you don't practice being passionate in all the other areas of your life, then you will never discover your true potential.

There is one great thing that all successes in any era have in common. It calls for no debate, it requires unconditional love, and it is the pinnacle of all emotions—it is the passion for life itself. When you have passion for every part of your life, things fall into place.

> *All successful people have one thing in common. They are all addicted to life.*

THE ENORMITY OF VISUALIZATION

> "Formulate and stamp indelibly on your mind a mental picture of yourself as succeeding. Hold this picture tenaciously. Never permit it to fade. Your mind will seek to develop the picture. Do not build up obstacles in your imagination."
>
> —NORMAN VINCENT PEALE

People continually visualize throughout their day. There are very few who embrace the present, but many who envision the past or the future. The issue is that it's of no benefit because those visions usually result in stress or worry. The same people have no idea how much power their visions have to become reality and that they cause them to experience the same emotions they so often complain about. As we previously read about neuroplasticity, constant repetition is effective in shaping who we are becoming. People get all spooked when they hear the word *meditation,* but they are missing out on one of the most powerful gifts mankind has. We are led to believe that when meditating we are thinking of nothing. Let me assure you, when you are thinking of nothing you are still thinking, because you're "thinking of nothing." It's an opportunity to take ourselves away from what we see with our eyes, away from space and time, and start using those thoughts to really create a feeling of success right now.

> "Why do we close our eyes when we pray,
> when we cry, when we kiss, when we dream;
> because the most beautiful things in our life
> are not seen but felt only by the heart."
>
> —UNKNOWN

Taking the time out for visualization is one tool that really successful people have used, even if they don't call it that. Meditation, prayer, and imagining are all the same thing. Successful people allocate time to completely focus on what they want, not what they don't want. I would get so strongly into visualization that the hairs on the back of my neck would stand up, because what I saw in my mind was just as real as if I were really there. Sure enough, they do happen.

Dr. Andrew Newberg conducted a study to check the neural behavior and physical responses to meditation by Tibetan monks and prayer by Franciscan nuns. The physiological changes in the brain and discoveries were outstanding.

Dr. Newberg found that the front part of the brain, which is usually involved in focusing attention and concentration, is more active during meditation. There was, however, a great decrease in activity in the parietal lobe.

The parietal area of the brain is responsible for giving us a sense of our orientation in space and time. He hypothesized that blocking all sensory and cognitive input into this area during meditation results in the sense of no space and no time. When this part of the brain, which weaves sensory data into a feeling of where the self ends, is deprived of sensory input through an individual's focus on inward concentration, it cannot do its job of finding the border between the self and the world. Dr. Newberg described how this affects consciousness:

> The brain had no choice. It perceived the self to be endless, as one with all of creation. And this felt utterly real. The absorption of the self into something larger is not the result of emotional fabrication or wishful thinking. It springs from neurological events, as when the orientation area goes dark.

Other experiments have also been performed, including those by Richard Davidson. He is a professor of psychology and psychiatry at the University of Wisconsin, and has led experiments in cooperation with the Dalai Lama on effects of meditation on the brain. His results suggest that long-term or short-term practice of meditation results in different levels of activity in brain regions associated with such qualities as attention, anxiety, depression, fear, anger, and the ability of the body to heal itself. These functional changes may be caused by changes in the physical structure of the brain.

With enough focus, your mind doesn't know whether what you are thinking about is real right now or not. When we daydream or close our eyes and drift off, we feel the same emotions as if we are actually living our dream. It feels so real, because for that brief moment your mind doesn't know the difference. The more energy we put toward something, the stronger influence it has on our life; it's the same with what we focus on in our mind.

That's the power of realization; those very images you choose to see in your mind on a daily basis, be they beneficial or not, are being attracted to your life. That's why things we don't want keep showing up—because we continually think about them! If we direct our mental images to what we want, it causes not just ourselves but everything else to surrender to manifestation.

> "Ordinary people believe only in the possible.
> Extraordinary people visualize not what is possible
> or probable, but rather what is impossible.
> And by visualizing the impossible,
> they begin to see it as possible."
> —DR. CHÉRIE CARTER-SCOTT

I don't care what you want to call it; closing your eyes, directing all your focus to one area as if you were really there, feeling the emotions, and even imagining how you would physically react is going to enhance your life. I used to sit in my room, close my eyes, and drift off. In that moment, I felt as if I could hear people telling me how much I'd helped them; I felt as if I already had a better relationship with my family. These feelings have since become reality. I would feel the warmth in a person's hand when they shook mine, or a hug from my nephew, just to inspire my day. I would do it anywhere and anytime I had the chance. **The power of visualization** has a weird way of speeding up time toward those things you desire. Things start to happen quicker, and I guess that's how you see some people's success and wonder how they achieved things in such a short amount of time. The more you visualize the qualities of life and what you want, the stronger your vision becomes. It will be a way of life and a means to take the appropriate action.

You can also cut time when something distressing displays itself by simply closing your eyes and drifting away to a better place for that short time. When you start practicing this, it might seem difficult to stay focused, but the more energy you put toward it, the better you become at it. Even when you drift off with your eyes closed, it is crucial to redirect toward things you appreciate, or an experience that would immediately make you happy. Have you ever noticed that the trip back from a journey always seems shorter? Why is that? The reason is that we have been there before. If we go somewhere in our mind, feel it, see it, and be it, then we obtain it at a much faster pace. If you don't believe that your mind is the basis of your creations, then ask yourself these questions: Why do we have a mind, and what is its purpose? Use it!

> "There are only two ways to live your life.
> One is as though nothing is a miracle.
> The other is as though everything is a miracle."
>
> —ALBERT EINSTEIN

No words I write could amount to the certainty I have in visualization. It is the key and foundation to all your dreams, and is the basis for your decisions and reactions toward life experiences.

Be different from the rest, and give yourself this wonderful opportunity. When doing this, it is crucial to feel every detail of the image, from the smallest to the largest. Embrace the power and the emotion of it and it will be the foundation of creating the life you desire.

VISUALIZATION EXPERIMENT

If you have ever played basketball or known a basketball player personally, you would know that many players choke when it's time to take a free throw. Even some of the best basketball players on the planet have this mental block. No one questions their ability to play the game, but they have trouble making those shots, and they will be the first to admit it's all in their mind. Dr. Judd Biasiotto at the University of Chicago reported about a study that was conducted to determine the effects of visualization on the free-throw performance of basketball players.

First, the athletes were tested to determine their free-throw proficiency. They were then randomly assigned to one of three experimental groups. The first went to the gym every day for one hour and practiced free throws.

The second group also went to the gym, but instead of physically practicing, they were told to lie down and simply visualize themselves successfully shooting.

The third group did nothing. In fact, they were instructed to forget about basketball. At the end of thirty days, the three groups were again tested to determine their free-throw proficiency.

The players who hadn't practiced at all showed no improvement in performance; many in that group actually exhibited a drop.

Those who had physically practiced one hour each day showed a performance increase of 24 percent. Here's the clincher: The visualization group, by merely imagining themselves successfully shooting free throws, also improved 24 percent!

It doesn't matter what area of life you apply this to: If you run a perfect scenario over and over in your mind with the inclusion of **sight, sound, and smell,** performance is sure to improve. Visualizing and taking physical action is a combination that is unbeatable.

TRAINING YOUR MIND

> "Give us a clear vision that we may know where to
> stand and what to stand for—because unless we
> stand for something, we shall fall for anything."
>
> —PETER MARSHALL

TASK

Visualize your updated appreciation list. Be still and make sure you are stationary. Once you fully focus and do it a few times, you won't want to stop. You will discover a shift in focus toward great things in life, rather than things that are of no benefit. The quality of your whole life will improve.

1. Start with focusing on breathing in and out through your nose. From the tip of your nostrils, follow the breath all the way until it flows back out. When you inhale, draw the air down to your stomach and back out slowly through your nose. You can count up to seven when exhaling to slow down the process. Do this until you feel light and weightless.

2. A euphoric state should arise in your mind; then start visualizing. I personally did this at night when I was relaxed, but still read my list in the morning. This addition to your daily ritual will transform your life—but you have to commit to it. Don't just do it for three days, stop, and then email me saying it doesn't work. It's an ongoing process, but results will be measurable immediately, especially in the way you feel.

3. You can visualize at any time during the day, and listening to music that inspires you is also a great addition.

Your visions will start to play out around you, awareness will rise, and you will notice things that are relevant to your success that once went unnoticed.

> Our mind is the canvas on which we create and imagination is its tool. Things once thought of as "just a dream" will turn into a vision so strong that your passion will see to its becoming real.

4TH STEP
Steer Your Relationships

17

Rocky, Docked, or Sailing Smooth?

"A loving relationship is one in which
the loved one is free to be himself—
to laugh with me, but never at me;
to cry with me, but never because of me;
to love life, to love himself, to love being loved.
Such a relationship is based upon freedom
and can never grow in a jealous heart."

—LEO F. BUSCAGLIA

Relationships play such a vital role in our daily life, so I knew I had to cover this topic. I went around to relationship experts, but my main focus was the everyday person. I wanted to know what people are really feeling; those who have overcome relationships that weren't working, couples who have been married for twenty years and are still going strong, and others who found their dream partner. I came to realize that it's in fact just like a ship—it all depends on how it's sailing. You could be on really rocky seas, nearly falling off; you could be sailing very smoothly; and you could be docked and waiting to be taken out. Let's start with the relationships that are . . .

ROCKY

These are the ships that sway from side to side and never seem to settle. I definitely found myself aboard this ship a few times in my life. A lot of it has to do with not being self-aware and not knowing exactly what you want—or knowing, but not taking appropriate action.

One guy in particular who seemed to be clashing with his girl-friend asked me what he should do. This one is very difficult, be-cause trying to get the truth out of someone is a battle in itself. Some people will defend their partner because they don't want to portray them as the villain. Sometimes they don't mention their own faults or they attempt to put all the blame on the other per-son. There seems to be a lot of attacking and defending on either end. It's also hard to get the truth out because many believe love is the sole reason they should be with their partner. I believe say-ing "But I love him/her" does not offer a strong enough reason on its own to stay with someone. I'm sure we are quite aware that we can fall in love many times, and on occasion with those who aren't right for us. It doesn't mean they're not right as people, it just means they're not right for us. We get sucked in by attraction and other things initially that get a good hold on us. But then every date with the person feels like a blind date, because we just don't know what is going to happen next.

I sat this guy down and I asked this question: "What do you love about her, and why are you with her?"

This was his answer: "She makes me laugh, she keeps me on my toes, I'm really attracted to her, she keeps me strong when I feel weak, she gets along well with my family, I love her, and I can communicate with her."

I went on to ask him what he loves about himself and he gave me only three answers and then struggled. How can we confi-dently give the best of ourselves if we aren't even sure what we can offer? How can we ever know what we want when we don't even know who we are? We must be the great person we wish to see in a partner, or else we will sadly never find happiness.

A couple of years ago on Valentine's Day, my mother asked me who I was going out for dinner with. I let her know that I was going by myself, but assured her I wasn't crazy. I wanted to go on a date with me and ask what type of person I am, what I want out of my life, and what's important to me. I'm so thrilled I did, because that night brought up a lot of answers and created many opportunities for change.

With regard to the first question I asked the guy, "What do you love about her, and why are you with her?" I explained that every single answer had "me" or "I" in it and was nothing short of self-ish. It seems that our relationships start to become all about our own desires, rather than being a paired force and helping each other grow. So I said to him, "Instead of saying 'she makes me laugh,' how about 'her amazing sense of humor'? So when she isn't there to make you laugh on a particular occasion, it's okay, because she is still funny and you will always recognize that. **Your partner has her own life as well.** It's not her full-time job to fulfill you; that's your own job. Instead of saying 'she gets along well with my family,' how about 'she is family oriented'?" Can you notice the huge difference this small shift in attitude could have on a relationship? You must focus on your partner's qualities, not only on what they can offer you.

So many relationships start becoming all about what one person wants, and one person taking control of the situation. You have to shift your focus to the other person and why you are really with them, because it's going to make you appreciate them on a completely different level. Acknowledging their great assets is the pillar that will hold you both up when challenges arise. Let's face it, as long as we are alive there are going to be some cracks, but if it's all about you, then you can bet it's not going to hold up too well.

"Consider how hard it is to change yourself
and you'll understand what little chance you have
in trying to change others."

—UNKNOWN

Another major breaking point I discovered through talking to many people about the topic, and through my own experiences, is that we believe our partner fills gaps within us that we don't believe we can fill ourselves. This seems to be the biggest unconscious issue many face. When that person isn't there to fill that part up for whatever reason, we start fighting, begin to doubt, and things crumble. Being an unconscious issue means we are not really aware that this is the case, but it warrants these deeper questions: Are you really in love with who they are, or are you in love with what you think they fulfill in you that you don't believe you can fulfill yourself? Did you have a clear indication of what you wanted out of a life partner when you met them? Did you really get to know them, or did you get sucked in solely by the attraction bug? **At the end of the day, no one can fulfill anything that you don't already have access to.**

When we truly believe that we need a person to live, it puts strain on the relationship. We make ourselves believe that if they are not around we are out of whack, can't function, are unable to get by or do anything in our life. I'm here to tell you now that everything you think you need you already have—it might just be qualities you are not yet using. Be with someone because you truly want them, not because you feel you need them or have to have them.

An expectation from others can really be an invitation for disappointment. When we expect things to happen and also believe that the other person has to do things, it prevents us from appreciating the great things they do for us. Realistically, they don't have to do anything, but if they do, it should be because they want to, not because they feel like they have to. If you have to keep asking them to do something and they eventually do it, but you just feel it's not coming from their heart, then it's only because you made them do it. No real satisfaction should be drawn from that and, to be honest, maybe that person isn't really your greatest match. If they're right for you, things just happen; you shouldn't feel like you are continually forcing them to. We must be at peace with ourselves and actually want that person for who they really are. You must respect they also have a life that should be lived. A partner's role is to help the other person with their aspirations and add as much value as they possibly can to their life. A healthy relationship is evident when both people seem to bring the best out of each other and shine simultaneously. **A life partner is not about battling each other, but overcoming life's challenges together.** Here are three ways to create a more fulfilling relationship:

- Command your own emotions, **not** your partner's. If you don't do this, your relationship won't stand a chance.

- Set up compelling visions together. If you don't have something to look forward to, you will burn out. Sometimes people are still together, but it doesn't mean their relationship is alive. What do you want your relationship to be like? How can you make it that way? What can you both do to bring that about? What would you like to achieve together?

- Create a strategy plan that you both work through to get those desired visions and outcomes.

IF YOU MUST, LET GO

> "The jump is so frightening between where I am and
> where I want to be . . . because of all I may become,
> I will close my eyes and leap!"
>
> —MARY ANNE RADMACHER

Our happiness as individuals will almost always be based on the decisions we make, or the ones we want to make, but aren't following through. **People experience unhappiness because the expectations they have set for their life haven't been met.** This goes for our finances, emotional state, and predominantly for our relationships.

It really does come down to what you want out of your life. If you know in your heart that your current relationship is something you don't wish to participate in any longer, you must feed your truth. There are many people who turn around after leaving their relationship and say, "I really want it back." It may be the fifth time they have attempted to end it, but every time the same story is repeated. The question must then be asked, "Do they want it back, or do they fear the unknown because they haven't yet built the inner strength to let it go?" By probing deeper, the answers I have heard over and over again are that they really want to get far away from the whole situation and have the feeling of being free from it. They just remind themselves of why they can't, not how they can. When they accept that "can't" is a choice, they automatically realize they can.

My truth was telling me for so long that I didn't want to be in my past relationship, and I would definitely have a lot more money if I saved a dollar for every time I ignored it. I would continually think, "This person isn't right for me, get out and run." I would then get down on my knees and say, "God, just give me a sign."

The funny thing was that asking for a sign was actually the sign itself! The signs are right there, we see them all day, and that deep voice inside will always be there to remind us. I now believe that if it's an "I don't know," then it's a "no." That goes for business, relationships, and everything else. Unless I am absolutely certain, it's a no-go zone. That's not to say I can't make myself certain or that I need to know instantaneously, but I won't fully commit my life to it until I am.

> "A sad thing in life is that sometimes you
> meet someone who means a lot to you
> only to find out in the end it was never
> bound to be and you just have to let go."
> —UNKNOWN

We are also able to build that certainty when we want to leave a partner. If you have ever been in a relationship where you were not fulfilled and finally gained the courage to leave, you would know that there comes a point when the pain is just too strong and the grass is too green on the other side. Just like anything in life, a shift of emotion caused you to act rapidly and you finally left. You hit that point in your life when you said, "That's it, I've had enough." That day came when you refused to continue living someone else's life. I'm sure you also became frustrated with trying to take control over their life, because that's not what it's about. It's not our duty to attempt to turn someone into us because that will surely create a clash. And essentially, who gives us the right to do that anyway? The reason we become involved with someone is so we can both add different elements to each other's life. Never attempt to make the other person live your life; they should respect yours, and you should respect theirs. Like I said, if they are right for you, then things aren't that difficult. You don't continually force them and they don't feel like they have to do something, they just do it.

When you attempt to control someone else's life, it only reflects the lack of control you have over your own.

Most of the time we drive ourselves crazy trying to figure out what our partner is thinking. Why did they do that, why did they hurt me, or why are they acting that way? How about you? **In doing this, we neglect to take accountability for our own life and realize it's never what they have done; it's what we allow them to do.** Once we take charge, the decisions to follow will bring the outcome we deeply desire. You must take charge of your own emotions and mental state! They are who they are, but you must be responsible for you and start making decisions accordingly. If they are not willing to make change, then you must. And in my opinion, a person can only give you as much love as they find within themselves.

In determining whether someone is a life partner or not, I think it's crucial that your core values do not clash with their values. At the end of the day, our values are the things we live by. I was speaking to a client of mine who always wanted to travel and eventually have children, but her partner's belief was that traveling was a waste of money, and he didn't want to have kids. Obviously, not really knowing what she wanted out of a life partner when she met him, she didn't probe those major details. By the time she found out, she had already built a love for him. He wasn't willing to compromise and he didn't want her to travel on her own.

The things this guy valued most in his life were obviously quite different from hers.

So I told this woman to write down everything she wanted to do or accomplish in her life and add up whether his traits would allow them to grow together. After she did the exercise, she discovered that she had put on hold nearly the whole list for him. She needed to take accountability for that and stop blaming him for her inaction.

He wasn't wrong; it's just not what he wanted out of his life. In order for her to live her life, she needed to leave him. After a five-year relationship, she ended it. She was hurting for a while, and assured me it wasn't easy, but it was the best decision she ever made. She finally visited her family overseas and started her own business. She also promised me that she would never be with another guy who didn't want to have children. That has now made the top of her **must** list. She has created clarity and learned from her past experience, and that's how we grow and attract what we want.

Don't lose yourself just because you found somebody.

If the things we value most aren't aligned with our partner, how can we ever expect our relationship to be successful?

Anytime you experience conflict with someone, it's because they have trodden on the things you value most in your life. No one likes the values they live by or what they stand for to be trampled on or questioned. Our values are our life, because we use them as the sole decider of our choices. If you have ever been uncertain when making a decision, it's because you were still unsure of what you valued most in that situation.

Many people settle for someone who has vastly different values than them, and who stands for completely different things. The importance of some things to them is lesser or greater than it is to their partner. Is it any wonder why these relationships continue to clash? Attraction, wealth, social status, loneliness, and emptiness are just a few factors that will make us hang around. I highly advise putting someone's core values at the top of your list if you want a fulfilling relationship. If you are unhappy in your relationship now because of this clash, and you know the person will never change (not that they have to or even should), then it's time to reassess and make a decision. Furthermore, people confuse lust with love. People obsess over someone they just met, or think they like someone they don't even really know. We then crave attention from them, and being ignored by the only person you want attention from is one of the worst feelings. We have all felt it! But when you look deep enough, you realize that the person you are really craving attention from is yourself. I think when we feel vulnerable to someone else's attention, it's life telling us that we aren't giving ourselves enough. It's usually a buildup of self-neglect that gets us to such a needy stage. And in essence, that person was the wake-up call: You need to learn how to love yourself again. Stop letting your happiness be dependent on someone else's mood.

The qualities that we value most, the standards on the top of our list, and the morals that mean the most to us shape our life. Some of the things you value most could be respect, communication, going on vacations with someone. However, someone else might have a different view of those things. They might consider texting you back three days later acceptable, when you feel like that is an unacceptable lack of communication. You might feel like following through on plans you've made with someone is a sign of maturity and integrity, where someone else may not really care or think twice about not following through. I believe there is a level of compromise, but I also think there is only so long we can live with things we don't really accept or respect. A partner should help you feel secure, not make you feel like you are constantly walking on eggshells.

Even though people have different values, we all have the same needs. One of those needs is to be loved for who we really are, not who we pretend to be. We need someone with similar values to help us grow. If we feel as though someone lives by a different charter of values, we will always have a lack of understanding and frustration toward them. We may even feel that the person is slowing us down. I'm not saying you should not be with someone who has different traits. What I am saying is to look hard at what values that person stands for in their life. The myth of "never going to find someone again" is just that, a myth. Don't be fooled—in time you will.

> *Ex-partners play a very important role in our destiny; they make us see what we definitely don't want, so what we do want becomes clearer.*

I think it's wasting your life being with someone that you don't really want to be with. **We make ourselves believe that it's so hard to follow our truth, but it is much harder living a lie.**

Continually remind yourself of the greater plan and why you have actually decided to leave. Your mind will play tricks on you, but essentially that deep voice inside will not hesitate to be brutally honest. I personally directed my thoughts and feelings to the notion of being free from the emotional chains that were holding me back, and I would visualize living my own life. The hard reality is that one person usually gets hurt a bit more than the other, but you are not really hurting them in the long run. In time they will know that, because it's far more selfish being with someone that you don't really want anymore. You will be doing both of you a massive favor, and it's okay if they don't see it right away.

If you have been on the receiving end of a breakup and have a broken heart, I have a message for you from my own experience: You are only really in a battle with yourself. You are more frustrated with the fact that you allowed yourself to be treated that way: upset with letting yourself go, losing who you are, and sacrificing so much. But I applaud you for your courage to wear your heart on your sleeve; it's the only way to truly experience love. The challenge is within you, not against the other. The mission is to regain your own trust, get yourself back, and rebuild the beautiful relationship you once had with yourself. And it will happen! All the best on your journey to find an even higher plane of being, a deeper fulfillment, and a better understanding of yourself.

> *We shouldn't have a partner to fill our emotional gaps with their presence. They should be there to complement the gaps we have already filled, and help us find a way to fill the ones we haven't.*

DOCKED

"You want to come into my life, the door is open.

You want to get out of my life, the door is open.

Just one request . . . don't stand at the door,

you're blocking the traffic."

—UNKNOWN

If you're just waiting to set sail, then you are at an absolutely great point. By making the right decisions and taking appropriate action you will attract someone like never before. That dream person won't be a fairy tale so much as a reality waiting to happen. As I mentioned earlier, what you focus on you will be sure to find. If we say, for example, "I don't want someone who is disrespectful," or "I don't want someone who is selfish," then you can bet you are going to notice it everywhere. Remember back in the "Focus and Find" section when we discussed the reticular activating system in your brain? The RAS is always working, but in order to make it work in your favor you have to direct your focus intelligently. We usually carry luggage from previous experiences that tarnishes any new ones. We will continue to focus all our energy on the particular traits that we now know we definitely don't want, but it still creates a block in front of us. How can we really be hugged if we have our guard up?

Let's give an example . . . You once had a partner with whom you didn't match too well, hence they're now an ex. Now you are thinking back and believing that all guys/girls are the same and you hold on to that belief. You think about it, dwell on it, and, more important, you reinforce it. You have an unconscious notion always ready to display itself with every person you meet. In truth, what hope do you really give someone new with that mind-set? Regardless of how they might act, it will totally change the way you approach the situation, so the situation will change. Your tone of voice, the types of people you are attracting, your body language, and your snap judgment all play a vital role. It's as if you wait in anticipation for someone to mess up so you can prove yourself right. They could say or do something very innocent, but to you it's catastrophic, because you will relate anything back to your belief. Then you wonder why the same challenges seem to arise and every person you meet has the same faults.

I don't believe in coincidence—we attract things. However, even if you believe in it, don't you think it's gone past the point of coincidence? If there is a constant pattern, are you the one who needs to start making changes? On the flip side, you could shift your mind-set. You could acknowledge that your ex wasn't what you wanted, so you now know what you don't want in a person, and more important, you now have clarity about what you do want. If you keep dwelling on what you don't want, all you do is replay your old relationship over and over again with everyone you meet. You might even turn bitter and cringe at the sight of a loving couple. With that attitude, who would want to be with you? You need to focus on the things you want in order to make the changes that will align with your dream partner. When you make change, the vibe you give off will scream, "I'm ready to embrace someone new." In saying that, sometimes we focus on what we want so hard it shows itself, and then we think it's too good to be true. Opportunities to grasp what you really want display themselves many times in your life; but it is up to you to grasp them. All change starts with you.

ATTRACTING A DREAM PARTNER

To create something different, you must do something different!

Before we go to the grocery store, we should write down a list of what we want. If we don't, then it seems we just walk around and settle for things that we never wanted in the first place. We will buy some chocolate, even though we went there to buy broccoli. We will get home, eat it, and then kick ourselves for buying it in the first place. Most important, we forgot the broccoli! If you're getting my drift, in order to get what we really want out of a life partner, we must make it real. We must have a clear indication of what we actually want in life to get it. All things manifested begin as a creation in our mind, which we should then seal by writing it down. This will allow you to refer back to that sheet and remind yourself of what you really want. That will enhance the reality by providing more visibility. Just keep in mind that we don't always get what we want, but there are certain things we *must* have. Never settle for less than the musts, but be lenient with the wants. I wouldn't reject someone because they didn't have the size eight feet I envisioned. And I wouldn't be taking my sheet along to a date. Don't be like a strict schoolteacher marking the sheet with every word they say.

Things don't always turn out exactly the way you create them in your mind, but make sure the fundamentals are in place and you get the same feeling. The present doesn't always come wrapped with a ribbon, but that's your chance to go and put one on, because you're going to help that person grow as well. It shouldn't be so much about what you can take from this person, but what you can give. Don't be one of those "love hoppers"—that's what I call them, anyway. All they do is jump from one person to another, just hoping the right person will pop up one day. I'm sure we all know someone who has barely broken up with one partner and is already with another. But you hear the same story, which is "I just can't find the one." Instead, have faith initially and use your power to be as certain as possible.

TASK 1

Clarification of what you want: Write down what you want and must have in a life partner—spiritually, mentally, physically, emotionally, and financially. Write down everything. Remember, an example would be "I want someone who is respectful," **not** "I don't want someone who is disrespectful." People always seem to write down what they don't want. Make sure you write down what you want.

Now that you have written down your perfect match, ask yourself these questions:

> Why would they want to be with me?
>
> What would I have to do in order to attract someone like that?
>
> If I was that exact person on my list and went on a date with me, would I want to go out with myself?

These questions demand that you are completely honest with yourself to get great answers and find areas for growth. If you have written down that you want someone who is fit and healthy, you can bet they are not going to want to be with someone who doesn't look after their body or who eats McDonald's every day. If you are out getting drunk all the time but you have written down that you want someone who is in touch with their spiritual side, that's a conflicting belief. If you must have someone who is happy, would they want to be with someone who has a permanent frown and doesn't enjoy life? These are just a few examples, but I'm sure you get the drift. We try to make ourselves believe that we can get things we want without making changes first. We must gain the balance of what we want and what we are going to do to get it, because that will ensure our confidence as well.

TASK 2

Making change: Go back to your list and note what you can do in order to attract someone like that. Find what you need to change to align yourself with those attributes on the list. For example, if you want someone who has a cheerful demeanor, but you're in a permanently sour mood, then you may have a conflict. Work on your attitude!

TASK 3

Pick your environment intelligently: I would also take note of the environment in which you wish to meet someone. We must pick our environment intelligently so we can increase the chances of meeting that person on our list. If you want someone who has a lot of mental strength and is family oriented, I don't think you are going to find them at the local sports bar on a Tuesday night. If you want someone who is healthy, your chances are slim of finding them dining at KFC. You would have a much greater chance at the salad bar down the road, but I wouldn't be taking the KFC bag along with you—just a tip. My friend always wanted someone who was spiritual while being very social. He was going to nightclubs and getting drunk beyond repair every week. He would then ask me why he couldn't find anyone that matched what he wanted. Simple: I told him that if he goes to a nightclub, maybe he shouldn't get drunk before looking for a girl who is sober. He should stay sober—that way he won't be attracting the opposite of what he is looking for, and he will be a lot more appealing to the girl who is sober. It's quite simple when you think about it, but that's exactly what you have to do: Think about it. If you want to find that person, make sure you're looking in the right spots.

The last and most important aspect is to be patient. Never settle because of impatience. That will surely bring unhappiness and isn't fair to the other person. Great things come to those who are great. In order to see something as great, you must understand greatness. Invest in your own growth first and make changes to become great within, and you will attract others accordingly.

FEAR OF GETTING SEASICK

Some people fear getting into a relationship because they believe they will be giving up their independence. We like to think we are independent, which means we don't depend on anyone or anything. Realistically, we are always depending on ourselves, so it means we are dependent creatures. We depend on the grocery store to have our fruits and vegetables, we depend on people to buy our products, we depend on family and friends when we want comfort, we depend on the rain so we can drink water—so we are always dependent throughout our life. It is okay to depend on others, because we are all in this together. The challenge is finding the balance between your independence and what role it has, and the role of your dependence. This is a common social challenge, as many people have the idea that a relationship is restrictive. Again, if you attract what you must have in a person, then you will truly complement each other. **Don't be scared to be dependent, but never base your complete happiness on another individual. You are the only one who can truly fulfill yourself.**

SAILING SMOOTH

If you are already steady on the ship and have been for quite some time, keep doing what you're doing. You can email me and give me some pointers; I'm always up for learning. There is always room for growth, though, so you can still use these tips and strategies from vibrant couples I spoke with. If you want your relationship to enter that calm sea, this next part is also for you.

YOUR AVERAGE PEOPLE

COUPLE 1

I asked this vibrant couple that attended the gym I used to work at if I could sit down and speak to them. They had recently gotten engaged and agreed to take part. I found out that their relationship had been on the rocks, but they were able to save it, and they said it was actually stronger now than ever. About one year before we spoke, they were about to separate over a miscommunication. I was surprised to hear that their relationship had nearly come to an end. The guy had put on over forty pounds in a matter of months and she felt as if she was caught in a dilemma. In a way she was, because her physical attraction to him had started to decline and she was concerned about his health. That might seem harsh, but being healthy and fit was something she wanted in her partner, so it's not wrong at all. The difference between a friendship and an intimate relationship is **attraction,** so it plays a major role. Looks might not always be the reason someone loses their attraction. It could be a shift in attitude, mood swings, inconsistency, or irrational behavior. She was also attracted to how in control and strong he was in his life, but that had diminished as well.

> "Anger repressed can poison a relationship as surely as the cruelest words."
>
> —DR. JOYCE BROTHERS

One day she decided to tell him that he should start getting healthy and fit again. Taking the advice the wrong way, he began to feel insecure and thought she might cheat on him. He became paranoid and stopped trusting her even to go to the supermarket. She said it was killing her because she loved him to death and never wanted to hurt him, but she told him that she couldn't handle the lack of trust anymore and was close to leaving. This caused his pain threshold to hit the maximum, so he decided to finally sit down and face what she had to say. After communicating properly, he said in a sarcastic voice, "I don't believe you are going to do anything differently." The next day she went and bought them both a gym membership. That's what I call enormous initiative. They began going to the gym twice a week, and now they are doing five sessions a week. It's a part of their life, and he assured me that he drags her out of bed most times now. They both look great but, most important, they feel great. He is soaring with confidence, their business profits have increased, and he told me that looking the way he had, he would have left him, too!

What a great way to share time together while also looking after their health. They motivate each other and have fun. They help each other grow and always try to find a way to push past their limits.

EMPOWERING TIP: Always communicate how you feel and exercise together.

COUPLE 2

This couple was about to get engaged, but they had hit a rough patch. Their relationship was built on trust, so they would spend a lot of time apart and with their friends. They noticed that their *engagement* with each other had declined, so they decided to sit down and communicate properly. They discovered that they had been seeing each other far less than they used to, and that their formerly frequent trips away together had been put on hold for quite some time. Both of them decided to get into action. They agreed to cut down on their separate social lives and save money for at least one weekend away every two months. They didn't say, "We don't have the money," but instead took appropriate action to get the money.

Going on trips with people has been proved to enhance many relationships and friendships alike. If you have ever been away with close friends, I'm sure you have experienced the bond that can form. Yes, some people do clash on trips—we are human, not perfect—but overall it does work.

This couple assured me that they would never take each other's presence for granted again and recognized that their effort really did get the right results. The tip here is to engage more with each other. Don't take the things for granted that once built your bond. Take action and do fun activities together.

One guy I was coaching in a similar situation with his partner told me that he didn't have the money for trips away, and then I found out that he was spending a minimum of $250 on alcohol every week. This is just an example, but seriously, how important is your relationship? If it's not more important than the beer you buy each week, then it's not that important. If you are committed, you will make the money and find the time. **There is always a way.**

EMPOWERING TIP: Go away with your partner or take up activities that are new to both of you. Do stuff that is fun and makes you feel great.

COUPLE 3

We all know that when a woman asks for your opinion on clothing, she is most likely going to do it her way anyway, but it's one of the great things we have to appreciate. When a woman tries on a new outfit that she just bought and asks her partner what he thinks, he'd better say it looks good, because he probably won't know the difference anyway. She will then ask again, causing her partner to rethink and say, "Yeah, but I like the other one, too."

Then she will say, "Why, what's wrong with this one?" and her partner might reply, "Nothing, it's nice, I thought you just wanted my opinion." Then the final say is, "Well, I like this one, so I'm going to wear it." The partner is left bewildered, and just as they are walking out the door, the question comes, "Are you sure about this one?"

I personally love this, because if women weren't like that, guys would probably be walking around the streets naked. Women will willingly go shopping alone, but men don't stand a chance. We are too scared to bring something home that our partner doesn't like, because we know we will be going straight back for a refund. Not by force, but because we accept their expertise in the matter, and if they don't like it, then neither do we anymore. All men know they need a great woman, and the saying "We can't live without them" is definitely a true one.

The last couple I spoke with have been married for eighteen years and are still going strong. They have three kids, and it's hard to see them without a smile. I desperately wanted to know what their secret was, and they willingly agreed to give me some of their time. The first quality that this couple has always been adamant about is honesty.

They assured me that they try their hardest not to tread on each other's toes, but will always be there to help the other grow. The husband totally respects his wife's role, and the wife respects his expertise in certain areas. Always willing to listen to each other due to their mutual respect, they are helping each other fulfill their dreams. They also let me know that both being highly involved in their children's lives has had a great impact on their marriage. They have never taken each other for granted, and said it was their honest communication, no matter how much it could hurt at times, that has given them a long, strong relationship. In order to have a great relationship, it's imperative that we openly communicate how we are feeling on a constant basis. Keeping issues to ourselves could cause us to act selfishly and irrationally, and that's usually how the battle continues.

EMPOWERING TIP: Be honest, communicate properly on a daily basis, appreciate even the smallest things, respect each other's dreams, and always be willing to lend a helping hand. Now that's what I call success.

SUMMING IT UP

These are just a few of many couples that all say the same things. So many people attempt to save a relationship by giving material gifts. Your partner might not want a Gucci bag or a new watch, but instead might want just a hug. They may not want a vacation, or to be taken out for dinner or bought roses. They might want you to actually listen to what they have to say and be present.

I wouldn't go into business with someone who lacks communication skills, I wouldn't build a friendship with someone who lacks them, and I definitely wouldn't get into a relationship with someone who doesn't make the effort to communicate. Why would I? It reflects the lack of respect and structure they have in their own life. To engage with your partner is absolutely crucial if you want a fulfilling relationship. If only more people were actually "engaged" in their relationship before someone got down on one knee to propose, there might be fewer breakups.

It's usually the things most people take for granted that build a strong relationship. **There is no greater relationship than the one between those who are self-aware.**

> *Friendships are such a beautiful thing. It is where one soul trusts another to find comfort and liberation on this journey.*

18

The Importance of Peers

"Keep away from those who try to belittle
your ambitions. Small people always do that,
but the really great make you believe that you, too,
can become great."

—MARK TWAIN

I was in a pet store to buy my nephew a fish, and I explained to the worker that I couldn't have one that would grow too large because it was only going in a bowl. He assured me that I had nothing to worry about, because most fish will **only grow in proportion to the size of their environment, and then stop.** What a great analogy for the way humans seem to adapt to the people they associate with and the environment they surround themselves with on a daily basis. Everything in the world survives by adapting to its environment. The horny lizard in North America is one of many animals that have proved this. It mainly eats ants, and has formed thick scales to prevent being bitten while having its platter of bugs. But the hunter can always be hunted, so when its worst enemy, a coyote, shows up, it needs to protect itself. Through evolution this lizard has developed the ability to shoot blood out of its eye at its attacker. The blood amazingly has canine repellent chemicals in it to irritate coyotes in particular. Humans are no exception in being able to adapt to their environment.

You don't have to be a genius to figure out that you will become like those you associate with, so it means you must choose whom you spend most of your time with intelligently. The reason is that the wrong choice of associates could prevent you from growing. What you feed your mind is what's going to come out of your life. If you feed it garbage all day, what results are you going to get? How are you going to feel? When I was thirteen and getting myself into trouble with some other teens, my grandfather told me, "When you hang around garbage, you start to smell." And I'm sure we are all quite aware that some of the actions of man are nothing short of that: garbage! It's one of the boldest but truest statements I have ever heard.

I'm not telling you to go and dump your buddies, but I would be seeing them in small doses if they contradict what you want to achieve. Some might need to be shown the door if your truth is telling you it's the best option. **If you really want to learn Chinese, but you hang around people who speak Spanish all day, which language are you more likely to pick up?**

"There are moments in your life
when you must act, even though you cannot carry
your best friends with you."
—MAHATMA GANDHI

Most times we condition ourselves unconsciously with mental, verbal, and physical actions similar to those of our peers. We also do this to satisfy our urge for social significance and acceptance. Sometimes we feel that if we make significant changes, our friends will think we are stupid or crazy. Guess what? Sometimes they do! We then have to ask ourselves: If they are seeing our positive changes that way, are they really reliable friends? Your dearest friends might also ridicule you, but they usually do it out of love. They feel as if they are losing you, or your positive change might make them feel insignificant. By beginning to excel in your life, it may finally show them how unproductive they are being in their own life. I understand that no one wants to do that to their friends, but you must acknowledge that it is no reason to stop living the best life you possibly can. At the end of the day, it's their personal issue, and all you can do is communicate properly. Some people find it most difficult to understand in the beginning, but they will eventually, if they are real friends.

I also love when so-called friends throw out the comment, "You only live once!" People say it in the face of smoking, drugs, or even criminal activity. Really what they should be saying is, "You only live once, so here, go and kill yourself, start a habit, or do something that could mean spending the next ten years in jail." I think nearly every time I have given in to that line I have known that it was a mistake, and I definitely paid the price.

Stop expecting a closed-minded person to have an open-minded conversation.

Do you ever wonder whether people are using that line for your benefit or for theirs? Something to think about, isn't it? An intelligent response would be, "Yes, I only live once, so why wouldn't I live the best way I know how?" Doesn't that just make a bit more sense? You might think that the options are fun in the face of that comment, but I ask you to have a deeper look and you will realize that what you might think is fun could actually be causing your emotional and mental torment.

I often hear people complaining about being pressured into doing something they didn't want to do. It's a pretty pathetic excuse, because they are only attempting to avoid their own accountability. They should be taking responsibility and finding out how to strengthen their mind. You are the one who has to answer to yourself when you lay your head on the pillow. Why haven't I achieved? Why did I do what I did? Why am I in a distressed state right now? No one but you can find answers that will satisfy you, so learn to take charge of your life and ignore outside influences that you know will make you doubt yourself.

> "A real friend is one who walks in
> when everyone else walks out."
> —WALTER WINCHELL

Who really cares what the people who judge the great changes you are making think? I'm sure they are not quick to lend you a helping hand on your journey. The people who ridicule your productivity the most are the ones who are jealous, have no clue about life, and, if you look carefully, are the ones living miserably with no sense of direction. Have you ever noticed how negative people spend most of their time with other negative people? Do you want to stop following your dreams and end up like them? I don't think so. Those who don't believe in you don't believe in themselves. As I mentioned earlier, I was teased, ridiculed, and told I was crazy on a daily basis just for loving life more than I used to. They said my ideas would never work, but they were soon very surprised. My vision and passion were far too strong to let anyone stand in my way. Yes, it crossed my mind to stop many times, but that's when you must be at your strongest, and when you get past one hurdle, the next one seems that little bit easier. Instead of curling up in a ball and giving up, I used it as fuel to drive me even further and create an even deeper hunger. **Sometimes people take the great things you are doing as a personal attack on their own life. Do not let their insecurities dishearten you.**

"Great people construct monuments
with the stones critics throw at them."
—ROBIN SHARMA

I discussed my change with a close friend one day, and this was his reply: "I know you are making changes, and I'm happy for you, but I'd prefer if you didn't discuss all this stuff with me. I'm always here for you, though." I respected that so much, and he is still a friend, because it was his choice not to hear about the lessons I was discovering with myself. I didn't storm off and get angry, but really appreciated that he was honest, and eventually he did come and ask for advice and I was more than happy to help. Tell your friends about your change, but don't try to force your beliefs onto others, because that will most likely send them the other way. If you are making great changes in your life, it will be evident to those around you, and they will come and ask you how you did it.

If you have modeled any successful person, you would see that they were always willing to pick their peers carefully. If you wanted to become a great painter, then you wouldn't hang around someone who is good at the drums and try to speak to them about how to paint. Hang around and get advice from those in the same industry. Don't be shy about going straight to the top or to the best person you know in the field.

A true friend is someone whom you can act like a complete idiot in front of and not be the slightest bit embarrassed. Try your hardest to keep this friendship. It is the closest we get to being a child again!

When I was doing personal training, I would notice that most times when two overweight people would sign up together, they wouldn't last very long. On the other hand, when I saw someone who was overweight train with someone who was fit, they would soon be looking quite fit. That's not being harsh at all; I am just stating what I saw. I got into that industry because I care about people's well-being, so the last thing I would do is ridicule someone. It's just the way it is, and if you want to be a certain way, then you must start associating with it.

If you want to achieve something great, pick the brains of those who you know have a clear history of achieving. Ask them what their secrets are. When asking, be humble, enthusiastic, and keen to learn. If you go up to those people with a big ego, you can bet they will probably show you the door. Let them know that you are driven and will do anything to learn the traits. Even if you are a millionaire, but having trouble breaking the barrier of hitting your next ten, ask someone who has. Read up on other success stories. They were probably in the same predicament at your stage but found a breakthrough. It doesn't matter how advanced we think we are, there is always someone out there we can learn from. When you associate with people who are great at what they do, you are forced to step up to the greatness. It's the same as adapting to our environment; we eventually learn to live that particular way to keep up. In business and networking, **be humble but never gullible!**

"Associate yourself with people of good quality,
for it is better to be alone than in bad company."

—BOOKER T. WASHINGTON

5TH STEP
Create a Healthy Physical Existence

19

Start That Engine

In order to see how the best of the best perform physically, you have to look at the best. Most top professional athletes have a personal athletic coach as well as a personal mind coach. The ones who don't have a mind coach do it themselves. But there is one thing for certain: Strengthening the mind is critical to their success. If these top athletes understand the importance of both mind and body, why don't we implement this in our physical training every day? The lack of this is the reason some stop exercising and others never begin. People train their body, but they forget to train the powerful force that is driving it. Most people I have trained make one crucial mistake: When they think about the body they want, or their desired level of fitness, they feel depressed because they don't have it now. As for the people who actually achieve it, they use the same visions as an empowering motive to get going. Don't be upset when visualizing your dream body, embrace it and feel good because you know you are going to get there.

If you don't respect your body, it will not respect you on your journey through life. Our body is the ship that carries us through this journey, and it must be held in regard. Would you put a hole in the hull of a boat you are traveling on? Of course not, because you would drown. Would you destroy a beautifully crafted piece by Leonardo da Vinci? How shocked would you be if you watched on the news that someone had deliberately done this? We may be very moved, yet we continue to wreck this beautiful piece of artwork called the human body. Our body is us, it is not separate. Our soul is one with our body and mind, so when one is out of balance, the other two are sabotaged and something is destined to break down.

WAKE UP AND LIVE

> *Motivation is what gets you started, ritual is what makes it habit.*

Our body cries out to us in a number of ways owing to lack of exercise or an unhealthy diet. We have aches and pains, feel drained, and get sick on a regular basis. To live a balanced life, our body demands that we respect it. I'm well aware that people have different lifestyles and wake up at different times. Being an author, I'm not always up early. At times I get inspiration at 2:00 a.m. and have to write it down. But when I do wake up, I don't drag myself through my day. Once I'm up, I'm up! Do you think highly successful people drag their way out of bed, hauling that uninspired mood throughout the whole day? No way. They begin their day without too much deliberation and switch on instantly. Have you ever noticed that when you are tired, you stretch and yawn in slow motion? This is our body temperature being cooled down. And when our body temperature regulates, our muscles receive messages that tell them, "It's now time to relax and to go to sleep." When we finish exercising, we should do static stretches (slow and relaxed) to rest our muscles—for example, sitting down and doing a hamstring stretch for fifteen seconds. These stretches are done in slow motion. Our muscles need to recover, so static stretches are ideal for this type of rest. Here is the big question: Why on earth are we moving in the same slow motion in the morning as we would before we go to bed or after we train?

Waking up isn't a time to let your body rest, it's the time for it to be active! If you watch any professional sports team nowadays, you will notice that they do very quick movements and fast breathing to warm up their body. This practice is called dynamic stretching and it has now fully replaced static stretching before games. The last thing athletes want is for their muscles to rest. If they do, they are more prone to injury and their performance suffers. Only after games do they perform static stretches to rest their muscles.

If you think about it, it makes far more sense to trigger the muscles you want to use rather than to put them to sleep beforehand. If you want to use your body like the best, then you must model the best. This is what top trainers teach and professionals do all around the world. If you want to be wide awake within thirty seconds, this is the key. This task has never failed me ...

WIDE AWAKE

As soon as you hear the alarm clock go off, jump straight out of bed. Open your eyes as wide as you can and begin taking deep breaths in a quick motion. While breathing, do dynamic stretches—move your body in any way, just make sure you do it fast. An example would be windmills with your arms, star jumps, or touching your toes. If you want, you can also take one deep breath in through your nose and exhale three short breaths out through your mouth while doing sharp movements with your body. You can add noise for optimal performance. If you're not going to wake anyone up in the process, I recommend doing that as well. If you think this doesn't work, prove it yourself by trying it the next time you wake up.

Deep quick breaths combined with doing fast bodily movements has been scientifically proved to start your engine. It gets your metabolism in gear, triggers your muscles, and ignites the cycle of energy creating energy. The only way to actually produce more energy in your system is to kick-start it with energy. If you're being slack, you will feel the lack of energy. This takes no more than thirty seconds to wake up, but three to five minutes for max performance. Go have two glasses of water and read your appreciation list, which takes five minutes. This morning ritual—which takes about as long as a snooze cycle—will shift your energy for the whole day. This should be done before you train, especially if you feel like you want to skip it for the day. Like the old way of turning on a light bulb, it requires kinetic energy. You must turn that wheel and set it into motion first.

TEN TIPS TO A SUCCESSFUL FITNESS REGIMEN

There are some broad steps for success in getting the most out of physical training. Everyone enjoys different things, and you should really mix it up every six to eight weeks to shock your body, but here are things that should be a **must** for every person.

TIP 1: GET STARTED

Get yourself a personal trainer if you can afford one, even for half an hour a week, so you can get some idea of how to train properly. Make sure they are good—references are usually the best way to find them. It's a pretty good indication when your friend calls you up puffing and says, "Phew, they're really good."

For now, just start being active and take immediate action. Walk, skip, run, or hop, I don't care, just do something. Regardless of what you may be thinking, there are no excuses! **Most aches and pains are caused by people's lack of action, not because of their action.**

TIP 2: MAKE SURE YOU HAVE FUN

Tell your trainer not to get overexcited and kill you in the first session. You will get scared off and probably find the energy to run home as fast as you can and never return. Push your body past the comfort zone, but remember that everything in life is progression.

TIP 3: MUSIC

Music is great when training. If classical music usually puts you to sleep, then I would advise not listening to it when training. Listen to something upbeat or that pumps you up.

TIP 4: HIIT

This stands for High Intensity Interval Training. Without getting too technical, HIIT has proved to be the best form of fat burning. An example is running for one minute, then power walking for five minutes, and repeating those for thirty to sixty minutes depending on your fitness level.

TIP 5: TABATA TRAINING

This form of HIIT is quick, constantly increases in duration and intensity, and produces absolutely amazing results. Most Tabata exercises can even be done at home, so there is no excuse for not doing them. The basis of Tabata training is four minutes of intense interval training/circuit training.

Here is an example:

1. Get two fairly heavy dumbbells and something to step
    up on.

2. Step up while lifting the dumbbells above your head in one motion. Step down while lowering the dumbbells to your side.

3. Repeat for twenty seconds, then rest for ten seconds. Repeat seven more times for a total of eight sets.

What you have is a total of four minutes of workout time.

Tabata training can be done with a number of different exercises, and the idea is to use an exercise that gets the whole body involved, or at least the major muscle groups. Tabata training can be done with barbells, dumbbells, kettlebells, or just bodyweight exercises. It would be a little difficult for me to try to explain all the different types of Tabata workouts, so I advise going on YouTube or browsing the internet to find plenty of visual examples.

Tabata training was developed by Izumi Tabata at the National Institute of Fitness and Sports in Kanoya, Japan. The institute did a study over a six-week period comparing the effects of moderate intensity endurance training (aerobics) and high endurance intermittent training (Tabata training intervals) on VO_2 max (the maximum rate of oxygen consumption during training) and anaerobic capacity.

To cut to the results of the study: The moderate intensity group training program produced a significant increase in VO_2 max of about 10 percent, but had no effect on anaerobic capacity. The high intensity group improved their VO_2 max by about 14 percent while anaerobic capacity improved by 28 percent.

TIP 6: MIND ON YOUR MUSCLE

If you focus your mind on the particular muscle you are training during the exercise, it is triggered far more effectively, and hence enhances strength. Example: Focus on your chest muscles when doing bench presses.

TIP 7: THINK BIG

Training time is a great time to think over your success. In your mind, reinforce empowering statements. During my jog or power walk, I would repeat the words *I am strong* in my mind the whole way through. When my mind would wander, I would redirect and focus back on that statement.

TIP 8: STRAIGHT BACK

Don't ever sacrifice great posture for heavier weights when lifting of any sort. As soon as you lose your good posture, you lose technique. This means you are not doing the exercise correctly and it increases the chance of injury. This also stands for walking and running. Shoulders should be retracted and chin should be parallel with the ground.

TIP 9: VISION

Set up a compelling vision and don't lose sight of it. See the body you want, feel being healthy and fit, and consume yourself with its presence right now. Visualize every day and experience the emotions of success, and it will motivate you like mad. Embrace it as a reality, get excited, and go and get it. Nothing is stopping you but you!

TIP 10: STEP IT UP

When you start feeling too comfortable with the exercises you are doing, push yourself once again. A term that is widely used in the fitness industry for this point is "plateau stage." It is said that this is a time when people feel as if they are standing still and not reaching new levels. In my experience with clients, this usually happens after eight weeks of repeating the same program. It's essential that we keep the same program for at least six weeks, and then mix it up. This keeps it fun and makes us hit new peaks. When you feel that your program is starting to get a little easy, step up the intensity.

Always combine weight training and cardio exercises in your program, and exercise at least three days a week to start off. Drink plenty of water and less caffeine (none is ideal). You need to stay hydrated during the day.

Something that is also very beneficial for the functioning of our body is an alkaline enhancer, which you can purchase from a health shop. I recommend a product that contains spirulina, chlorella, and barley grass, which should also be 100 percent vegetarian. It usually comes in a powder that you mix with water. Himalayan salt mixed with water works the same way. If you own an aquarium, you know that if you do not get the pH level correct in the water, your fish will die. Your body is also made up of water, which requires you to gain a balanced pH level. This is a process where the acidity and alkalinity in your body reaches 7.35. You can tell what you are currently at by getting a simple mouth swipe from your local pharmacy. Too much acid in your body means your health will suffer, so start balancing.

TASK

What beliefs would you have to build about exercise and your diet to live a healthy life?

Why do you want to be healthy and fit?

What does your health mean to you? What is it worth?

Focus on how much you are benefiting from doing this. Never think of the sacrifices, because there are no sacrifices when it comes to getting your health in check, only benefits.

20

Losing Weight vs. Becoming Healthy and Fit

"An active mind cannot exist in an inactive body."

—GENERAL GEORGE S. PATTON JR.

If your mind is set on the idea of losing weight, you are focused on a negative notion and that builds a constant fear. As long as you think of wanting to lose weight, that's all you will ever want to keep doing. We are inundated with marketing campaigns that shove such an ideal right in our face. We all know that fear is the number one seller, and what better way to instill it than based on appearance?

In the instance of having a weight-loss mind-set, we surround ourselves with the words *lose, lose,* and *lose.* We get into the belief of losing and never seem to be winning, which is why most are never satisfied. The obsession with losing weight becomes a never-ending story.

The majority of desirable people shown in magazines are malnourished, airbrushed, or take extreme health risks in the hope of getting work. Having been in the fashion industry, personal training, and now coaching has given me a fair amount of insight into models and other media-related personnel. I have met extraordinarily good-looking people and high-profile models throughout my life, and some of them have the biggest insecurities with the way they look. Believe it or not, some are also the unhappiest and most unfulfilled individuals I have ever met. Don't get me wrong, looking good is great; but **you will never think you look good unless you feel great about your choice of lifestyle.** You go from being happy one day to being upset because you want to lose a little more weight off your right butt cheek, or your right arm is smaller than your left, and this craziness continues on forever. In so many cases it consumes someone's whole life to the point that they forget how to live!

Full focus on feeling (FFF) is the key to success in any aspect. We have to shift our mind-set to focus on being healthy and fit. It's about the feeling, not the visual appearance to others. Everyone has different opinions, so you are going to be pretty unsatisfied if you are just doing it for that reason. When you start getting a little wrinkly or your body doesn't seem to keep in shape as well as when you were younger, are you going to hate yourself? That's why this world is filled with appearance challenges, because we believe that feeling great starts with outward appearance. Your body should be loved for the highly technical machine it is. It deserves respect for housing the only thing that is ever permanent: your soul. When we exercise, we **must** amplify the importance of how it's making us feel, because that's what keeps us motivated. Reverse "looking good, then feeling good" to "feeling good, then looking good," because that's the key to remaining happy.

Bathroom scales are something that I believe should be smashed with a baseball bat, as they should not be the measure of your success. First of all, if you are training, you will be building muscle, which weighs more than fat. Scales can definitely screw with your mind, so I suggest you get rid of them. You are not going to see results overnight if you go for looks, but you will immediately notice results when going for feeling.

A bodybuilder I knew had an amazing physique, but all I would hear him do was complain about his body. To him, there was always something wrong with it, and his appearance soon became an obsession. It took control over every area of his life. He saw his relationship diminish, his finances go down, and his emotional state hit its lowest point ever.

We are all imperfect if you wish to look at it that way, but I like to see it as we are all perfect. Our imperfections make us perfect, because if we were all the same this world would be pretty boring. We all have different perceptions of what we find appealing, but the point of feeling great makes you appealing to everyone. Your glow is contagious, and you will notice that when you go for the feeling, the physical shape comes rapidly along with it. I have personally trained hundreds of clients, and the ones who go for the looks to make them happy never last or are unfulfilled. Those who go for the feeling acknowledge that being healthy and fit is a lifestyle to drive them to their peak and help them attain that balance for a great life. **Losing weight is an activity that drives us crazy; striving to be healthy and fit is a lifestyle that lasts forever.**

6TH STEP
Awaken Your Mind,
Unchain Your Heart

21

The Infinite Human Spirit

There's more to you than meets the eye;
it's your soul. I can't see it, and neither can you,
but we can feel it.

Your greatness lies in the spirit that waits patiently within your being. If you have yet to tap into it or listen carefully to what it tells you in the face of decisions, that's the reason your dreams seem so far from ever coming into existence.

I've had many people tell me they don't know if they have a soul, and others who think they might but have no real grounds for their belief. I would just like to sum it up the best way I can. We see our human body like a machine. The brain thinks and visualizes through chemical responses, the heart pumps blood, and our lungs help us breathe. From the outside it appears very technical, scientific, and easy to explain our physical existence. But have you ever wondered who is observing the surroundings you see with your eyes? **Who is controlling your machine (body)?** Who's aware that you're thinking? Look around the room, and think about who is actually directing that focus. We cannot just get up off the chair and walk automatically; we are obviously being commanded by something. Who calculates what you are going to say before you say it? Most would answer these questions with "I am" with a bit of confusion, and that's exactly right. Me is only your physical existence; I is your spirit that is in control. We can't see it, but we can feel it every day, and it's the voice we are in constant conversation with. I guess that's why when our soul passes on from this earth we are no longer able to control our body.

> "Man struggles to find life outside himself,
> unaware that the life he is seeking is within him."
>
> —KAHLIL GIBRAN

Once you let that conscious voice take over your life, that deep wisdom that is quite aware and knows what's right for you, then you will discover your greatness. It's an invisible force that lies deep within you, the person you know you really are. It is the person that most of us never let other people see. We become too caught up with reacting to our environment or fulfilling what we believe other people expect. A great spirit lies within all of us and that's why many men and women have defied the odds throughout history. Every single person has a great calling and purpose in life that no one else is called to do. We are all designed to fill a spot that no one else can fill. When every person realizes that, they live the life of their dreams, but more important, the world will truly be united. As long as those spots continue to be ignored, it leaves big holes, which I guess is the reason so many fall through the cracks.

The human spirit is so fascinating and infinite that it overcomes what many in society would regard as impossible. We have seen it throughout history. One man can change the course of the whole world and implement a revolution; we can survive under the most horrific situations, or create what would have once been perceived as unbelievable.

I find inspiration in men who have the courage to walk the path of truth. One man in particular is Nelson Mandela—a perfect example that man's will is far greater than all the odds put against him.

He created a passion so strong that he was able to successfully rally for peace and equal rights, which was a major part of the fall of apartheid in South Africa. Mandela grew up in a small village with hardly any of the resources we have today, and he was repressed by white supremacists. Because of his vision to help his people, he was jailed for twenty-seven years in total. How many of us would have given up on our dream after six months or one year, without half the challenges such a man had? His greatest pleasure and most private moment was watching the sun set with the music of Handel or Tchaikovsky playing. That was denied him in prison, and he noted that simple moment in life was the thing he missed most.

Three years after being released from jail, Mandela was elected president of South Africa. This is one story of many about how the human spirit is used to utmost glory. We seem to forget that we are human and have that same spirit within us. When one has a compelling vision, determination to overcome any obstacles, and, most important, a passion for life, the possibilities are endless.

"There is no passion to be found playing small—
in settling for a life that is less than
the one you are capable of living."

—NELSON MANDELA

22

A Spiritual Journey Through Thailand

"If we are facing in the right direction,
all we have to do is keep on walking."

—BUDDHIST PROVERB

As I began to write this book, I had been thinking about going to Asia to talk to a Buddhist monk. I knew I had found an inner peace here in the West, but I was always interested in how at peace monks were. I wanted to get away from the West to do it, because I wanted to see if someone from the East, with a completely different religious and cultural background, social status, and environment, could have similarities to what I had found within myself. I declared that before I finished my book I would go and feature that part in it. I remember discussing this topic with my mother. I had no money or job at the time, but I knew it was going to happen. I wasn't really concerned with how or when; I just knew I was going to make it happen before I finished the book.

About three weeks later, while writing by the beach, I received a text message from one of my friends. Katie, who works in the travel industry, and whom I hadn't known for very long, told me that work was sending her to Bangkok, Thailand. She was going to inspect hotels over there and asked if I would like to go. It was for one week and everything was paid for. I instantly got goose-bumps all over my body. I asked her why she offered to take me. Her explanation was that she felt a great energy, and even though she hadn't known me for long, she felt a very friendly connection and trusted me.

A question then dawned on me: Was it that mysterious what had happened, or was there more of an explanation? A light-bulb moment arose once again. I knew that the only reason this happened was because of my change. If I had met Katie through my previous thoughts and actions, this opportunity would have never come up. People told me that I was lucky, but I was quick to remind them that I created it far before it had happened. It had been there in my mind! Katie had no idea that It had the thought of going to Asia, so I decided to leave that detail out. It crossed my mind that she would think I was crazy and take back the offer.

When you act great, you get great experiences. Great experiences create extraordinary opportunities, while extraordinary opportunities create great experiences.

I thought it was now time to step it up, so off I went on the internet to track down a monk I could meet with. Not just any monk, mind you; I wanted a master, and I knew it was going to happen no matter what. That's why this opportunity arose, to fulfill what I already knew. I emailed many people but got no replies. I didn't let it faze me and persisted. I had seen online that people had had a quick chat with some monks while visiting the royal temples in Bangkok. It was now a week before the trip, and Katie had sent through the week's plan to see if I wanted to change anything. This is how it read:

DAY 1: Arrive in Bangkok, dinner at PP hotel

DAY 2: Shopping at MBK, lunch, etc.

DAY 3: Breakfast, Siam Paragon, etc.

DAY 4: Royal temple tour with English-speaking guide

Bingo! Again I was overwhelmed: It sealed it one more time. This was happening to fulfill my vision. I was a cocreator in all of this, and at that moment, I remember knowing I had found the key to life—**the ultimate power between mind and matter.** I got down on my knees in my bedroom and screamed out, "Thank you!" This all started with a strong vision, and it was beginning to play out around me.

After seeing the email, I decided to call Katie and let her know what was going on. She was pretty amazed and told me that she would contact her connection, Panja, in Thailand to see if he could arrange a monk to meet with me.

We met with Panja for dinner the night before the tour. I had told him about my situation, and we began to get into a pretty deep discussion. Panja opened up and told me about his life. We became friends instantly. He said he was shocked to see a young guy from the West think and talk so deeply to him. He also mentioned that I didn't look like the type to embrace life in such a manner. After having laughed it off, he told me he learned not to judge a book by its cover; how ironic.

After seeing my genuine feelings on the topic, Panja told me he would try his hardest to make the experience with the monk a great one. We also spoke about Panja's remarkable story, which he gave me permission to share. If you want to hear about persistence and someone who pursued his dream, then this story is it.

ONE OF MY FAVORITES

> "A man with many riches and no inner peace is like
> a man in a river, dying of thirst."
>
> —YOGANANDA

Panja grew up in a small village in the south of Thailand with twelve siblings and his parents. Living in an area where money didn't have a major role, they lived off the land. We in the West would classify this as poor, but to most of the people who live there, this is a rich lifestyle that they wouldn't give up for big-city life. As a child, Panja would catch fish with a bamboo stick so they were able to eat. They didn't have a clock to tell time, so every day Panja was sent outside to watch for the one airplane that used to fly over, because they knew it left around the same time each day.

He told me that through it all, he believed he wasn't meant to stay there. He wanted to go to Bangkok to study, but Panja's parents had a misconception of city life and didn't want him to leave. He would be the first family member to ever leave the village. With this playing on his mind, he decided to head for the city to pursue his dream. When he arrived he had no money, nowhere to live, and his village background had not equipped him to get a city job. So Panja became a temple boy for four years just so he could be fed and sheltered while he studied. His duties were to be of service to the monks, garden, clean, prepare food, and do anything else that needed to be done. He told me that people were compassionate toward him when he told them he was from the South, and he would quickly assure them that his people were happier than anyone he had met in the city. When he was unhappy about the smallest things, he would instantly remind himself that at least he had food to eat.

After finishing studying, he got a job in the travel industry. He later became the head of World Travel Service and lives what he considers a great lifestyle. When he visited his village years later, his father was worried and asked where he had been, as the last train arrived at 9:00 a.m. and Panja hadn't shown up until 12:00 p.m. He told his family that he had flown there, and they were overwhelmed that he had been in an airplane.

As a child looking up at a plane to tell the time, Panja would envision himself sitting in one. His job now sends him all over the world, and most of the year he is in a plane, traveling. To top it off, he is one of the most humble gentlemen I have met. A great man that contributes to the world, acknowledges he had success far before his achievements, and is grateful for his life when he was a temple boy struggling to get by.

How we take things for granted sometimes amazes me. I think of this story when I find myself complaining about the most insignificant things. So many of us let opportunities pass by or cease to create them because we waste our life whining. A story like this really makes you want to start living the best possible life you can, doesn't it?

ANOTHER STEP FORWARD

"To the mind that is still,
the whole universe surrenders."
—LAO-TZU

The day of the temple tour arrived and our guide, Sam, greeted us. The funny thing about this situation is that Sam had just found out he was taking us for the tour the day before. He has a "brother" in one of the temples we were set to visit. After speaking to Panja, he had tried to organize a meeting for me with one of the most respected monks in all of Thailand, who was stationed at that same temple. The monk had just returned from giving seminars overseas and had arrived only the day before. He was an extremely busy man and getting him to have a one-on-one wasn't going to be easy. Sam continued to remind me that he was waiting for a phone call to see if it was going to go ahead. I assured him that it would, I just knew it. I was creating this, and this was the reason I was there. Ten minutes before we were to visit the last temple for the day, he got the call, so off we went.

I knew that it would work out. I had declared that I would meet a monk that was a master, and he was: Dr. P. Boondham, a PhD in philosophy with multiple other master's degrees to his name. He is also the teacher to all other monks. He is on TV and radio, and travels the world, including to the United States, to give seminars about the power of the mind and inner peace. The doctor has his signature quotes printed on key rings. He represents Thailand at a number of world peace summits and is well known by national leaders. He told me he had met the prime minister of my birth country, Australia, only a few weeks earlier. Above all, I wanted the meeting to be in private, with no one else around.

After being told that he was a busy man and would only have about half an hour, I tried my hardest to think through what I was going to say to him, as I knew I needed longer. I decided to walk in with all restrictions aside. We ended up speaking for over two hours, and he invited me back two days later. We spoke for another few hours, exchanged gifts and contact details, and became "brothers." In my explanation of the meetings I have preserved exactly what was said. Dr. Boondham does not speak English fluently, but I am transposing straight from the text I wrote in the original exercise book so I don't mix up the genuine meaning of his message.

MASTER OF THE MIND—DAY 1

"Minds are like parachutes.
They only function when they are open."
—SIR JAMES DEWAR

When I walked into the temple, excited but a little nervous, I was greeted by a frail older man whose presence blew me away. I was told to sit down in front of him. Another humble monk came in to give us both some water, and we continued. Just being in his presence I could feel his calm nature and inner peace. I couldn't help but be rapt with every word he uttered, as his demeanor was like nothing I had ever come across in the West.

First we went through some basic ritual explanation of Buddhism, with the lighting of candles, incense, and so forth. At no time was he trying to convert me to his religion or sell it to me; he spoke from the heart about all mankind, which gained my full respect.

The words were subtle, yet every one was powerful and full of meaning. Here is some of my unedited transcript of his words, in his accent, exactly the way I experienced it:

> A person should not believe blindly. No superstition. You should be able to properly reason with your belief. True happiness only comes from within.

> If you do not train your mind, it becomes weak.

> The correct way is the way for everyone, peace and love. This is the only way you will find happiness.

Next was Eightfold Path:

Right understanding

Right thought

Right action

Right speech

Right effort

Right livelihood

Right mindfulness

Right concentration

RIGHT UNDERSTANDING

Understand the things happening correctly, not just how they appear in an instant.

Maintain right understanding at all times.

If you love yourself, you love others because you understand more.

We are human beings, we are feeling the same. Right understanding creates you to act correctly.

RIGHT THOUGHT

When you think, you have to think correctly. Not out of hate, but love, no matter which situation, to stay strong.

Purified mental state.

Mind is controlled by the anger, ill passion (greed, envy, resentment), and ill power. Must eliminate these.

Man becomes slave to materialism. The mind of man is not free this way.

Liberated by only controlling the mind, meditate, make strong.

RIGHT ACTION

Help only in truth, good intent, act correctly.

RIGHT SPEECH

Talk the truth, not lies and deceit. Talk properly, no cursing to others or yourself.

RIGHT EFFORT

Maintain legally, morally for money, the right way.

RIGHT LIVELIHOOD

When you maintain family life, you must do it correctly, rightly. Not against the law of rules and regulation of society. No breaking the law. Not breaking the law of that good society.

RIGHT MINDFULNESS

Must maintain and train the mind.

Control the mind with mindfulness, wisdom. When you're feeling trouble, you try to maintain mindfulness.

Focus the mind.

Concentration of the mind. Mind should always be strong, feeling normally.

Mindfulness and wisdom, strength should be maintained.

RIGHT CONCENTRATION

When your mind is not happy, your mind is in trouble. You should concentrate by maintaining meditation.

Follow anapanasati—breathing in and out through nose, sit to control the mind. Concentrate on breathing and thinking of only that.

I just want to highlight the final notes he told me for day one:

We are feeling only from the matter of the mind. Nothing externally.

Mind is the master of body, mind is the master of action, mind is the master of life.

Man gives in to lies–ill passion, greed, anger, hate, sadness. Try to destroy these things.

At the end of our talk we exchanged contact details, and I was glad to hear that Dr. Boondham was interested in having another chat a few days later.

MASTER OF THE MIND—DAY 2

Being self-aware is not the absence of mistakes, but the ability to learn and correct them.

When I arrived in the temple at about 1:30 p.m. I was nodded and smiled at by all the monks who had seen me there a few days before. I'm not sure what Dr. Boondham had told them, but they all seemed so friendly, and it was quite breathtaking. To have these humble men get me water and sit me down was totally different from anything I had experienced. I felt so much tranquility, peace, and love in the temple garden; the energy was quite astonishing. It was 40°C on the day so it was scorching hot, yet the humility I was surrounded with made me forget the temperature. A monk took me into the temple where the doctor was sitting in the same spot as a few days ago. He was underneath the shrine with his legs crossed, wearing an orange robe. As I sat down, he got off his thin cushion and came right up in front of me, sat on the hard surface as I was, and began speaking.

GIVING CORRECTLY

If a man comes up and asks you for fish to eat, do not just give the fish. If you do this, the man will continue to come back for more, again and again. When you give the fish, you must teach him how to catch the fish, so he can depend on himself, learn, catch many fish, and teach others.

LEAD BY EXAMPLE

A learned man may teach and write many books, but never put into action. Do not be this man who just lives a life of serving spoon. Spoon serves apple, spoon serves banana, spoon serves orange, but the spoon never tastes the fruits of life. The life of man should not be serving spoon.

We get the knowledge, a concept, then must bring it to action.

A man knows a lot of things but never put into positive action. Learning by doing.

Some things are not easy to understand, you have the right to criticize to get the truth. Believe the things which are wisdom.

Man's action by right or wrong depends on the action of man.

When a man acts wrongly they don't ever fully accept inwardly what they have done, unless spiritually liberated.

HAPPINESS

Momentary happiness—eating something nice, sit on a comfortable chair.

Access happiness—buy a new watch, nice clothes, good car, family member make you happy.

Attained happiness—from within, awakened, must be concentrated. This is true happiness.

- Material convenience is not real happiness

- We must get the mind right, clean, and purified. The less angry someone is, less greed and ill passion. We must always control our passion with thoughts and action, don't let passion control you.

- When you lose something, illusion starts to take over and you begin to worry.

- We never came with a watch, and we don't take it when we die. We do not need the watch, so it can never make us fully happy and should never make us sad.

Everyone needs peace, in and out. External peace is easy, new car can make you feel happy only temporarily. This is easy to duplicate. Inner peace is hard to attain. Only with mindfulness can you sustain happiness.

We must all get mindfulness first, which is training mental strength in all situations and use our wisdom as guide. Someone who gives in to anger has no mindfulness, no strength.

————

Dr. Boondham then went on to explain how youth in southern Thailand are taught a moral subject at school. After monitoring them, he said it has had a fundamental impact on their growth and learning. It was quite surprising that he brought this up, as this has been one of my visions to implement in the West for a long time. We began speaking about youth and other daily affairs such as news and the amount of negative energy that is being portrayed on a daily basis only to generate fear in people. This is all contributing to the destruction of people and the world.

It came up that parents, older siblings, and many others teach youth about their belief systems, yet it is quite evident that they don't even help themselves. Will people listen, especially kids, when you say one thing yet they see you act in a contradictory manner? They will do as you do, not as you say. Teaching peace for humanity is the approach the world is taking.

Until recent times, it was thought that war was a way of gaining prosperity for a nation. Now, it is undeniably true that peace is the only way for everyone to prosper. We have even managed to come together as one world and create the Global Peace Index (GPI). The GPI is used to monitor how peaceful each country is. It shows that the more peaceful the country, the more productive it is. With this information, strategists have discovered that peace and prosperity go together. The world is now focused on bringing peace, because once that is achieved we can focus more intelligently on bigger issues. Curing disease, maintaining nature's essence so that we can live in better conditions, harvesting crops so more people can eat, regulating the world's temperature, and advancing technology deserve far more energy than wasting it on a ridiculous war created by egotistical men and women. We all play a major part in bringing peace to this earth and setting up an environment that our children deserve to live in.

I went back to the hotel that night after spending the day with Dr. Boondham, and I was staring out the window. I was looking over the lit-up city of Bangkok and had a feeling of absolute comfort. I sat there and really embraced what had just happened and the questions that were answered on this day. They would definitely affect my life forever. I found what I was looking for, and that's the same love that dwells within all mankind. It doesn't matter where you are in the world, what your religious background is, or any other social limitation, the truth remains the same for all. We are all human beings, and we all have the same feelings and emotions.

I found it amazing that someone from the East, a Buddhist monk probably three times my age, had the same feelings as a young man from the West. I have had completely different experiences throughout my life, I come from a different religious background and social group, yet human love was so strong that we created a bond and mutual respect. When you open your eyes and let your ego fall asleep, you discover the connection that makes us all one, and the power that could turn this world forever. I always used to think, "What can one man do?" Now I realize that this was affecting my own life in the process. Imagine if everyone had that thought—the world would be finished.

I guess I was just looking on the outside to try to comfort the inner. I finally noticed that the opposite way around really opens the door to life.

23

It's Not Just Your Life

LIFE STARTS WITH YOU—ANYWHERE, ANYTIME

Living in someone else's dream is like being a bird with clipped wings. It looks up to witness freedom but can only sluggishly walk around and attempt to fly. To its anguish, it is picked up by its owner and placed back in its cage. Live your life!

There is this notion that we have to hit rock bottom to ever see the other side of our life. Maybe this is true to an extent, but only because we keep on believing it is. In feeding such an idea, does it mean that someone who doesn't think they have been as low as others cannot progress and be awakened to their greatness? I hear it all the time, and that's why I had to add this part in.

One guy said, "I haven't been through half the stuff you have; maybe if I do I will realize it then." He is only one of many, and I couldn't think of anything further from the truth. Some people will even reassure me that I must have been through a lot of "life experience" to obtain the knowledge I teach. Who hasn't, though? I just decide to probe my experience until I am inundated with answers that I can grow from.

It's sad that some of us have to wait to hit that low point in order to wake up. We have all had our individual experiences, and I'm sure there have been times in your life when you have felt lost and confused. It may be that way now. The reason I know it's not a must to hit rock bottom is that one of my best friends discovered his greatness and he said his life was pretty enjoyable before he decided to go deeper.

Yes, it rocked him a bit when he would ask questions and certain beliefs would be tested, but it helped him grow. He would text me at 3:00 a.m. sometimes because he questioned himself so deeply that he needed a second opinion on the answer. I always replied with, **"If it seems that it can enhance your life, regardless of how much it tests your old belief—if it is reasonable, makes proper sense to you, helps you to display a more loving nature to everyone and everything, then yes, go for it."**

Just by opening up his mind, letting down limitations, and gathering knowledge from other sources, he was able to find his truth. As we have discovered, rock bottom is only a perception, so I choose to see it is a POA (point of awareness).

Everyone has wants, and the only way they are accessible is if the changes start with the individual. To be awakened to your power within is a personal choice. Even when faced with really difficult challenges through life experience, it is up to you to grow in those times. That's why when people tell me about their problems, I reply with, "Problem or choice?" Think about it: Are they really problems, or do we have a vast array of choices to make in those moments? The word *problem* is far too restrictive. We are always faced with numerous options to direct our focus. Next time you say, "I have a problem," change it to "I have a choice," and see how different you feel.

THAT KID!

> "I've learned that people will forget what you said,
> people will forget what you did, but people will never
> forget how you made them feel."
>
> —MAYA ANGELOU

One unexpected event can really shake you, and at the same time remind you that you are on the right path. When you start to feel more love on the inside and that starts to project outwardly, the truth of who you really are begins to display itself. We are tested, not in a way that sets us up to feel failure, but instead to the point of recognition and growth. Your views become stronger, they advance, and certain things start to cement that. One of those situations took place on a rainy night only to help shape my destiny once again.

The supermarket became a place for yet another awakening. As I was entering I saw a child no older than ten. He was alone at 11:00 p.m. and smoking a cigarette. It was evident that he was limited by social beliefs and had no real sense of direction at such a young age. I noticed about four people walk past him and ignore a conversation that he tried to start. He was very polite in his approach, but no one seemed to take notice of him, or they were just too busy feeding their egos.

I believe we can learn a lot from children. As we grow older, we like to believe we are getting wiser. I have found with children that when they burn their hand on something hot, they know never to touch it again. How often do we adults get burned, yet continue to act in the same way and get the same results?

As I was leaving, the boy asked me if I played soccer. I replied that I didn't but I played other sports. I had a strong urge to talk to him. I wanted to explain that love is within him always, that he had an important role in the world, that he was special, and that no matter what anyone believed of him, all he had to do was believe in himself and he could do anything. All these thoughts were flowing through me, but I got in my car and drove off. As I was driving, the thoughts became stronger and the feeling was overwhelming. I turned my car around and went back to look for him. He was gone.

The immediate feeling of neglect I felt toward this child put me in such a state that I had to hold back tears. The powerful message this event taught me was that that kid might never hear that again. My simple words may have had the power to ultimately change his life forever. Just through that short message, who knows where he might have ended up?

Perhaps those other people had a preconception of where that would be and so they ignored him. Instead of showing him that he was a human being they contributed to another possibly sad story. I realized that boy could turn to drugs next, having no guidance, and by a few words could have been saved. That's the power of it.

"Courage is what it takes to stand up and speak;
courage is also what it takes to sit down and listen."
—WINSTON CHURCHILL

I was disappointed until I realized the change that I am able to make. I gathered a great purpose and empowering direction. I'm not going to let these limitations hold me back. When I feel the urge to help, it's the world telling me to step up to the plate. It's an opportunity to allow us to see who we really are, and the only way to gain fulfillment. We must be the change we wish to see in the world, and **we are just as much the things we don't do as the things we do.**

Are those people failures for just walking past? Of course not, but we must acknowledge that displaying that type of energy toward one person contributes to their inner turmoil. If we realize this and are able to make a difference, then we are saving not just those around us but ourselves as well. We are on a journey of getting to know ourselves, and such acts will help us. People who use their intelligence identify that helping others is actually helping themselves.

SET UP YOUTH FOR REAL SUCCESS

"Children need models rather than critics."
—JOSEPH JOUBERT

It is quite clear that the youth are in desperate need of proper guidance. Our generations revolve around teaching kids how we think they should react to things, or our own individual beliefs. As we have already discussed, some beliefs we have are not always the truth, so how do we know we are teaching them correctly? Just because we are adults doesn't mean we haven't been negatively influenced and are passing that down to the younger generation.

There are some children who won't hold back from telling us when we are taking a turn for the worse. My sister receives no shortage of lectures from her four-year-old for smoking; sometimes kids know better than we do. But the majority of times, we are the role models, so here are a few tips for how we can monitor whether we are teaching them things that will empower their lives. The first point is that we must be able to make sure that what we are teaching them is aiming toward a true love. We must also question what we are teaching them and ask how this could benefit others or affect their lives. **"If I do teach them about love and real success, do I practice what I preach? What detrimental effect could this particular belief have on their well-being when they have**

**to be out on their own? Is it leading them toward more hatred
and belief in failure, rather than enhancing and enriching the
quality of their lives? How has this belief negatively affected my
life? Are they in fact limiting beliefs?"** This all goes back to really
looking deeper into what you find with your own beliefs that will
help you empower youth and set them up for a quality life. While
doing this, you will equally enhance your own life.

So often we teach children our own individual belief systems,
which are significantly different from what they might see on TV,
learn from their friends, or hear at school. With all this confusion
going on, can we ever change the course of the world? It is increas-
ingly crucial to find a common way for all mankind. I think we
are neglecting the greatest lesson at school and at home, which is
one of love, respect, appreciation, and abundance for all people; a
subject that teaches children that limitations spring from hate, disrespect, judgment about people's looks, social status, and religious
background; a subject that teaches that we are all part of the same
team and promotes a common reverence for our fellow humans.
Children must be made aware of how those things drastically affect their own lives.

As an adult, you have a duty to make sure that teaching about
love and kindness is at the top of your list. But more important,
you must practice what you preach.

Regardless of cultural differences, imagine if someone asked
what we are, and we all answered, "Human." That one word has
the power to change the world. Rather than separating ourselves,
could you picture what a difference that one-word answer would
make in the world? Being a black belt and state gold medalist in
tae kwon do, Bruce Lee was always one of my inspirations when
I was growing up. In an interview I saw, he was asked if he considered himself Chinese or American. His reply was, "You know
what? I want to think of myself as a human being, under the sky,
under the heavens, like one family." If we could prepare ourselves

and our youth for the challenges that we face on a day-to-day basis, the results would be astounding. We must teach them a universal respect for all things and allow them to see that they are part of this world, and the world is a part of them.

I was inspired to write about this topic when I witnessed a child accidentally hit his head on a seat at a local mall. He began crying, and his mother called it a stupid chair and told him to hit it back. Once the child started striking back, he stopped crying and smiled. There were people around laughing because they thought the situation was cute. I think that what this child was taught did nothing but satisfy his mother's selfish desires. She just didn't want to be embarrassed anymore by his wailing. Although this might seem like a trivial incident, that child will grow up to believe that when he is faced with physical or emotional hurt, revenge is the best option. That will be his subconscious reaction. What a misconception and a lie. This is why I repeat, **it is absolutely crucial what we teach the next generation,** as belief systems create us to make decisions and hence sculpt our life accordingly.

Proper education is the only way to enhance the quality of people's lives, and that's why I say you don't have to hit rock bottom to make change. We can make subtle changes and educate children on fulfillment and love, rather than waiting for them to be taught through life experience. They will definitely have challenges along the way, as we all do, but proper education for you and for them will set us all up for real success.

24

The Mystery of Life

When you really think about this infinite galaxy and this sphere you are walking on, it makes you wonder about the mystery that surrounds us. Trying to figure out all the answers would drive us insane and stop us from really embracing what we know as life. Through my journey, I have had some awakenings that I would like to share, which I believe are very important to understanding and enriching our life.

PAST, PRESENT, FUTURE

> "What we are today comes from our thoughts of yesterday, and our present thoughts build our life of tomorrow: Our life is the creation of our mind."
>
> —THE BUDDHA

In order to experience wholeness, we must conclude that the present moment is the only thing that is real and therefore complete. Have you ever wondered where yesterday went? Take a look around—can you grab it? It didn't just disappear, as we know nothing in life ever does. How does a part of the world leave the world? It ultimately can't. So if your experience still exists somewhere, then where is it? Only in your mind! It is yet another thing stored in the vast and infinite realm of your consciousness. That means it's accessible, re-creatable, and believable, just like the thoughts we have of our future. We become so entrenched in the notion of past or future that we forget the most important time of all: now. When a thought about the past comes into reality again, or a thought about a future desire comes about for the first time, we are still experiencing it in the present, aren't we?

An example of a past thought being re-created would be to organize a family dinner similar to one you had a month ago where everyone thoroughly enjoyed themselves. A future one would be to create an experience you have never had. But how often do we get the experience we desire, yet not appreciate it enough because our mind is too busy wandering rather than being present in that moment? That's a life that is far too common for most.

There are certain people who try to hold on to their past or a happy experience they once had and base their fulfillment on that. This could be a good tool to get some quick satisfaction, but the only way of being truly fulfilled is to embrace the beauty of now. No matter what challenge I am faced with, I always come back to right now, and a sudden peace manifests itself. I do this to clear my mind at times when it feels like it is racing around or wandering. Once that is done, you will be in a prime position to put something that will benefit you in its place.

Seeing that all experience is in the mind means we have control over it. I'm certain there have been times when you have looked back and shifted your mind-set over an experience. The experience itself then seems to change altogether—like those times when you have looked at something that you initially interpreted as being bad, but after further assessment the same experience seemed great. We must be aware that the situation was always available for that other perception, as the situation itself has not changed. It was your choice to attach a different mind-set to it and draw a benefit. This can be done for any situation or experience if we focus on it.

Living in the moment is not the absence of care for the future; it actually creates the future with awareness.

People often talk about a past and a future. **The past is only a mental image, just like the future; however, they are pictures that affect how we act in the present.** You are the editor of the photo album in your mind. Would you repeatedly look over a photo album that brought up shocking emotions? Then why do you do it in your mind? If we acknowledge this control, it allows us to really embrace our decisions right now, as we know nothing else is essentially real. Let me put it to you more simply. Most go about their day worrying about something that has happened or stressing over something that hasn't happened yet. It's a ridiculous and insane thing to do. They are creating imaginary scenarios in their mind and killing themselves in the process. It affects what they are creating and attracting in their life because they make it a priority. The funny thing is, they never needed to worry or stress, because neither of those events are real, but by continually thinking about them, they make them a part of their reality.

As we have been told by many great people in history, our thoughts become real.

I have a little exercise for you to do. **Right now, take one of your hands off this book and repeatedly move your fingers up and down. Watch them closely and concentrate on their movements for about thirty seconds.**

Now look at your whole hand. Touch it, embrace it. **You are in the now.** Did you think of anything that made you worry while you were doing that exercise? Of course you didn't, because you were focusing on the present moment. You came back to reality. Where are the things you once stressed about? Take a look around. Exactly—it is only a story that you are replaying in your mind.

Being one with your mind means you have the power to manipulate it any way you like. Who's in control of your thoughts? You are. Truly successful people have a strategy with this knowledge. By acknowledging they are the only ones who have the power to create scenarios or stories in their mind, they think of ones that are beneficial to them. Other stories that have a detrimental effect are quickly attacked and overpowered. This is one secret fulfilled people know.

I once read that a good way of finding the now is to look up at the clouds. When you see just clouds, you are in the now—but as soon as you start seeing faces or shapes in the clouds, you know your mind has wandered. We can't always stay in the now. Our mind will certainly wander, but by knowing you have the ability to come back to right now to clear your head when something is affecting your life, you have power. Most times, our mind should wander only to make sense of past experiences or create an empowering path for our future. When it's not doing either of these, find comfort in the now.

> "The art of life is to live in the present moment,
> and to make that moment as perfect as we can
> by the realization that we are the instruments
> and expression of God himself."
>
> —EMMET FOX

Whatever we choose to think about now, whether it's an unpleasant experience or the great life we envision, will certainly have an effect on what we do next. This acknowledgment really altered the way I approached my life, as I began embracing the moment and using my time productively. It stopped me from procrastinating, because I became aware of the enormous power that my present thoughts, words, and actions have in creating my life. **Every new moment creates new opportunities: a fresh slate offered by life.** You can think what you want, feel what you want, and create what you want. The next time you find yourself fixated on a past experience or a what-if scenario that is negatively affecting your state, ask yourself these three questions:

> What do I want to think?
>
> What do I want to feel?
>
> What do I want to create?

Who's in control of how you think? Who's in control of how you feel? Who's in control of what you create? These three important aspects of life are solely your choice in every moment. You are in control of all of them, so choose intelligently.

To create things that are worthy of looking back on, you have to change your decisions in the present. The scenarios you replay in your mind and the stories you tell yourself shape your life.

YOUR GIFT TO CREATE

> "Whether you think you can,
> or you think you can't—you're right."
> —HENRY FORD

Life is a plane of endless possibilities, and what you choose to do now creates what will come next. It starts with our thoughts, comes out of our mouth, and then reflects through our actions. **Manifesting our visions into reality is just like a puzzle. First we take a good look at a picture of the end result, hold on to it, and then set out to fit the pieces together.** We have also been given the gift of free will, so what you decide to create next is entirely up to you. If you decide to think and believe strongly about something, whatever it may be, you will create it. Everything that exists in the world is someone's creation. It began as a mental image, a strong vision, followed by a passion that caused action to create it. A table, a bridge, a book, or a painting all follow the same principles in order to be created.

It's also evident that we manifest most things throughout our day. The mind is so powerful that we are able to focus on one thing and make it real among so many choices. Let's say you choose to go to a store at 10:00 a.m. to buy a new outfit you have been waiting for. It began as a thought, you told people where you were going, and you created the scenario in your mind. Even though it was only in your mind at the time, you knew that's where you were going to go. You planned to wake up at 8:00 a.m. to get ready, and you took the appropriate steps to manifest it into reality. It then became your creation.

You automatically deviate from the masses by merely realizing your power to create.

On the other hand, if you decided not to go to that store, then it would never have become real, and what you chose to do instead would have taken its place, right? Does that mean your ability to create going to the store didn't exist? No, it did exist—you just chose not to go. It existed as a realistic option you may have taken. Your consciousness offers you a vast array of possibilities in all moments. You could have washed your car in that time, watched TV, read a book, or begun working. And if that were the case, going to the store would have never been a creation in your reality. **It's quite fascinating how most of our life is created by our choices!**

Every moment we are creating our life. We create as we go.

DESTINY—THE CHOICE IS YOURS

> "Shallow men believe in luck,
> strong men believe in cause and effect."
>
> —RALPH WALDO EMERSON

Most people live their whole lives believing that their experiences were due to a mysterious force of luck that circles the universe and chooses random people to have certain experiences. If we know anything about how the world and nature operate, it's that everything has its place. Too regularly, people use the concept of luck to escape accountability for their own actions. The universe and everything in it has been proved to be a wonderful energy that connects us all. All the experiences that have recently happened in my life and to others around me have made me reject that limiting belief in luck.

If you do believe in coincidence, explain it. If you believe that things just happen out of luck, what is the basis on which you allocate experience? It's absurd to pick and choose what you think is luck, and if you do, what's the reason behind all the other experiences? If we believe in luck or mysterious coincidence, that explanation must hold up for every single thing that happens in our lives, and we all know believing that is just a cop-out, an excuse for not taking responsibility. It would mean we have absolutely no control over our life, which is a lie. By that reasoning, even waking up in the morning and not getting hit by a car on the way to work is good luck. Dropping a pen would be bad luck. If you get my drift, in order to believe in luck, you must adapt it to every little thing that happens. It's not okay to say something is luck when it suits you but not say it about everything. We all know that we are in far more control than that.

Reason cancels out coincidence. Cause and effect cancel out luck. If you want control over your life, look to cancel both of them out with those substitutions.

People want to believe that things happen for an unknown reason because they don't want to believe they had any control over the outcome. Most times we say something was bad luck because of a failure to see that opportunity as one for growth and a means to act differently. We may not see the reason or the cause instantly, but with enough thought, we will in fact see that every experience has meaning and is a basis for learning. I'm not sure about you, but I find it hard to believe that there is a man up in the sky rolling dice on our life. Everything that happens in nature is due to cause and effect, and we are no exception. This is a hard concept for some to grasp, because our ego stands in the way of taking responsibility for our life.

The stars may look scattered from where we are, but they are exactly where they're meant to be.

We all hold the paintbrush for the canvas of our lives. It's not until we truly understand and take hold of this that we are able to make clear decisions. It all depends on how you look at your experience. If you refer to luck or coincidence, the true meaning of an experience seems to go past with no benefit. Taking accountability and gathering knowledge from an experience that can benefit your life helps the whole world. We are not in this alone, and if everyone took accountability this world would be a much better place. If someone slips on a banana peel on the floor and breaks their back, would that be bad luck? I would have to say that it was due to the inconsiderate and stupid act of another person who dropped the peel, and also due to others acknowledging that it could be dangerous and walking straight past it. **Luck has no grounds for growth or action; accountability does.**

"Nothing happens by chance, my friend . . .
No such thing as luck. A meaning behind every little
thing, and such a meaning behind this.
Part for you, part for me, may not see it real clear right
now, but we will, before long."

—RICHARD BACH

There is a God-given path for all of us and it's the path of love, which opens up all the doors to our life; but then again, it's our choice whether we wish to walk it.

We attract what we focus on. I have always been a massive fan of the old saying "Everything happens for a reason," yet most times I couldn't put my finger on what the reason was. It would confuse me even more until another, similar event took place. When I really started questioning everything about my life, I came to a rude awakening about that saying. The deeper I went looking for those reasons while trying to be honest with myself in the process, I found that the reasons were all pointing to me.

I definitely had to let go of my ego when doing this, because that's the only way the truth seems to arise. We become confused by always looking on the outside to find a meaning, unaware the answer is actually right here within us. Was it me that was attracting these things in my life? Was I the reason they were happening? The answer would keep falling back on me. I would calculate the way I had been thinking, and it was quite true. I was attracting these things in my life through the attitude I was taking to it every day. The way I thought, the words I spoke, and the physical actions I took were all contributing to my downfall. I would try to believe that things just happened, but that belief leads to no benefit. Do we really believe that, or are we just scared to face the truth? When a certain situation arises, are we taking any accountability? I discovered that the reason something happens is subject to whatever we wish that reason to be. If things happen for a reason, make sure you make the reason an empowering one that you can grow and learn from. **An experience means whatever you want it to mean.**

It wasn't until I began really taking control of my life that I became aware of the power I had to shape my destiny. It was in fact me the whole time; and it makes sense, considering I've been given free will. Funny that it took so many experiences to finally have a light-bulb moment on the matter. As I began taking sole accountability for the position I was in, my position turned around radically. Doing this is the only way you are ever going to gain that control and make everlasting change. As long as we blame everything and everyone else for the position we are in or the experiences that arise, we cannot excel. Don't get me wrong, **we definitely can't control everything outside, but we can control the significance it has on our life and how we react to it.**

"Destiny is no matter of chance.
It is a matter of choice: It is not a thing
to be waited for, it is a thing to be achieved."
—WILLIAM JENNINGS BRYAN

One of the greatest examples of this was from a young woman named Bethany Hamilton who had her arm bitten off by a shark when she and her friends were night surfing. She was an aspiring professional surfer at the time, and even after such a challenging experience she decided to pursue her dream and won many titles. She has inspired millions of people around the world with her book and movie *Soul Surfer,* starring Helen Hunt and Dennis Quaid. Bethany is someone who sees her experience as a means to teach others—not as bad luck. She said she would not take back what happened to her and regrets nothing.

Our truth will always display itself throughout our life, but given free will, we have a chance to grasp it or live a life far from it. We know that if we are not following our true path, it is usually indicated by the emptiness we regularly feel. Taking accountability and relating your current thoughts, words, and actions to what position you are in is crucial for allowing your spirit to tell you the truth. You will be shocked at times, but the deeper you search, the closer you get to that gift in every experience.

UNCERTAINTY VS. CERTAINTY

There are times in our life when we feel so certain about something, but it soon becomes obvious that life has something else in store for that moment. Thinking about it, though, it's life's uncertainty that makes it worth living. If we knew all the answers, there would be no point, and it would take away any experience or emotion. There would be no thrill, challenge, love, or appreciation. It's like when we go watch a movie with a friend who has already seen that film. We read up on it, we get a fair idea of what it's about, and we go to experience the rest. How annoying is it when your friend starts telling you what happens? You're like, "Shut up, I came to watch it." We don't want to know all the answers; if we did, life wouldn't be worth living.

Don't think about life's uncertainty until it shows itself, and then deal with it intelligently. When uncertainty shows itself, I still make certainty out of it. Until it's displayed, just be certain, because there is no reason to be otherwise. What chance do you give yourself if you're reminding yourself of uncertainty before it's even happened? Even when it comes to the smallest things in life, I find people are so uncertain. It's no wonder their goals seem unreachable. We say things like, "I might," "I'll try," or "Maybe." With that attitude, nothing is ever going to get done. When you make the decision to actually do something you will always find a way. We just need to make the decision. We say things like, "What if . . ." or create scenarios that aren't real and tarnish our decisions right now, usually attracting the very things we tried to avoid in the first place. Acknowledge that life has its uncertainties, and you won't be shocked when they arise. In the meantime, focus on creating certainty where you can and eliminate all barriers in your mind.

WE ARE ONE

> "If we have no peace, it is because
> we have forgotten that we belong to each other."
>
> —MOTHER TERESA

Humans don't know all the answers. Throughout history we have tried to find out what the truth is, but everyone has something different to say. Various religious sects, scientists, and even the guy at the local convenience store all claim that they have the truth. There are more than **45,000** different religious factions in the world. It's bad enough to fight against other religions, but many even manage to fight within their own religion. Christians versus Christians, Muslims against Muslims, and Hindus with Hindus. In all seriousness, what on earth is going on? Where is basic human respect? Was that really God's plan—to give certain people permission to destroy something he created out of love? I don't think so; that sounds more like a selfish human act, don't you think?

Someone once asked me, "Well, what is God?" To be honest, the answer I found going through my journey satisfied me. I replied, "We are all God evolving." You see, our concept of God changes as we change. In history, many different cultures have believed in multiple gods—the Romans, Persians, Egyptians, Assyrians, and others. To them, their gods were so real that they helped these societies conquer the world. If you were preaching about there being one god back then, you would have been seen as crazy. The Roman Empire was incredibly powerful. And most of that was due to the belief in their many pagan gods. Today we look back and think that belief was ridiculous. We have evolved!

In my opinion, thousands of years from now humans are going to look back at us and say, "Can you believe they were crazy enough to believe in one god that was separate from us?" We are all god-connected, doing our part in creation. We are forever changing, forever evolving, and the more we delve into who we are as humans, the more we find out about our connection with the whole universe.

What is the truth? Who's right and who's wrong? There has to be a truth that everyone can accept—one that allows us to live peacefully at this time of our existence. Once a mind is fully awakened and a heart unchained, that truth becomes clearer. It has no limitations or restrictions. It's not a matter of gaining any selfish satisfaction of ego by saying, "I'm right and you're wrong"; it's just the truth.

That truth is love. That's the special feeling. The truth is your truth, that deep voice inside that always shows how you can give more love. Some believe that voice will give them nothing but disappointment, but those who are truly rich in life know it's that exact voice that makes their dreams a reality. It is the voice we rarely dare to reason with because it would expose how we lie to ourselves all too often.

Love is the essence of all creation, and that is the truth. All great leaders who have led their nation out of suppression and into liberation did it through love. Nelson Mandela, Mahatma Gandhi, Martin Luther King Jr., and Mother Teresa are great examples. Their message was clear and concise: Put down your arms and give love—and it worked! The same goes with finding liberation in our daily lives. Apply it and you will prove it to yourself.

We were never meant to separate ourselves from any part of creation, but I guess that was the human pride factor. The "I'm this" and "you're that" notion has been in the foreground of every war or obscenity in history. Love is pure and not prideful—and it definitely does not wish to be separated from anything it dwells in. That is why the great teachers never asked for a religion to be based around them. Others did that of their own accord. All these masters came to do was teach about love for all creation. I am a major believer in God, but I don't believe the higher power is separate from me or any part of creation. If I stuck to that concept, I would never be able to understand or feel the creator's presence. I know this because I used to claim I believed, but never acted as if I did. Further to that, my inner self was not at peace, and that is a sign that we have not yet grasped the true nature of the higher power that exists in everything.

As we are all one, the universe and everything in it is at the mercy of our actions. We affect everything and create anything!

If you believe that the creator is separate from you, then I ask, "Where is God?" Is he really up there? Where's "up there"? Up there is infinite! If you are able to feel the higher power (love) within you, then doesn't that mean that power exists in you? If God is all, doesn't that mean we are one with all creation? If we feel emotions that are so far from explanation, and we understand there is a much deeper level to life than what surrounds us with our eyes, it seems it is within us. We are not separate from anything or anyone. If we were, it would mean we wouldn't have the ability to affect things, and we have now learned that is untrue. Everything exists within our own conscious realm, even the very concept of God. That's why we have the ability to influence and affect everything, even if it's only through perception.

Where did consciousness originate? No one knows, and I guess that's why most of the world's population acknowledges that there must be something greater. There's a simple reason I have no choice but to really believe that all this was created: **I can't come**

to terms with how something could come from nothing. If you ever find the answer, I would like you to email me instantly. But then I'd reply with the question, "Where did that come from?"

Scientists say it was the big bang theory; well, what created the big bang? Then they will come up with another answer, but then what created that, and what created that? It's a never-ending cycle, and if you attempt to comprehend it, you will realize there is actually no reasonable explanation. It's like asking, "What came first, the chicken or the egg?" The human mind is clearly incapable of discovering such a finding. If you don't believe we have a creator, then all I will ask you to do is **think of what created thought!**

Most people wait in anticipation for a miracle to happen in their life, unaware that the miracle is actually life itself.

I'm sure it is quite obvious that when something is created, it has a part of its creator in it. We can all comprehend that much. That means if all this started from something—and it had to, because something definitely doesn't come from nothing—there is a part of our creator within all of us. Call it God, higher power, Allah, Yahweh, ether, plasma—it doesn't really make a difference. It's still within you, and it's the same for all of us. Just like a painter and his painting, or a sculptor and his statue. A part of the painter or sculptor remains in their creation forever. It starts with passion and love, and most important it is a means of expression. Those attributes will be evident for eternity. Don't you have your mother's DNA within you? Of course, because she took part in creating you; a part of her has to be in you. As for the connection among us, well, that's just evident in everyday life. Take a good look at just how much other people affect how you act in one day, and they don't even have to say anything half the time.

Science has proved that everything in the universe comes from the same source and is made up of the same compounds. Matter exists in everything! The common definition of matter is anything that has both mass and volume (occupies space). For example, a table would be said to be made of matter, as it occupies space and has mass.

Matter consists of protons, neutrons, and electrons. **Electrons** are tiny, very light particles that have a negative electrical charge. **Protons** are much larger and heavier than electrons and have a positive charge. **Neutrons** are large and heavy like protons, but have no electrical charge. What I find fascinating is that our positive charge is larger than our negative. I wonder if that has anything to do with hearing that **love conquers all,** light will put out the darkness, or happiness will win over sadness.

You are made up of this matter, along with your TV, your car, the tree on your front lawn, and everyone you know. The world and everything in it truly comes from the same source. Isn't everything created from the earth? Take a look around. From dust we came, to dust our bodies return. We will be entangled with everyone and everything forever because everything is held together by a common element. Even the events that take place in outer space influence what happens on planet Earth. If one thing did not play its part for one moment, nothing could survive.

Most major religions state that God is above everything else. Well, is there something that exists in everything? Yes: energy. And if God is greater than this, then it means that our creator, too, exists in everything and more, right? Being one with all means we have the power to influence everything.

> "So powerful is the light of unity
> that it can illuminate the whole earth."
>
> —BAHÁ'U'LLÁH

You might be thinking, "Well, what is the creator, and what shape or form does it have?" It's ultimately unknown. It's like asking the same question about consciousness; no one can answer that, and even quantum physicists are stating that it's easier to do work leaving it as the unknown. The most intelligent people in history have tried to figure it out and failed miserably. We will never get to the bottom of it as humans because, like I said before, there is no bottom. That's how you know there is a greater meaning to life. How do you truly embrace such a mystery? You consume yourself with it every time you project love. It's evident when you have a person that you really love next to you, when you're in a mode of total appreciation, or when experiencing those overwhelming emotions when contributing. The best way to know our creator is to understand the creation. Once you understand yourself and the world, its magnificence will show itself.

There is definitely a mystery to life because we don't know all the answers. We look up in the sky; there's a sun, a moon, all these planets, this galaxy. Each of us has wondered what it's all about, and what it all means. We are as tiny as a speck of dust in the universe, so we know there's more to life than the petty complaints we surround ourselves with on a daily basis. Life is to be enjoyed.

We have a tendency to bog ourselves down with things that we will never find out. It then feels like too much, we begin to doubt ourselves, and we forget the most important thing—to **live!** Some will attempt to know all the answers and will put limitations on the unknown. They consume themselves with the idea of past lives, or the afterlife, yet neglect the most precious time of all: right now. I have found a new comfort in not knowing exactly where I will be next, or what I was before, but I know I am getting closer to love in this, and that will carry on and on to whatever comes next. Understanding there is more to you than meets the eye and realizing there is a major purpose to this mystery we call life is extremely important to your happiness. It allows you to search deeper, accept your greatness, and use the once-slumbering power within you. This will ultimately help you defeat what society has branded you as being and prevent you from falling back into insignificance. It's also very important to not get caught wandering in a daze all day about these mysteries. You may just bump yourself on things nearby, and it's going to hurt! Searching for more is great, but make sure you always remain conscious of the reality of the present moment.

Realistically, all you have to do is ask the question "What am I doing here?" and you are thrown into a massive realm of possibility that is far greater than you alone. Do you really think that whatever it was that created this world only did so to obtain praise? Isn't that selfish? I think it's an insult to believe that a God who dwells in all things would need anything from us. Life is our gift; it is not meant to be lived in fear of love. A recent study showed that 88 percent of the world's population believes in a higher power. This figure is higher in the United States, where it is estimated that 95 percent of the population do. We understand that there are lots of questions we don't have answers to and that there is a far greater meaning to life, which is why I think so many believe. We want to continue to have hope and faith, because we know it has seen us through on so many occasions. We just need to learn how to really amplify the qualities of the creator that dwell within us.

> "A wise man sees himself in everyone
> and everyone in himself."
>
> —THE BUDDHA

FINDING THE CONNECTION . . .

The wind that circulates through the world is the same air we breathe. The sun gives us energy. The planet we live on is mostly water. What is your body mostly made up of? When we blow on a leaf, it has the same effect as when the wind hits it. The water that drops out of the sky is the same water we drink to stay alive. It's so amazing that I can walk into an old building and feel its history and the energy in the room. You don't have to be Einstein to figure out that we are all interconnected and one in essence. I feel people's pain and I don't even have to see them. I would also like to note that whichever man or woman created the word *universe* was definitely inspired by collective consciousness. *Universe* derives from the Latin word for **one version.**

In being one with this endless universe, we are built with infinite intelligence and we have a higher power that most have yet to tap into. This is why there are individuals who seem to be on a completely different level than others. They have discovered a hidden source of power and connection to their soul. There's a great mystery going on in the world, but we seem to be blind to this phenomenon. The most important aspect of this realization is that God has always been with you, yet on occasion we choose not to listen to the wise voice that lies deep within our heart. If you fight the thought that the qualities of a higher power reign with you, you will never discover the essence of life. You will not express one love for all creation, and therefore you will never be at peace.

"You menace others with your deadly fangs.
But in tormenting them,
you are only torturing yourselves."

—MILAREPA

This next revelation that I discovered was basically the foreground of my permanent change. How does being connected with the world and everything in it affect my life? Well, **if I harm you, I'm only harming myself in the process.** By harming myself, I'm harming you and this world. If I disrespect the environment, I'm only doing it to myself and it will distance me from ever discovering my greatness.

If we do bad things or act with negative intent, the world will answer back ferociously. Some people like to think they can get away with treating others poorly, but the effects are immediate in their own life. Every time they do, it penetrates their soul and an inner peace becomes harder to grasp. They will battle their inner demons until the day they die unless their actions are liberated. On the other hand, if you are pure, respectful, loving, and give of your true self, the world will answer accordingly.

Those who bully and tease others are a great example. How do you think they feel? Short-term satisfaction is no means of gaining true happiness. They are scared because they haven't yet discovered their greatness because of their constant decisions that go against reason and truth. When they go home and lay their head on their pillow with no one to bully, they realize they are empty. Others usually submit to their energy, which then affects their own life and the people around them. It's like the continuous ripples caused by dropping a pebble in water. We are never going to eliminate such people or situations in our lifetime, but it is our choice about what significance they have in our life. If you hate back, are you any different? But if you feel compassionate to these people and realize that they are unaware of how their actions are affecting their own life, then you will be able to interrupt the energy pattern.

The lack of understanding that we are all one is what separates us.

All giants that have come before us have spoken clearly about this unity in the world and the effect it has. In Hinduism and Buddhism, karma holds extremely high importance. The core meaning of **karma** is **action.** Karma is the direct effect your actions have on your own life. As soon as you commit an action with a certain intention, you are immediately affected. Whether that's in a positive or negative way depends on the action and the intention you choose. Dr. Wayne Dyer summed it up beautifully when he said, "How people treat you is their karma; how you react is yours." In the Bible, in Galatians 6, it states, "Each one should test his own actions, then he can take pride in himself, without comparing himself to somebody else, for each one should carry his own load. . . . A man reaps what he sows. . . . Let us not become weary in doing good, for at the proper time we will reap a harvest if we do not give up." Clearly this is not just talking about what is to come, but this life right now. The message is quite clear, I think; **the energy you give off is the energy you get back.** Everything you do emanates energy, including your thoughts. If you doubt this notion, just review previous actions you have taken and see if your attitude (energy) has anything to do with the experiences you have had. In relation to that, notice how those actions made you feel. Even if some brought short-term satisfaction, did they really fulfill your life and purpose, or create a deep inner peace? The way we feel after we take action is usually the best indicator.

Don't just treat others how you would like to be treated; treat yourself how you would like to be treated.

The challenge I frequently hear is when people tell me they have tried being nice and loving, but they feel that if they continue they will be taken advantage of. If that is your motto in life, then you are actually only giving to obtain something in return. No one can walk all over you unless you let them, so the giving of your true qualities should require nothing in return. If you give only to receive, then you have given nothing. When you emit love and kindness to everyone and do not expect a response externally, the reward is apparent. Do not wait to fill yourself up with their gratitude, but embrace the fulfilling feeling you attain from giving. If you are faced with this challenge you will realize these people are trampling themselves for having a heart that is not yet filled with love. Be compassionate in this situation, but be even more grateful and proud of your choice of action. **No one can take your happiness unless you let them.**

*The way you treat yourself is more important to your life
than the way others treat you.*

The greatest thing that inspires me to push my vision forward and enhance the power of my passion is when I hear people speak disparagingly about life. I know from experience how sad it is to resist life. We will never reach our full potential, nor will we live the life we envision with that mind-set. Most times all it takes is shifting your focus onto something you love, and you will see how easy it is to free yourself from that imprisoning thought or emotion. This leads to the great question, **"Are we slowly dying, or are we beginning to live?"** It seems the world has been caught up in trying to find a cure for death, which is inevitable. We are blinded by the fact that the only cure for death is life, so we'd better start living. You really live when you truly live as you are; not how you think you have to live.

HARD-TO-GRASP NOTIONS

"And we have come to know and to believe the love
that God has in us. God is love, and the one who resides
in love resides in God, and God resides in him."
—1 JOHN 4:16

When we comprehend that we are all one, other notions about the source from which we originate are called into question. A common one is the word *he* that gets used to replace God. If it's used to narrow the higher power down to something that is absent from this world, then I disagree. Most people take the word *he* literally, even though when you ask them, they reject that God is a *he* or a singular, separate entity. This is due to not being able to ultimately explain what God is.

The concept of God is used by many people as a tool to separate from each other. It's a contradiction, considering all major religions claim to be followers of love. In my opinion, using the word *God* to separate ourselves from one another is the greatest blasphemy. It doesn't matter what religion you are, there is no excuse for treating another human like garbage or believing yourself superior to them. If you follow beliefs that enforce those notions, then you have been sadly deceived and will never experience true fulfillment.

I know many spiritual people who say, "I'm not religious, because that is separation from the world." I am quick to remind them that categorizing themselves as "spiritual" is equally separating. When you think you are superior to someone else, and you use religion as an excuse for your ego, you actually contradict the very religion you claim to protect. Was the true message to ever separate ourselves from the world or place ourselves on a higher pedestal than others? Doesn't that display a form of hatred? I'm sure these great teachers just came to teach love, but some people use the grand message as a means to fulfill their own selfish desires and emotional gaps.

When people ask what religion I am and are getting ready to throw me in a category like a piece of meat, I always answer with, "I am who I am." When they ask what organization I am part of, I answer, "Life. My religion is love." Yes, some people do think I'm crazy but I get a good laugh out of seeing the expressions on their faces.

Many people have built a concept of fear around God. I truly believe to fear God is the biggest insult. When you fear your human father, you may do things that he wants, but not because you truly want to. It's not coming from your heart because you feel as if you have to, right? In fact, no satisfaction should come to your father, and if he were intelligent, he would not want you to continue to feel that way toward him. But when your father shows you love, and you have that same love for him, you will do things from your heart. And that's where meaning and depth come into action.

At times we get down on our knees and call out to God for something. I know I have done this many times myself. Some are brought up to believe that asking is enough. We say things like, "God, can **you** please comfort my auntie at this time," or "Please give me more money." It's as if we deliberately ignore the resources we have within us that have the ability to answer our own prayers. We then never get what we want and doubt that there is a God. Have you ever heard that voice telling you that you can have everything you have ever wanted if you are able to work for it with the qualities you already have? Those moments when something tells you to get up and go for it. How many times have you ignored that voice in the hope that what you want will magically appear if you get on your knees and ask for it? Well, God is that voice telling you that you can have it all, but you must use what you have to get it. **Underachievers are too busy asking while the great achievers are doing.** I wonder if it has ever occurred to people that everything they have ever wanted or desired will come about from their own actions; that in fact we are here to create with the gifts that have already been given. We must take accountability and responsibility for our life.

We have been socially conditioned to think of humans as being incapable of godly acts. We are cocreators in all of this. After asking for money, opportunities, happiness, and so on, we suddenly realize that living a successful life doesn't happen that easily. Is there really nothing you can do to enhance the chance of fulfilling your prayers or your dreams? I remember watching an inspirational interview one night in which John Conteh, a former world boxing champion, discussed the spiritual aspect of his success. He mentioned that once he realized that **God helps those who help themselves,** his attitude in life and commitment toward his dreams were never the same. For a brief moment, I want you to think about how you pray or even converse with yourself in a day. Ask yourself this question: "How many times do I say 'please,' rather than 'thank you'?"

Every key to our life has been given, the master key being love. In prayer we must have faith that the gifts are already there, like wisdom, power, energy, love, respect, happiness, patience, and fulfillment. It's not like we can just go to the local supermarket and buy these qualities off the shelf. We must unwrap everything that is stopping us from expressing these qualities. We must rejoice that our inner voice will really light up the path, and trust that the events that take place are the result of our creations. They may not always be controlled physically, but we can control what certain events mean in our life. Situations take place to help us harness learning and growth, especially those that you think are the lowest points of your life. Have faith in yourself, but above all be thankful in prayer and meditation.

And in recognizing that the point of life is to learn, it brings to light the stereotypical notion of heaven and hell. I couldn't imagine a God that is unconditionally loving damning us to hell for eternity. Have humans interpreted this notion of their own accord? Has anyone been to hell or heaven and back to tell us what it is like? I know one thing—we experience hell on earth when we don't tap into our awareness and fail to experience more love. That's all I can really understand in this human body, so that's what I'm going to work with.

I don't believe God is something to be feared, but to be embraced as love. When you fear God, you fear yourself, and that is no way to live. When you do something that is considered a sin, you run and hide, scared that the ground is going to open up and swallow you. That's not life. We are human, and this is a journey of self-discovery. We must take those events as learning opportunities and use fear the best way we can—as a chance for new action.

"Such love has no fear, because perfect love expels
all fear. If we are afraid, it is for fear of punishment,
and this shows that we have not fully experienced
perfect love."

—1 JOHN 4:18

Then there is the thought that God chooses individual people to do his work. But if God chose that person and broke their free will, then why didn't he choose everyone so that we could all live happily ever after? Well, that's the whole point: Everyone is chosen because the qualities are already there; most just choose not to use them. God doesn't choose or want certain individuals, he does not favor some and not the rest—**God already is.** So does that mean God created us with a want, as if he needs something from us? Does that mean God has ego? What does God look like? God doesn't choose and shouldn't be limited to our human concepts of wanting or characterizing. It's an insult in its truest form, as God does not need anything from us.

You don't have to be a world-famous speaker, an author, or what others deem successful. In your daily affairs, just show love and let your truth guide you, because you will get it back, and that's contributing. It's funny what a smile can do. When you see people in the supermarket or wherever you are, just smile and be extremely nice, and you will notice the power of it. You may get the odd person who doesn't appreciate it, but don't stress about those guys; it's just that they don't appreciate life themselves. You are the decider of how your life is created, and essentially we are our own judges. But remember, the great gifts reign within you, and they have always been there.

People say that we must believe in God, yet what most forget is that God also believes in us. The only way you can believe in God is if you believe in yourself. I don't believe that God is loving; I believe that **God** is **love.** They should never be separated. When we feel love in our heart, that is God. God is love and love is life. That's what unites the world and helps us to discover our greatness. Love (a higher power) cannot be seen or limited, it has no shape or form, it dwells in all things, it is forever in existence, complete fullness, and the ultimate truth, but above all, it's that special feeling.

> "For beautiful eyes, look for the good in others;
> for beautiful lips, speak only words of kindness;
> and for poise, walk with the knowledge
> that you are never alone."
> —AUDREY HEPBURN

7TH STEP
Find Fulfillment: A Real Success

25

A True Happiness

"If an Arab in the desert were suddenly to discover a
spring in his tent, and so would always be able to have
water in abundance, how fortunate he would consider
himself—so, too, when a man, who as a physical being
is always turned toward the outside, thinking that his
happiness lies outside him, finally turns inward and
discovers that the source is within."

—SØREN KIERKEGAARD

There is one particular myth when it comes to happiness that
leads to disappointment for all who embrace it. It causes us to
become confused, to continually question who we are, and it sends
us around in a circle never finding everlasting happiness. These
points in our life derive from the notion that true happiness can
be obtained.

Have you ever bought a new car or a watch and then after a
month or so you realize that it's **just** a car, or just a watch? Those
materialistic purchases only bring short-term satisfaction and do
nothing but drive us crazy trying to figure out how we are going to
get our next fix. We go on a vacation to make us happy, find a partner, eat some food that we like, sit on a comfortable chair, or make
some more money. When we spend the money, come back from

the vacation, or eat the food, it seems we are unhappy once again. All these external aspects of life are restricted by other people's behavior, environment, social status, time, appearance, and so on. With so many limitations, is it any wonder that your so-called happiness seems to come to a halt on a regular basis? Shift your focus toward things that really matter in life and you will notice your power to create true happiness.

When I was in Thailand I met a multimillionaire who had twelve stable businesses across a few countries. He was also the owner of a number of suit shops there, and I bumped into him while he was on vacation checking up on the stores. If you have ever been to Thailand, you will know what I'm talking about when I say that the guys at the suit shops are pretty hard to get away from. But it was all in good fun, because I ended up liking them and buying three suits.

I was discussing true happiness with one of the workers there, and he said, "That's what makes you happy," pointing at a screen saver of a Lamborghini on the store laptop. The other guy, who I didn't know was the owner of the store, and of that very Lamborghini, said, "That hasn't made me happy." We began chatting and he offered to take me to lunch.

I found out that this great achiever who had millions of dollars was one of the unhappiest people I had ever met. I discovered that this man had been chasing what he thought was happiness his whole life, only to be faced with nothing but emptiness. No matter what he obtained, it never fulfilled him. I totally shifted his focus to allow him to see that happiness was right there within him the whole time. The attitude he takes when going to buy a new car should be the same one he takes out to life every day. I'm glad to hear that his progress is outstanding and that he is contributing to his country for the first time in his life.

Thinking about it, this makes sense when we hear about millionaires being addicted to drugs while poor kids in Asia are doing the same thing. What's the difference? There is none, because they are both sectioning off their happiness. When it comes to finding happiness in addiction, it is important to realize that in doing it you will not find happiness, and in not doing it you might still be unhappy. This is due to, again, believing that your happiness lies in something outside of you and not a choice within that you are able to produce at any time.

The only way to true happiness is to recognize that it has always been attained. It was never those particular things that made you happy; it was always your choice of attitude in the face of them. If you believe that your happiness lies in certain circumstances or things, how could it be if they also bring you pain? You hear a strange noise coming from the car engine, scratch the new watch, or the food isn't as you expected, and your outlook changes instantly.

The greatest gift a person can discover within is to acknowledge that they have always had the power to produce whichever emotion they like, including happiness. Let's take going away on a vacation, for example. We plan it, we tell people about it, and we get absolutely excited about what's to come. The funny thing is that we are actually not on the trip yet, so our happiness cannot be the vacation itself. Even a month leading up to it, we seem to be much happier throughout our day. Workdays don't seem too hard anymore; we ignore insignificant hiccups and choose not to focus on the worst in life, because *we are going on a vacation!* **Create a vision, a projection into the future, or something to look forward to. It will increase your willingness to keep that same feeling and use it to overcome and create a different outlook on challenges along the way.**

"A happy person is not a person
in a certain set of circumstances, but rather
a person with a certain set of attitudes."
—HUGH DOWNS

Once you finally go on the trip, everything seems amazing. The people are the nicest you have met, the buildings are extraordinarily beautiful, and you even seem to appreciate things that you would have tried to avoid back home. In reality they were just buildings and people like anywhere else. The reason they look like the best bricks you have seen is that your attitude toward life is different.

You then come back home and meet a tourist in your town. They begin to tell you how amazing your city is, but you can't figure out what all the fuss is about. The truth is that when you shifted how you felt about life internally, it created everything outside to shift with you. Without argument, we will always see on the outside how we choose to feel on the inside. This means your happiness was always attained and is accessible anywhere at any time. Just like on vacation, I urge you to walk around your town with the same enthusiasm and happy feeling, and you will see it reflected instantly. If I told you right now to close your eyes, drift away, and imagine a time where you were at your happiest, you would be able to feel the same emotions. Are you really there? I don't know, open up your eyes and tell me. The point is that no matter where you are or what your situation in life, a sad or happy feeling has always been there for you to grasp.

I would personally close my eyes in times that I felt were about to shift my happy mood and go to that place or envision that special something that I love. **If we shift our focus toward happiness, our energy will flow in that direction.**

If you decide to look at the worst things in life, you are choosing to be unhappy. If you command your focus toward what's great in life, even in the face of challenges, you will produce emotions accordingly. As time goes on, the more you do this, the stronger and more emotionally intelligent you become. However, as we all know, this is life, and it's just not that easy at times. My theory about happiness is simple: **I am content with knowing that I will not always be happy. That is my happiness!**

I have come to accept that life is not made up of the stereotypical happiness that society has created. To reach the pedestal that social happiness is put on, it must mean we are in a bubbly, enthusiastic mood—or that's the common notion, anyway. If we are not, it means we are sad. Nothing is further from the truth. How about when you are in a mood of complete concentration and don't want anyone to interrupt you? Would you say you are not happy then? I wouldn't, because life has never been just two emotions: happy or unhappy. It even gets to the point where friends and family will ask you what's wrong when you are just sitting there. Do I have to be sad or does something have to be wrong if I just sit on my own for five minutes? You must eliminate the concept that society has created of happiness and accept all emotions as a part of life.

Our main mission in life is not to try to hold on to the concept of happiness, but rather to pursue and discover self-worth. Embedded deep in every soul, a thirst for self-love waits to be quenched. Once the source is found it can never be abolished, even in times of unhappiness.

26

To Find a Heart Filled with Love

"Love gives naught but itself and takes naught
but from itself. Love possesses not nor would it be
possessed; for love is sufficient unto love. When you
love you should not say, 'God is in my heart,' but
rather, 'I am in the heart of God.' And think not you
can direct the course of love, for love, if it finds you
worthy, directs your course."

—KAHLIL GIBRAN

First we are awakened through the power of change, and then the enlightenment of love comes knocking on the door. I highly advise you to open and embrace it, as it's true life in the purest of forms. As you have probably already noticed, at the start of your awakening (self-discovery) you are judging others not on a social level but on a consciousness level. The reason this happens is that you are starting to live life as an observer of cause and effect. I know you have probably heard the words *conscious awakening* before, but they just refer to the **self-awareness** that finally allows you to discover the massive impact **you** actually have on your own life and the world at large.

If you are fan of *The Oprah Winfrey Show,* I'm sure you will remember the segment when her crew went to assist the Hawk family, who were all heroin addicts. The two sons, the father, and the mother were all addicted, and they had a baby whom they were desperately trying to look after. Mike Hawk, the father, was separated from his family during rehab. The follow-up show months later revealed some astounding changes. I saw a man who was enlightened, with an inner peace that was truly breathtaking. He spoke like a true master and someone who had been like this his whole life. But he wasn't—it had only been a few months! Many of the things he spoke about were the same exercises we have completed throughout this book. His inner journey completed his outside world. He even deliberately walks past the drug dealers that he once scored off of in the streets to prove his strength. By adding meaning and purpose to his life again, he was able to create the life he so often dreamed about. If a man who was a heroin addict for years turned his whole life around in a few months, then anyone can. Being consciously awakened to your true potential is the only way to ever be spiritually free and experience true fulfillment.

Going through my own journey, I would describe it as being like having a bucket of water thrown over me and waking up after years of sleepwalking. I stopped looking at the world through a cylinder. My mind was opened, which allowed me to finally discover the meaning in every experience. Every time I left my phone at home and had to go back and get it, all the times I tripped, all the missed opportunities, the bad times, and the great times led me up to this point, right now. I began to fit together the pieces of the puzzle, and it started making sense.

After you experience such a realization, you feel as if you need to go and shake everyone into it, and that's caused by the love that is starting to emanate from you. As time goes on, if you choose to go deeper, you are enlightened. You will notice that you appreciate other people's differences as judgment fades. Instead of feeling like you're on a higher level than the rest, you bring everyone around up with you. I guess that's why it's so infectious. It sets you free from the mental, physical, and emotional chains that enslaved your heart for many years. The beauty of it lies in the one love you attain for all creation. Your heart knows how to free itself from resentment and hate, and you finally see life as it was intended to be.

Once I was awakened, I realized I had the option of stopping there. Being awakened to who you really are allows for a good life to be lived, although nothing is more fulfilling than being enlightened by that master key that opens up all the doors to our life: love.

I went so deep that I questioned and challenged everything about my life. It went on for months, and there were nights when I felt as if I was in the dark. Everything about your reality starts to shift. When you decide to fully jump into the ocean of love, its ferocious tide will rock your whole world. It will force you to shift beliefs you had forever, cry about things you once laughed at, and become a true child of life itself. Your heart is not weighed down, and your mind is not surrounded by darkness. As the sea starts to calm, your heart fills with love's light and free-flowing water, which makes you never thirst again. As it fills up and starts to overflow, it radiates to everything and everyone around. You will notice that same love that dwells within you is in all creation, and you finally realize you are a part of it, and it is a part of you.

"Love is patient, love is kind. It does not envy, it does not boast, it is not proud. It is not rude, it is not self-seeking, it is not easily angered, it keeps no record of wrongs. Love does not delight in evil but rejoices with the truth. It always protects, always trusts, always hopes, always perseveres. Love never fails."

—I CORINTHIANS 13:4–8

Surprisingly, I would wake up day after day to mysteriously find new answers and create more strength. My inner peace became overpowering and my whole attitude toward life had changed. I discovered my connection with this world and aligned with my spirit to be the greatest person I knew how to be. The process was so intriguing, tireless, and fascinating that the deeper I went, the more I was overwhelmed with awe. After a while of monitoring your thoughts and directing them back to love, it seems new growth happens constantly. You are always reaching new levels.

Many people in history have died trying to find the tree of life hidden by God in the Bible. They thought it was an actual tree, and to their constant disappointment they never found it. They were oblivious to the fact that the tree of life is within all of us, but it is hidden because of our separation from love and unity with the creator. Finding the tree of life is to discover the unity between your soul and God, and the ego and higher self.

The process of discovering the essence of your being and using it with intent for the good of the world has been called many things in history. It's been called the "Great Work" and even saints such as Saint Francis of Assisi, Saint Teresa of Ávila, and Saint Augustine have spoken about this phenomenon. Mahatma Gandhi, Mother Teresa, Orison Swett Marden, Albert Einstein, Martin Luther King Jr., and nearly every other influential person spoke about our higher powers. It is also the core message of every major religion. It is a truly rare gem to find, but if you don't stop on your quest of self-awareness you will be aligned with new answers.

At one stage as I was on my journey of self-discovery, I was curious to know if I was the only one experiencing this. I felt alienated from the rest of the world. It was playing on my mind one day, and as I was walking down my corridor, I looked up to where the set of encyclopedias was. I hadn't looked up there in years but my attention was drawn to it on this day. I saw a little white book in between all the other large ones. It was the only book that wasn't in the set, and it was no bigger than my hand. It had no pictures on the front and no big title, just a plain and simple white book. I opened it up and had to immediately sit down from being so overwhelmed. It was a book on those saints and other people in history who had experienced this connection with their soul. It mentioned how some were persecuted and killed because they couldn't explain in words what it was exactly. I totally understood their situation and couldn't help but sympathize with their predicament. It's one that cannot be explained in words, as it's far too great to be restricted. A love so pure is a feeling that is not bounded by finite words. It is to see the world in the eyes of God, and to be surrounded by beauty.

As we begin to understand ourselves more—and I'm sure you have made some great progress after completing the tasks in this book—we enter the never-ending cycle of self-growth. With it, we spiral upward, and we find ourselves in love's direction.

When you can close your eyes and fall back into love anytime you like—even at the times that seem the most distressing—and then open them up and see the world that way, its enormous power is displayed.

> I'm only really in love with one thing. I'm in love with the feeling of love. I have felt that love in everything.

27

The Beginning

"The ideals which have lighted my way, and time
after time have given me new courage to face life,
have been kindness, beauty, and truth."

—ALBERT EINSTEIN

After so many years, I finally began to live. I discovered that I was actually slowly dying before. Most people believe they are getting closer to death by physically growing. They feel aches and pains; they fear the number of their years as they start to increase. They think that every year that passes is another step toward leaving this earth, and they get depressed. But why would you be depressed about leaving when you don't even make the most of it when you're alive? When you are aware of your actions, it is the complete opposite. You acknowledge that every year that passes is another year you have learned how to live!

We surround ourselves with stress, worry, selfishness, sadness, hate, and every other feeling that kills us—not just physically, but mentally, financially, and spiritually. It attacks every part of our life, directly and indirectly, and it affects most people around us. Seeing you only have one shot at this life, why on earth wouldn't you give it the best shot you possibly can and be the greatest person you know how to be? Don't just live because you were born, embrace that you were actually born to live. Just because you are alive doesn't mean you are living. This is why it seems so many only begin to live when they finally stare death in the face.

I have come to a point in my life where I appreciate every part of its existence. The joy, the sorrow, the uncertainty, the laughter, the crying, and the love—all have equal respect and importance. It didn't take long to condition this embracing of life, which truly changed every aspect of its direction. I know I must show as many people as I can for as long as I can, because it truly does open up all the doors to life.

The explanations I have given in this book were the best way my spirit could pour out the strategies to find ultimate fulfillment. It is still a journey, but I have faith that you will persevere. I trust that by doing these tasks you have had a pretty good taste of the other side, which I call life. The ultimate advantage of success is success itself, and to find fulfillment as you are now. Inner peace must come first, so read this book and complete its tasks ten times if you have to. Use it as your guide and not a "read and put down" story, because that's not what it's about.

Never give up on the life that flashes before your mind, as that is the true path the creator intends for you. We are meant to be great, experience emotions like never before, and continue to grow through any challenge. We were built with the gift to create our own life any way we choose, and we have a source of infinite intelligence to gather from.

Love yourself, love others, love life, and the world is yours.

Follow these tasks and let them consume every part of your life. Let your mind work overtime on your success instead of working on your disappointment. I'm not sure about you, but I am not, under any circumstances, throwing life away on being the victim. I will not waste it on hating, judgment, or selfishness. I want to win for myself, for everybody around me, and for the world. Take a leap of faith, push yourself, and live the life you dare to dream.

Feel those same emotions and attitude that you know you will have when you obtain that money, are able to share love with that person, or attain that inner peace, and it will happen.

The choice has always, is always, and will always be yours. Be true to yourself and persist for those visions, no matter what. You will make mistakes, but get on with life and it will become your cause.

Acknowledge that some experiences in life happen without us ever really knowing why. Why are there earthquakes that kill thousands of people? Why does someone get stabbed to death while trying to help someone else? Why does a baby have a deformity from birth? These are the events in life that make us search deeper. If anything, they should make us want to strive to be a better person.

In life we get thrown curveballs, but it's not how quickly we can move out of their way, it's how well we learn how to hit that home run that counts. Experiences are there to shape who we are, even though at times they seem too much to bear. Isn't it true that some of your hardest experiences taught you the most? In time we may know why certain things happen, but even if we never do, it is no excuse for not being the best person we can be.

I don't care how much I think someone has mistreated me; I have come to appreciate the massive role they played in my life. For that I do not hate them but love them.

In order to create an outstanding life you must have two things: a great SOM (state of mind) and the ability to command your own emotions.

This book offers you insight into both these goals, yet your individual and unique journey will go on. The blueprint of your greatness is just like your fingerprint—it is one of a kind.

In conclusion, I really hope you enjoyed walking this self-journey and sharing it with me. I was inspired to write this book because of so many people displaying their confusion about how to actually go on a self-journey. Most wouldn't even know where to start, so I thought this would be a guide.

Congratulations on completing this book, as it is a massive accomplishment. But do not stop here. You have many experiences and challenges to come. I really hope one day we can meet and exchange stories. I thank you humbly for allowing me to share your emotions, your mind, and your life through this journey. I know it's been a roller coaster of emotions throughout this book, because I have felt it, too. I consider us friends, wherever you are on this earth—and friends help each other spread their great message! It gives me great pleasure to know that we have connected. Funnily enough, even though we have never met, I feel as if I know you personally, and I'm sure you feel the same about me. Until we connect again, dream big, act extraordinarily, and live with purpose.

I find myself asking the same questions I did at the start of my journey:

Looking up high, I wonder, what is all of this? What does this all mean? What am I doing here? A new comfort seems to arise now, which puts me at the essence of all creation. I am a part of it all, and it is a part of me. I guess the best answer is:

LIFE IS TRULY WHAT YOU MAKE IT.

It would be great to hear from you. Send me your feedback or your story, or write just to reconnect. You can contact me at:

EMAIL: info@danielchidiac.com

WEBSITE: danielchidiac.com

INSTAGRAM: @whosaysyoucantyoudo

ACKNOWLEDGMENTS

How does someone who has been emotionally touched by so many people in life ever have the words to express how they feel? These words are like a drop of water in an ocean compared to the enormity of the gratitude I feel toward these amazing people.

To my unconditionally loving mother and father, thank you for always encouraging me to be the best person I can be. Your support, belief, and faith have driven me to levels I once dreamed about.

To my brother and mentor, Matthew, I appreciate the life chats and the support you have given me throughout my life. We are in this together.

To my sister, Jeannie, thank you for giving me unforgettable Saturdays with my beautiful nephews. To raise children the way you have says it all about the qualities you attain.

To my second mother, Auntie Helen, I would definitely not be where I am today without you. I don't need to explain; you know how much you mean to me.

To my grandparents and Auntie Adele, thank you for the support you continue to give me throughout my life. And especially to my grandfather, even though it has been many years since your passing, your spirit continues to inspire me.

I would also like to thank all my friends who have been there through thick and thin. You know who you are.

To the rest of my family, thank you for always being there. Our family is so special because of the morals we have been raised to value. Let's never forget them.

I would also like to thank all the people who said, "No, you can't." You have been the fuel that drives me to prove that I can.

Last, to all of you who want to dump the word *can't* and go on a journey that will empower your life forever, I salute you for having the courage to master your life.

I believe the true meaning of our experiences is not just to learn but to teach others what we have learned.

—Daniel Chidiac

ABOUT THE AUTHOR

DANIEL CHIDIAC is a writer from Melbourne, Australia, committed to sharing his message that life should be lived freely. Daniel went on a journey of self-discovery after becoming awakened to his power over his own life and wrote this book to share with others what he had uncovered. *Who Says You Can't? You Do* was first published in 2012 and became an Amazon best seller in six different countries. His writing has changed countless lives around the world and he inspires hundreds of thousands of people every day on Instagram. Find him online at danielchidiac.com and instagram.com/whosaysyoucantyoudo.